Welcome to the *Teacher's Resource Book* for *Network Now A2.2*

Your course: *Network Now A2.2*

- *Network Now A2.2* provides 24 ninety-minute lessons, covering a one year (2 semester) course.
- Each of the 6 units has 3 steps (18 lessons), followed by a revision lesson, *Now I can* (6 lessons).
- If your course has more than 24 lessons and you need **extra lessons,**
    - use the ***Zero lesson*** on pages 5–7 of this book for your first course contact.
    - use the ***Globetrotter*** pages. There are two *Globetrotter* pages – a *Globetrotter Work* and a *Globetrotter Travel* page after Units 2, 4 and 6, and you can find ideas on how to use them in class in this *Resource Book* (pages 122 ff.). Each of these pages provides forty-five minutes of classroom material and a further forty-five minutes of activities are available on the Internet.
    - use the ***Christmas lesson*** at the end of this book.

Your students

Many of your students will have just completed *Network Now A2.1*; some of your students may have joined your course from another institution which possibly used a different coursebook series; and some of your students will have decided to return to learning English after a long break. So how does *Network Now* help these learners?

- *Network Now* recognises the benefit of a **relaxed classroom atmosphere** and friendly interaction between students. There are many opportunities for students to work with a variety of partners and in different groups, thereby allowing students to get to know each other quickly and communicate without inhibitions.
- Inevitably, you will find a **range of abilities** in your class – and *Network Now* offers some solutions to make the group more homogeneous.
    - In the coursebook, you'll often find elements of 'refresher' grammar ***(You already know)*** before the new grammar ***(And now)*** is introduced. This can be seen on the classroom pages (see page 11) and, in more detail, on the ***Language study*** pages (see page 12). You can advise students to look at the ***You already know*** grammar before the next lesson if they feel unsure of themselves.
    - Refer students to the **online codes** next to the ***Language study*** headings (see page 12). Here they can easily access more practice of the structures which are being revised and introduced.
    - In the *Resource Book*, tips are given on how to **adapt classroom exercises** to suit the needs of weaker classes (↓) or more able classes (↑). In addition, some exercises can be offered to students at three different levels: simple (*), standard (**) and complex (***) and they can determine how challenged they want to be – see ***Part 1: Lesson notes*** on page 4.
    - Apart from the traditional *Selfstudy* exercises (see page 17), there's a personalised writing page, ***Now me***, at the end of each unit (see page 26). This gives students the opportunity to read a blog about the unit topic and write a blog of their own. It also sets students a related straight-forward Internet task for them to accomplish. This is to encourage students to do their own Internet research – in English.
    - Students will find tips on how to improve their learning skills on the Selfstudy pages – ***FAQ*** (see page 13) – and a collection of more tips on pages 198/199.

Your *Network Now A2.2* lessons

- Each step of the 3-step unit is designed to last for 90 minutes.
- In Steps 1 and 2 there's a reading input (which can be read again and listened to in the first exercise on the *Selfstudy* page: *Read and listen*), a listening input, grammar, vocabulary and functional English.
- The final activity in Steps 1 and 2 is ***Talk about it***, giving students the opportunity to talk freely about topic-related themes.
- The third step of each unit has a focus on coping in everyday situations, e.g. understanding language on realia. There's a topic-related reading passage and a section on writing tips: ***Write it right.***
- The fourth lesson in the unit, ***Now I can***, is a review lesson and it mirrors the list of learning aims on the introductory page of each unit – the *Photo page*. To facilitate the different levels of ability in the class, there's a ***Now you choose*** activity where students can choose whether they want to try an easy, standard or challenging task.
- If your lessons are longer than 90 minutes, or if you want to have **something extra for your lesson**, you can find materials here:
    - In every step, there's a reference to the ***Language and culture*** section – texts and tasks about linguistic and cultural aspects of life in English-speaking countries – and this can be done in class or set for homework as the tasks have →

keys. Recordings of the texts can be found online. The final task on this page is ***Listen in***. Students hear an unscripted conversation and are encouraged to understand the gist of this conversation. This is a confidence-builder to get them used to authentic situations and to learn not to panic if they don't understand every word – they can understand more than they think! (The transcripts of the *Listen in* tasks can be found online.)

- The ***Reading*** pages, which are part of the *Selfstudy* for each Step 3, can also be used in class. Ideas for exploiting the *Reading* texts can be found in this *Resource Book* (pages 120/121).
- This ***Resource Book*** provides ideas for more activities in each step (pages 81 ff.), and has a resource section of photocopiable materials and templates (pages 102 ff.).
- Download the extra *A2.2* materials from the Internet – see **www.klett-langenscheidt.de/networknow/activities**.
- Download extra materials from the *Network Teachers' Club* – see **www.klett-langenscheidt.de/network/club**.

Your *Teacher's Resource Book* for *Network Now A2.2*

The ***Teacher's Resource Book*** (TRB) is divided into **three main parts:**

Part 1: Lesson notes

- The lesson notes give detailed **instructions** on how to organise activities and teach the structures.
- Approximate **timings** are given for each activity – and what to do if you're short of time.
- There are **keys** to the activities on the classroom pages, where appropriate.
- If an activity involves a listening exercise, you'll find the **audio script** framed on the page and the **track numbers** are given with the relevant activities: 2/13 = CD number 2, track 13. The ▶ indicates when the track is to be played.
- Some of the information in the notes is printed in grey – this means it's an optional activity.
- Suggestions are made on how to make some exercises simpler (↓) or more complex (↑).
- Some activities offer the students a choice of complexity. The one-star* option is slightly easier than the standard, two-star** option, and the three-star*** option is more challenging. Each students can decide for him- / herself the degree to which he / she wants to be challenged.
- And look out for these useful elements:
  Tip – a teaching tip which can be used at this particular stage of the lesson (see page 8).
  ! – a reminder about some aspect of what you're about to teach (see page 8).
  NB – a relevant piece of information for this step (see page 9).

Part 2: Optional & additional materials – Getting ready for Unit (1)

This section provides extra activities for each step and each *Now I can*. It should be looked at before the lesson as some of the activities require preparation.

- **FYI (For Your Information):** This guides you to topic-related information on the Internet. It isn't intended for the students, but as background information for the teacher.
- **Preparing Unit (1) (Step 1):**
  - Extra activities for the step or for *Now I can.*
  - Notes on dealing with the *Language and culture* texts and tasks in class.
  - A link to the downloadable activity for this step or for *Now I can.*

Part 3: Optional & additional materials – Photocopiable activities

- There are **photocopiable materials** to accompany the extra activities for the **steps** in Part 2.
- And there's also a **template** to accompany the extra activities for the ***Now I can*** of each unit. These templates can be filled in and used in a variety of ways at different levels – so you can have a 'tailor-made' activity for your class.

So all it remains for the *Network* team to say is: Enjoy your teaching with *Network Now A2.2.*

The Zero lesson

You may find that, in the first lesson, not all students have the coursebook, so here are some ideas for classroom activities which you can do without your students needing a coursebook. The times given are approximate – it depends on the number of students in your class. The aim is to encourage students to get to know each other and get used to working together. The activities are also confidence-builders and help learners to overcome their inhibitions in speaking.

In this first lesson, there will, inevitably, be some German spoken. The golden rule about German in the lesson is: *As little as possible but as much as necessary.*

For some of the activities on this page, each student will need a copy of the **worksheet** (page 6). And if you want to find out more about your students, their linguistic backgrounds and their expectations, ask them to fill in the **Learner profile**. For this, each student will need a copy of page 7.

1 **Introductions:** Introduce yourself to the class and / or greet students you know:
Hello, my name's (Eva). Nice to see you again. / Nice to meet you.
If there are several students in the class who know each other, get them to introduce each other to the new students, giving the person's name and saying something they know about the person. New students then introduce themselves and volunteer one piece of information.
Students make a name card by folding a piece of paper in half and writing their first name on the front and back of the paper (so that classmates in front of them and next to them can read it).
Time: About 10 minutes.

2 **Getting to know you:** Hand out a copy of the worksheet to each student and refer them to ▸ worksheet activity A and give them time to read it through.
Demonstrate the activity by choosing a topic you'd like to talk about and inviting students to ask you questions.
Students work in small groups and talk about their chosen topics. After ten minutes, invite volunteers to tell the class one piece of information about someone in their group.
The aim of this first activity is to give students an opportunity to speak, to get to know each other, and to feel comfortable working with people in their class. Monitor the activity, joining in when appropriate and correcting only if communication breaks down.
Time: About 15 minutes.

3 **Learning English:** Check that everyone has a copy of ▸ worksheet activity B.
Ask the class to tick the reasons that they want to learn more English and then tell the class about them.
Time: About 15 minutes.

4 **Your coursebook:** Refer students to ▸ worksheet activity C. Give students time to read the section about *Language study* and *Selfstudy*. Then ask the class to try to complete the titles:
1 **Home** and away, 2 **Learning** and working, 3 **Travel** and transport, 4 **Going out** and staying in, 5 **Sickness** and health, 6 **Saving** and spending
Then get them to match the photos to the unit titles:
1e), 2c), 3a), 4f), 5d), 6b)
Ask them to work in groups and speculate what is in Unit 1 and then compare their ideas in class.
Look at page 9 of the coursebook: *Unit 1 Home and away.* Tell the class that each unit begins with a photo page. Show them page 9 (they can open their books if they have them), point to the Learning aims in the bottom right-hand corner and read them out. Finish by saying: *Please have the book with you in the next lesson and we can start with Unit 1, Step 1.*
Time: The coursebook activities should take about 25 minutes.

5 **Learner profile:** Finally, ask students to fill in the Learner profile page (page 7). This is particularly useful to find out about students' previous language experience as there may be students in your class who haven't come directly from the *Network Now A2.1* course. As people finish writing, collect their sheets and chat to individuals about what they've written.
Time: This is an open-ended activity, minimum 10 minutes. Leave five minutes at the end of the lesson to say goodbye.

6 **Goodbye:** As the lesson draws to a close, write on the board, as appropriate:

Board: Goodbye (Tina). See you (next week / tomorrow / on Thursday).

Get students to say goodbye to you and each other.
Time: About 5 minutes.

The Zero lesson

Worksheet

A Getting to know you

Tick two topics you'd like to talk about.

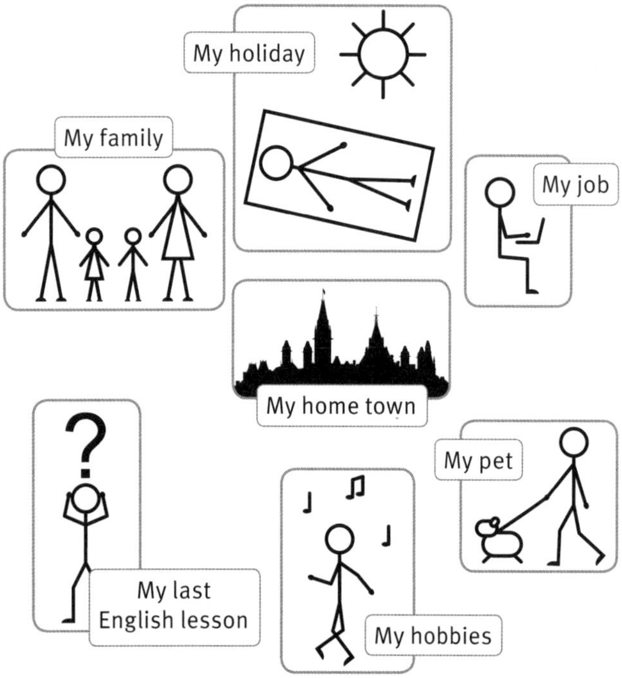

In groups of three or four, take turns to talk about the topics you've chosen. Other people in the group will ask you questions.

B Learning English

Tick the reason(s) that you want to learn more English. Then tell the class a bit about your motivation:

I need English for ...
I want to improve my English because ...
I'd like to be able to ...

- ☐ for my job
- ☐ for my holidays
- ☐ for social reasons
- ☐ to keep my brain active
- ☐ to be able to help my son or daughter with English
- ☐ to be able to communicate with someone on my family
- ☐ just as a hobby
- ☐ because I like languages
- ☐ ....

C Your coursebook: Network Now A2.2

Ihr Kursbuch heißt *Network Now A2.2*. In jeder Lektion lernen Sie, sich in verschiedenen Situationen auf Englisch zurechtzufinden. In jedem *Step* gibt es eine Seite *Language study*. Hier können Sie die Grammatik üben, die Sie im Unterricht gelernt haben. Manchmal gibt es auf dieser Seite zwei Abschnitte: *You already know* (mit der Grammatik, die Sie schon von früher kennen) und *And now* (mit der neuen Grammatik aus der Unterrichtsstunde). Außerdem gibt es eine Seite *Selfstudy* mit Übungen für zu Hause. Wenn Sie lieber online lernen wollen, finden Sie diese und weitere Übungen auch im Internet unter www.klett-langenscheidt.de/networknow/selfstudy. Damit Ihnen das Lernen immer leichter fällt, enthält das Buch auch zahlreiche wirksame Lerntipps.

There are six units in your coursebook.
Try to complete the titles with these words:
Going out | Home | Learning | Saving | Sickness | Travel

Network Now A2.2

Unit 1
________ and away

Unit 2
________ and working

Unit 3
________ and transport

Unit 4
________ and staying in

Unit 5
________ and health

Unit 6
________ and spending

Which unit do you think these photos are from?

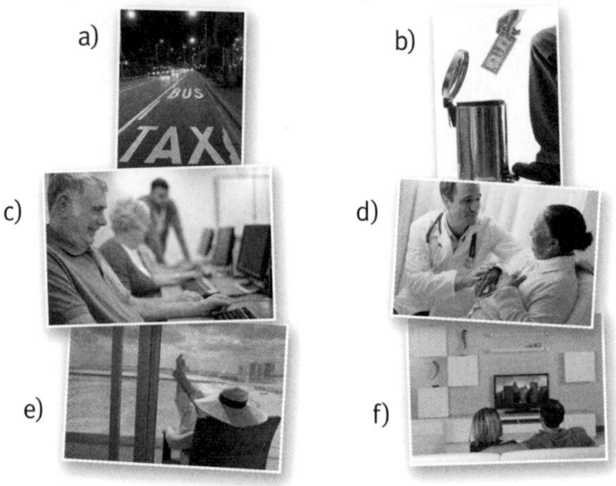

In groups, talk about what you think you're going to learn in Unit 1 *(Home and away)*. Then compare your ideas in class.

The unit might be about ...
I think we're going to learn about ...
Maybe there are photos of ...

Learner profile

Ihr Lehrer / Ihrer Lehrerin möchte gerne mehr über Sie und Ihre Erwartungen an diesen Kurs erfahren. Daher wäre es schön, wenn Sie das folgende Profil ausfüllen. Lassen Sie die Fragen, die Sie nicht beantworten möchten, einfach aus.

Name: ______________________________

Geburtsort: ______________________________

Nationalität: ______________________________

Muttersprache(n): ______________________________

Wenn Deutsch nicht Ihre Muttersprache ist, welche Aussage trifft auf Ihre Deutschkenntnisse zu:

- ☐ Ich kann vertraute, alltägliche Ausdrücke und ganz einfache Sätze verstehen und verwenden.
- ☐ Ich kann einfache und häufig gebrauchte Ausdrücke verstehen und mich in einfachen routinemäßigen Situationen verständigen.
- ☐ Ich kann die meisten alltäglichen Situationen bewältigen und kann mich einfach und zusammenhängend zu mir vertrauten Themen äußern.
- ☐ Ich kann mich spontan und fließend mit deutschen Muttersprachlern ohne größere Anstrengung auf beiden Seiten verständigen.
- ☐ Ich kann mich spontan und fließend ausdrücken und mich strukturiert und ausführlich zu komplexen Sachverhalten äußern.
- ☐ Ich kann mich sehr spontan, sehr flüssig und ganz genau ausdrücken und auch bei komplexeren Sachverhalten feinere Bedeutungsnuancen deutlich machen.

Welche anderen Sprachen sprechen Sie? ______________________________

Haben Sie Englisch in der Schule gelernt? Wenn ja, geben Sie bitte an, an welcher Art Schule, für wie lange und wie lange es her ist.

____

Das hat mir gefallen: ______________________________

____

Das hat mir nicht gefallen: ______________________________

____

Haben Sie schon einmal einen Englischkurs besucht? Wenn ja, schreiben Sie bitte ein paar Worte dazu:

____

Ich habe aufgehört, weil ______________________________

____

Das hat mir gefallen: ______________________________

____

Das hat mir nicht gefallen: ______________________________

____

Warum möchten Sie Englisch lernen? ______________________________

____

Was möchten Sie am Ende des Kurses alles können? ______________________________

____

Unit 1 Step 1 Home

Contents

Text topic	An article about the twin towns Swindon and Walt Disney World
Functions	Describing your town and local area
Vocabulary	Things you find in and around town
Grammar	**You already know:** How to make questions **And now:** Subject questions with *Who*

Lesson notes

Additional material

For optional and additional material for Unit 1, Step 1, see pages 81/82.
Refer to this section before your lesson as some of the materials require preparation.

Optional stages

Optional stages of the lesson are written in grey in these notes.

Tip: Learner profile If you haven't done the *Zero lesson*, you can copy the *Learner profile* (p. 7) for each student and ask them to fill it in at home.

Starter: Where are you from?
5– mins

- Introduce yourself to the class and demonstrate the task briefly by telling the class where you are from and how long you have lived in this area.
- Ask students to introduce themselves in the same way.

Tip: Getting to know your class You may want to extend this stage of the lesson, particularly if there are a lot of new people in the class, by doing a *Getting to know your class* activity. You can find an idea for this on page 81.

Photo page
5– mins

- Hold up your open book at page 9 and introduce the topic of the unit by looking at the pictures with the class. Ask the questions to individual students.
- Refer students to *In this unit, you will learn to: …* . Give them a minute to read the learning aims.

NB: The learning aims of each unit appear again in the revision section, *Now I can.*

1a Vocabulary: In and around town
5+ mins

! The *Info box* highlights some possible false friends for German speakers. Remind students that some words may look and sound the same in English as in German but have different meanings.

- Look at the photos on page 10 of Walt Disney World and Swindon with the students. Ask them what they can see. (Fairytale castle, trees; block of flats, houses, city.) Ask them if they know where these places are. (Florida USA; Swindon UK.)
- Read out the first part of the instructions. Students read the text silently and find the words.

! Check students know how to pronounce *museum* [mjuːˈziːəm] and Swindon [ˈswɪndən]. Say the words and ask students to repeat them.
A lot of British towns end in *-ton / -don,* e.g. Paddington, London. The *ton / don* syllables shouldn't be 'swallowed' – they should be pronounced [tən] or [dən].

- Board:

town or city	area around …

Students call out their answers. Add them to the correct column. Then ask the class if they can think of more words for each list. (town or city: school, shops, parks, cafes, bus station, swimming pools, …; area around: airport, mountains, football stadium, …)
! You can be flexible with the answers which students provide as many towns / cities also have lakes, woods / forests, castles.

1 railway museum, arts centre, castle; 2 theme park, lakes, forests, castle, countryside, villages, woods, fields

1b Comprehension
10 mins

Tip: Task complexity (1) When you see an arrow like this ↓, there's a suggestion how to make the activity a little easier. When you see this arrow ↑, there's a suggestion how to make the activity a bit more demanding. These suggestions are optional – it depends on the ability of your class whether you choose to use them or not.

- Read out the comprehension questions. Students look at the text and write down their answers.
- ↓ Students work in pairs and work out the answers.
- Check the answers in class.
  1 They have become twin towns. 2 Disney. 3 … because Swindon loves fun and magic (exactly like Walt Disney World). 4 It's in Florida about 20 miles south-west of Orlando. 5 Swindon has got a railway museum and an arts centre. 6 Possible answer: **They both have beautiful countryside nearby. / Nothing. / Not a lot.**
- Students write one extra question about the text and ask the class.
- ↑ Students write two extra questions to ask the class.
  Extra question examples (with answers): **How many visitors does Walt Disney World have a year? (46 million.) / How many people live in Swindon? (200,000.) / Where is Swindon? (In the south of England, about 40 miles east of Bristol.) / What's one nice thing about Swindon? (The beautiful countryside nearby.)**

Language and culture

In every step, there's a reference to the *Language and culture* section at the end of the unit. Students can read these texts and do the related tasks at home. There's a key to the tasks in the coursebook. However, if you have extra time at the end of the lesson, you could look at the relevant *L&C* in class. The first *L&C* focuses on the differences between a city, town, village and hamlet, *City, town or village?* (coursebook p. 25). For more information on this, look at pages 81/82 of this TRB.

2 Grammar
10 mins

NB: The Grammar section is often divided into two parts: the *You already know* section and the *And now* section. *You already know* focuses on grammar which students should have come across at the A1 or A2.1 level or, in later units, grammar which they have done earlier in the A2.2 book. The *You already know* structures are used as a stepping stone to the new *And now* grammar which is being introduced in the lesson.

You already know: How to make questions
- Read out the questions from the *You already know* Grammar box. Have students repeat them in chorus.
- Board: Present simple / Past simple / Present perfect / *Going to* future
- Ask students to match the questions in the *You already know* Grammar box to the tenses. (Present simple – Where does Rebecca Warren come from?, Past simple – Why did Disney choose Rebecca's presentation?, Present perfect – Has Rebecca ever been to Walt Disney World?, *Going to* future – When is Rebecca going to travel to Florida?)
- Then ask students which words you need to make questions in the Present simple (do / does) and write them next to the tense.
- Do the same for the Past simple. (did)

And now: Subject questions with *Who*
- Read out the questions from the *And now* Grammar box. Have students repeat them in chorus.
- Board: Who lives in Swindon? Ask the class to answer the question. (Rebecca)
- Say: *Can you see the difference? With subject questions we don't need do / does.*

NB: If you have time, and if you feel your students need more consolidation of these grammar points, there's an explanation in German and some example sentences in the *Language study* (p. 12).

2a Questions and answers
5+ mins

- Students work in pairs to ask and answer the questions in the Grammar boxes.

Where does Rebecca Warren come from? – Swindon.
Why did Disney choose Rebecca's presentation? – Because it showed them that Swindon loves fun and magic – exactly like Walt Disney World.
Has Rebecca ever been to Walt Disney World? – No, she hasn't.
When is Rebecca going to travel to Florida? – Next month.
Who lives in Swindon? – Rebecca Warren.
Who organised the online competition? – Disney.
Who is going to travel to Florida with Rebecca? – Her six-year-old niece.

2b Who won the online competition?
5+ mins

- Read out the instructions up to ... *match the answers*, and read the example (question and answer) to the class: *Who won the online competition? – Rebecca.*
- ↓ Students work in pairs and write the questions.
- ↑ Students write an extra *Who?* question to ask the class.
- When the activity is finished, ask individual students to ask their questions to the class.
  Disney bosses: Who chose Swindon / Rebecca's presentation?
  Rebecca and her niece: Who is going to travel to Florida next month?
  Rebecca's niece: Who hopes that Mickey Mouse will come back to Swindon with them?

2c Now you: Your classmates
10 mins

NB: The *Now you* exercises appear in each step. They give students the opportunity to personalise the language items they have just learnt.

- Students work in groups of four or five.
- Read out the first part of the instructions.
- Students write the name of one student from their group in each sentence.
- Then they ask their group questions with *Who?* to see if they were right.

3 A street survey
1/2–3
10 mins

- Read out the first part of the instructions.
- Play ▶ 1/2. Students listen and tick the true sentences.
- Check answers in class.

  ✓ 1, 3, 4
- Read out the second part of the instructions.
- Play ▶ 1/3. Students listen again and correct the false sentences.
  Corrected sentences: **2 The woman doesn't think Swindon has got a lot of attractions for families. 5 The woman and her husband go walking in the hills.**

(I = interviewer, W = woman)
I: Excuse me. Do you have a couple of minutes to answer a few questions?
W: What about?
I: We're doing a survey about Swindon and the local area.
W: Well, OK, but I've only got a couple of minutes.
I: Great. So, the first question is: Do you live in Swindon?
W: No, I don't. I was born here, but I've lived with my husband and our little boy in Hodson for three years.
I: Oh, I know Hodson. It's a lovely little village! How often do you travel into town?
W: Oh, about two or three times a week. Mostly for shopping.
I: And do you come into town for a day out with the family or to go out in the evening?
W: Well, there isn't a lot to do here, especially with a young child! Our son loves trains, so when my husband goes to watch the football – he's a big Swindon Town fan – we sometimes visit the railway museum.
I: So how do you think we could make the town more attractive for you?
W: Well, we need more things for families to do. Now that we're twinned with Walt Disney World, maybe we could have a small theme park, or a Disney festival. Our son would really like that.
I: That's a good idea. OK, now, about the local area. You live in Hodson, so what do you do in the area around Swindon?
W: Oh, we love being in the countryside. It's so beautiful around Swindon. We're an active family, so we often go for walks. When our son's with us, we often go to a lake to walk – he likes watching the boats.
I: Oh, that's nice. The lakes *are* beautiful.
W: Yes, they are. Or if my son's at his grandmother's and it's just me and my husband, we go walking in the hills. It's so lovely there!
I: OK, thank you, that's everything. We'll use the information to try to make Swindon a better place for everyone. Thank you for your time.

4a How to say it: Describing your town and area

- Play ▶ 1/4 and have the class repeat the phrases in chorus.

Tip: Listen and repeat With every *How to say it*, students are asked to listen and repeat. This choral repetition gives each student a chance to practise the phrases. It also allows more hesitant students to practise speaking without doing it in front of the class.

1/4
5+ mins

It's a big city. It's in the east of Germany. It's about 200 kilometres south of Berlin. About five hundred thousand people live there. It's got a lot of old buildings. It's famous for its *Stollen*.

Dresden

If short of time

If you notice you're getting short of time,
- do ***Exercise 4b*** as a class activity. Ask students to tell you three things about the town / local area.
- do just one of the ***Round up*** activities.
- do only one or two questions of ***Exercise 5b*** as a class discussion.

4b Now you: Your town and local area
5 mins

- Students work in pairs to describe their town and the local area.
- After the activity, ask volunteers to tell you one interesting thing they heard from their partner.

Round up

NB: The *Round up* activities consolidate the structures which were introduced and practised in the lesson. They also facilitate time flexibility at the end of the lesson. If you have enough time, you can do both *Round up* activities. If you're short of time, students can choose one or the other *Round up* activity.

5a Who is it?
5– mins

- Ask the class the questions.

The Queen (lives in Buckingham Palace). Bram Stoker (wrote Dracula).
- Then ask individual (confident) students to ask their own questions with *Who?* to the class.
- ↓ Give students time to write down one or two questions first.
  Board: lives, plays, sings; played, sang, won, wrote

5b Talk about it
5– mins

Tip: Free speaking activities It's important to provide students with the opportunity for free-speaking activities where the main focus is on fluency rather than accuracy. These *Talk about it tasks* provide an ideal opportunity for students to 'chat' and practise the language in small groups / with a partner in a relaxed manner.

- Students work in small groups or in pairs, and choose one or more of the questions to chat freely about. They can just talk about one, or two, or all of the questions.
- If communication seems to have come to a standstill, join the group / pair and ask additional questions.

And finally ...
5+ mins

Point out the following features of the cousebook and give a short explanation:

- **Language study** (p. 12): An overview of the grammar in the step with exercises – the *You already know* is revision grammar, the *And now* is the grammar that is introduced in the step. Students can do this in their books or online. Tell them to go to www.klett-langenscheidt.de/networknow/selfstudy and type in the Language study code which is given at the top of each Language study page. Online they can find – in addition to the exercises from their books – extra practice of the A1 and A2.1 level grammar.
- **Selfstudy** (p. 13): There is one page of homework after every classroom step which provides consolidation and practice of the areas which have been covered. Students can do this in their books or online and check their answers at the back of their books.
- **Keys** (p. 129) to the Language study and Selfstudy exercises.
- **Language and culture** (p. 25), Step 1: *City, town or village?* and the corresponding task.

And point out ...
- The **FAQ** *What can I read that's not too difficult?* at the end of the Selfstudy page (p. 13). FAQ reflects the kind of questions that more advanced learners may ask in order to improve their independent learning. Students can find more questions with more detailed answers on pages 198/199.

Unit 1 Step 2 Away

Contents

Text topic	An advertisement for the Chicken Hotel
Functions	Asking for hotel information; Talking about hotel facilities; Booking a hotel room
Vocabulary	Hotels and facilities
Grammar	Passive (Present simple and Past simple)

Lesson notes

Additional material

For optional and additional material for Unit 1, Step 2, see pages 82/83.
Refer to this section before your lesson as some of the materials require preparation.

Optional stages

Optional stages of the lesson are written in grey in these notes.

Starter:
Your last holiday
5 mins

Tip: *Starter* exercises The aim of the *Starter* exercise is to sensitise the class to the topic, to provide an opportunity to talk freely and to allow possible latecomers to pick up on the theme immediately without fear of having missed something vital to the lesson. Often you can choose to do the *Starter* exercises as a class, or as group or pair work.

- Students work in pairs to complete the *Starter* task.
  ! Remind students that *What was ... like?* asks for a general description of something.
- Ask individual students to tell the class about their partner's last holiday.

1a Comprehension
5 mins

- Ask students if they have any pets / what they do with their pets when they go on holiday.
- Tell students they are going to read about a very special hotel.
- Students read the text silently and tick the true sentences.
- Check answers in class.
  ✓ 4
- Students then correct the false sentences.
  Corrected sentences: **1 Chickens can stay at the Chicken Hotel when people want to go on holiday. 2 Four to six chickens can stay in one room. 3 It costs £7.00. ((4 chickens x 75p = £3.00) + (2 nights x £2.00 = £4.00) = £7.00)) 5 The chicken butler can visit your home to give your chickens food and water.**

Language and culture

Students can read the text *Pets* (p. 25) and do the related tasks at home – or you can use this as a 'filler' if you have time at the end of the lesson. For more information on this, look at page 83 of this TRB.

1b What services are offered at the Chicken Hotel?
5 mins

- Students look back at the text, underline the matching sentences, then read them out.

1 ... rooms are designed for four to six chickens. 2 The rooms are, of course, cleaned every day. 3 And where is food served? 4 ..., meals aren't served in the rooms. 5 Your chickens are brought from your home to the hotel ...

2 Grammar
5+ mins

Passive (Present simple and Past simple)
- Read out the sentences from the Grammar box. Have students repeat them in chorus.
- Board: Food is served in the dining area.
  Ask: *Do we know who serves the food?* (No.) *Is it important who serves the food?* (No.)
- Board: The chickens are given fresh water every day. Ask: *Is this about the present or the past?*
  Say: *To make passive sentences in the present, we need is / are plus the third form of the verb.*
- Board: The chickens were brought to the hotel yesterday.
  Ask: *Is this about the present or the past?* Say: *To make passive sentences in the past we need was / were plus the third form of the verb.*

2a Hotel information
10 mins

- Read out the instructions and the example.
- Students write the passive sentences. Ask individual students to read them out.
  2 The front door is locked at midnight. 3 Internet access isn't provided in the rooms. 4 The rooms are cleaned every day from 10.00 am. 5 Towels are changed if you put them on the floor. 6 Towels aren't changed if they are left on the rail.

2b Now you: Your last stay in a hotel
5+ mins

- Demonstrate the activity using the example questions.
- Ask student to work in pairs and do the activity.
- ↓ Elicit the questions and write them on the board. (When was the door locked? ...)
- Ask individual students to report back to the class and tell them one piece of information.

Tip: Task complexity (2) When an exercise can be made easier for the whole class, you see ↓, and ↑ means it can be made more complex. This is a decision the teacher makes for the class. Now, for some exercises, we're introducing a system whereby the student can decide for him- / herself how adventurous he / she wants to be! All the class does the same basic exercise but to varying degrees of complexity, signalled by a star system. It involves writing three short tasks on the board. The first task (*) is easier than in the coursebook; the second task (**) is the standard task as in the coursebook; the third task (***) is more complex than in the coursebook.

2c Holiday problems
1/10–11
10 mins

- Ask individual students if they have ever had a bad holiday. If yes, where? What happened?
- Tell students they are going to listen to Kevin talking about a bad holiday he had.
- Read out the instructions. Play ▶ 1/10. Students listen and choose the correct information.

  1 taxi, 2 credit card, 3 front door, 4 a restaurant, 5 some money
- Explain the 'star system': *Maybe you had a hard day at work today and you're tired? You can do an easier task – a one-star task. Most of you can do the standard task that you read in the coursebook – the two-star task. Do you want to work a bit harder? – Then do the three-star task.*

  Board:

*	Answer questions 1, 3 and 5.
**	As in the coursebook.
***	Do ** and then tell the class one more piece of information which you heard about Kevin's holiday.

- Say: *Listen again. Answer the questions*. Allow students time to read the questions. Play ▶ 1/11.
  1 Because their plane was half an hour late. 2 He had to leave the restaurant and find a bank. 3 They thought it would be safer. 4 It was ten minutes walk away. 5 A hundred and fifty euros.

(S = Susannah, K = Kevin)
S: Hi, Kevin! I haven't seen you and Ruth since you got back from your holiday in Mallorca. How was it?
K: Oh, don't ask!
S: Why?
K: Well, you know that we found a really cheap holiday on the Internet? We know now why it was so cheap. It was a complete disaster from start to finish.
S: What happened?
K: It started at the airport in Palma. Our plane was half an hour late because of bad weather. The hotel said that they would pick us up from the airport in their shuttle bus. But when we got out of the terminal, it wasn't there! So we had to take a taxi – and that cost a hundred euros because it was so far to the hotel!
S: That's expensive!
K: I know! And things didn't get better. On the first evening, we went out for dinner at a restaurant nearby. We had a lovely meal, and at the end of it I wanted to pay by credit card. But they weren't accepted, only cash! I had to leave the restaurant and find a bank. It took me about half an hour!
S: Oh dear!
K: And when we got back to the hotel, the front door to the hotel was locked and we didn't have our key with us. We thought it would be safer to leave it at reception, and they didn't tell us that the front door was locked at eleven-thirty.
S: So what did you do?
K: Well, there was a bell for reception, so we rang it for about fifteen minutes before someone came and opened the door for us.
S: That's not really a 24-hour reception, then!

→

K: No, it isn't! Then the next morning, we found out that breakfast wasn't served in the hotel. We were sent to a restaurant about ten minutes walk away!
S: That's a long way when you've just got up!
K: It certainly is! And later in the week, the worst thing happened. Some money was stolen from my bag!
S: Oh, no! How did that happen?
K: When we were on the beach. We were there all day, sunbathing and swimming. We didn't notice anything. It was only when we got back to the hotel room and I wanted to get some money for dinner that evening that I noticed. A hundred and fifty euros gone!
S: Oh, my goodness! That's a lot of money.
K: Yes, it is! We were just happy to leave at the end of the week. So our cheap holiday turned out to be a lot more expensive than we thought!

3a Vocabulary: Hotel facilities
5 mins

- Read out the instructions to the class. Students match the two halves.
- Check answers in class.

1d), 2a), 3b), 4h), 5g), 6c), 7e), 8f)

If short of time

If you notice you're getting short of time,
- do ***Exercise 3b*** as a class activity.
- do just one of the ***Round up*** activities.
- do only one or two questions of ***Exercise 5b*** as a class discussion.

3b Now you: The facilities you need in a hotel
10 mins

- Demonstrate the task.
- Students work in small groups and talk to each other.
- Ask one student to report back to the class on the top three facilities from their group.

4a How to say it: Making an enquiry to a hotel
1/12
5 mins

- Play ▶ 1/12 and have the class repeat the phrases in chorus.

I'm calling to ask for some information.
I'd like to stay for three nights from 1st to 4th June.
Do you have a single room with balcony?
Is breakfast included in the price?
Is parking available?
Does Internet access cost extra?
Thanks for your help.

4b An email enquiry
10 mins

- Students write a short email with a partner and then give it to another pair to read.
- If time permits, ask students to make any corrections to the mail they receive.

Round up
5a Role play
5– mins

- Read out the instructions. Students work in pairs and role play the conversation.

5b Talk about it
5 mins

Tip: Learner autonomy (1) – student choice It's a good idea to promote student choice / learner autonomy in class. One way of doing this in the *Talk about it* sections of the book is to encourage students to decide in their groups which questions they want to chat about.

- Students work in small groups or in pairs, and choose one or more of the questions to chat freely about. They can just talk about one, or two, or all of the questions.
- If communication seems to have come to a standstill, ask additional questions.

And finally ...
5+ mins

Remind students of the following:
- **Language study** (p. 16): An overview of the grammar of the step with exercises. Students can do this in their books or online.
- **Selfstudy** (p. 17): Students can do this in their books or online.
- **Keys** (p. 129) to the Language study and Selfstudy exercises.
- **Language and culture** (p. 25), Step 2: *Pets* and the corresponding tasks. Encourage students to do the Internet task at home.

Unit 1 Step 3 Staying over

Contents

Realia	Hotel information brochure
Functions	Talking about different types of holiday accommodation; Comparing things
Vocabulary	Abbreviations in emails and letters
Reading	Couch surfing
Grammar	**You already know:** Comparatives *(cheaper than / more expensive than)* **And now:** Comparatives *((not) as ... as ...)*
Write it right	Abbreviations

Lesson notes

Additional material

For optional and additional material for Unit 1, Step 3, see pages 83/84.
Refer to this section before your lesson as some of the materials require preparation.

Optional stages

Optional stages of the lesson are written in grey in these notes.

**Starter:
Somewhere to stay**
5 mins

- Ask the class the *Starter* question. Write their answers on the board (e.g. hotel, bed and breakfast, motel, camping, caravan).

**Places to stay
1a Everything you need?**
5+ mins

NB: In Step 3 of each unit, there's always a piece of realia as the main focus. So students are presented with something they might actually experience in real life. It's important that students realise that, although they may encounter unknown words, they shouldn't panic! They will still probably be able to understand enough to cope with the task and this is good practice for coping with English in real-life situations.

- Direct the students' attention to the Holiday Inn Hotel's brochure (top right hand corner of page 18). Say: *Look at this information about the Holiday Inn.* Assure students that it isn't always necessary to understand every word of a text – they can still cope in everyday situations.
- Ask: *Where is this hotel?* (Swindon.) *How many stars does it have?* (Three.)
- Say*: Read the information about the Holiday Inn and tick the true sentences.*
- Check answers in class. Students then correct the false sentences.

  ✓ 2, 4, 6

  Corrected sentences: **1 It isn't difficult / It's easy to get to the centre of Swindon from the Holiday Inn. / The Holiday Inn is located within easy reach of Swindon town centre. 3 It's a three-star hotel. 5 The hotel has a health and fitness club.**

1b A trip to the US
1/17
5+ mins

- Read out the instructions to the class. Play ▶ 1/17. Check answers in class.

✓ 1, 2, 4, 5, 6

(C = Clare, J = Josie)
C: So have you got the tickets for your trip to the USA, Josie?
J: Yes, we have – we got a really good deal on the flights. We're flying to San Francisco on 30th June – and then we're going to spend two months travelling round California and the West Coast.
C: Wow! Fantastic! So, have you decided where to stay?
J: That's a bit of a problem. My mum says we can stay with her friends in San Francisco, but I don't really want to. After that, I think we're going to decide as we go.
C: Well, staying with friends is better than going to a hotel. Hmm ... my aunt and uncle rented a camper van when they went to the US.
J: Well, that would be great, but we can't afford it. We thought about hiring a car and sleeping in it ...

→

C: Ooh! That sounds very uncomfortable! That's not as nice as sleeping in a proper bed.
J: Yes, but they have very big cars in the States – and sleeping in a car is a lot cheaper than hiring a camper van.
C: What about camping? Camping is more comfortable than sleeping in the car!
J: Ooh, yucky! All those insect and things! And it can be dangerous ... you know ... you hear about ... bears ... sometimes camping isn't as safe as people think!
C: Could you stay in motels?
J: No, staying in motels every night would be as expensive as getting a camper van.
C: Have you thought about couch surfing?
J: Is that where you contact people on the Internet and stay with them? My mum doesn't like that idea ...
C: So where are you going to visit? I'd love to see the Grand Canyon one day.

2 Grammar
10– mins

NB: There's only a minor grammar element in Step 3 – the main focus is on the realia tasks and reading.

You already know: Comparatives *(cheaper than / more expensive than)*
- Read out the sentences from the *You already know* Grammar box. Have students repeat them in chorus.

And now: Comparatives *((not) as expensive as)*
- Read out the sentences from the *And now* Grammar box. Have students repeat them in chorus.
- Board: motel $20, hotel $20, camping $10
  A: The motel is ___ ________ ___ the hotel. (cheap)
  B: Camping isn't ___ ________ ___ the hotel. (expensive)
  Ask students to complete the sentences. (The motel is as cheap as the hotel. Camping isn't as expensive as the hotel.)
- Ask: *Which sentence shows two things are the same?* (A) *Which sentence shows two things are different*? (B)

2a What's best?
1/18
5+ mins

- Tell students they are going to listen to Josie again. Read out the instructions.
- Ensure students have understood they only need to write the letter not the whole phrase.
- Allow time for students to read the phrases and the sentences. Play ▶ 1/18.
- Students do the task. If necessary, play ▶ 1/18 again.
- Ask individual students to read the sentences out to the class to check.
  1d), 2b), 3e), 4f), 5c), 6a)

Audio script: see above in *Exercise 1b*.

2b Now you: Your holidays
5 mins

- Read out the instructions.
- Students chat in small groups about the topic using the questions as prompts.

Couch surfing
3a Reading
10 mins

- Tell the class: *You're going to read a text about couch surfing. What do you think that could be?*

Language and culture

Students can read the text *Web addresses* (p. 25) and do the related task at home – or you can use this as a 'filler' if you have time at the end of the lesson. For more information on this, look at page 84 of this TRB.

3b Talk about it
5 mins

- Allow students time to read the text silently to find out what couch surfing is. Then ask individual students to tell the class about the text.
  NB: Students shouldn't be asked to read this text aloud. They need the opportunity to digest the information without being distracted by pronunciation and new vocabulary.
- Ask students to cover the text and answer the questions.
- Board: * Don't cover the text.
  ** As in the coursebook.
  *** Do **. Then write one more question about the text and ask it to the class.

- Students ask and answer the questions with a partner. Check the answers in class.
- ↑ Write these extra questions on the board for faster students to discuss.
  Board: Would you couch surf on holiday? Why / Why not?
  Would you offer couch surfers accommodation in your flat / house? Why / Why not?

  1 The chance for visitors to a country to stay with someone for free. 2 Casey Fenton started it when he emailed students at the University of Iceland to ask for a place to stay. 3 Possible answers: **Advantages – You can make friends around the world. It's cheap. Disadvantages – It's dangerous. You don't know the people. You might not like the people. The house might be dirty.**

If short of time

If you notice you're getting short of time,
- do ***Exercise 3c*** as a class activity.
- ask individual students to read out the sentences in the circles in ***Exercise 5***. Students don't write their own sentences.

3c Now you: Your guests
10– mins

- Encourage students to work with a different partner from the one they worked with in *Exercise 3b*.

Tip: Pair / Group work (1) Changing pairs / groups in class is important as it not only allows the students to get to know each other better, but also gets students used to a range of different voices / pronunciation / speed of speech / accent etc. Try to ensure that students work with different people each week. It's a good idea to use activities and games to allocate pairs / change groups. For some ideas on this, see page 84 of this TRB.

- Students chat with a partner about the topic, using the questions as prompts.

4a Write it right
5 mins

- Students read the email silently and then answer the question.

She wants to stay at Anna's house.

4b What does it mean?
5 mins

- Board: bzw.
  Ask students what this means / stands for. (beziehungsweise)
- Say: *These short forms are called 'abbreviations'.*
- Ask students to work with a partner to explain the abbreviations in Julia's mail.
  1 television, 2 post meridiem (it's Latin and means after the middle of the day, so it's used to talk about any time after 12pm), 3 for example, 4 as soon as possible, 5 Here's some more information. / I've forgotten to say.
- Ask students what the *x* in Julia's mail means. Refer them to the answer on page 127. (Kiss)
- Students then match the German abbreviations to the English ones.
- Check answers in class by asking individual students to write an answer on the board.
  a) GmbH, b) ca., c) usw., d) u.A.w.g., e) Abt., f) d.h., g) b.w., h) Betr.
  ! GmbH = Gesellschaft mit beschränkter Haftung, ca. = circa, usw. = und so weiter, u.A.w.g. = um Antwort wird gebeten, Abt. = Abteilung, d.h. = das heißt, b.w. = bitte wenden, Betr. = Betreff

4c Write now
10– mins

- Read out the instructions.
- Each student writes a short mail and then gives it to another student to read.
- ↓ Students write a short email with a partner and then give it to another pair to read.
- If time permits, ask students to correct the mail they receive and hand it back.

5 Travelling in circles
5+ mins

- Read out the instructions. Students complete the task.

Couchsurfers live all over the world. It's a great way to travel and meet people. You can even visit Antarctica. There are nearly three million members.

And finally ...
5+ mins

Remind students of the following:
- **Language study** (p. 20): An overview of the grammar of the step (both *You already know* and *And now*) with exercises. Students can do this in their books or online.
- **Selfstudy** (p. 20): Students can do this in their books or online.
- **Keys** (p. 129) to the Language study and Selfstudy exercises.
- **Language and culture** (p. 25), Step 3: *Web addresses* and the corresponding task. Refer students to the *Listen in* task. (For more information on this, look at page 84 of this TRB.)

And point out ...
- **Reading: First night in London** (p. 21): A story 'just for fun' with a glossary of unknown words. If you want to use this story in class, there are some ideas on how to exploit it on page 120.

Unit 1 Now I can

Contents — **Review of vocabulary, functions and structures in Unit 1**

Starter	Talking about hotel facilities
Part 1	Describing my town and local area; Talking about hotel facilities; Talking about different types of holiday accommodation; Comparing things
Part 2	Describing your town and local area; Talking about hotel facilities
Part 3	Asking for hotel information; Talking about hotel facilities; Booking a hotel room
Part 4	Graded writing tasks

Lesson notes

Additional material

For optional and additional material for Unit 1, *Now I can*, see pages 84/85.
Refer to this section before your lesson as some of the materials require preparation.

Optional stages

Optional stages of the lesson are written in grey in these notes.

Now I can pages
5 mins

Tell the students that the *Now I can* pages revise and consolidate what they've learned in the previous three steps. There's no new language to learn. The *Now I can: ...* at the top of the pages can be used as a checklist. Next to each newly learned skill or vocabulary item there's a symbol. These symbols can be found again next to each task and tell students which skill or which vocabulary item is being practised. They link back to the unit aims on the photo page. Most of the tasks in *Now I can* focus on more than one skill or vocabulary item.

Starter: Look back
5 mins

- Point to the picture from the Chicken Hotel text and ask students the *Starter* questions.

  Possible answers: **It's a hotel for chickens. It was opened in 2010. It has four-star rooms. It costs 75p per chicken (+ £2.00 per room per night). There's an all-you-can-eat buffet for breakfast, shuttle service and butler service.**

Starter: Now look forward
5 mins

Tip: Grouping students When grouping students to work on longer tasks, it's a good idea to mix the groups so you have more able and less able students working together within each group. This ensures you will have groups working at a similar pace, and that the more able students can help the less able ones.

- Read out the *Now look forward* instructions and ask students to work in groups of four to five.

Part 1:
1a Designer accommodation
5+ mins

- Read out the first part of the instructions and the types of visitors.
- Each group chooses one target group from the types of visitors.
  ! Ensure that the groups choose different target groups so that there will be a variety of presentations later in the lesson.
- Demonstrate the second part of the task.
  Board: a group of foreign teenagers
  Ask the class what type of accommodation would be best for this group. (campsite / hotel / youth hostel)
- Students then decide on a type of accommodation to suit their target group.

1b What do they need?
10 mins

- ↓ Create a spider diagram on the board by eliciting hotel facilities from the students (e.g. sauna, pool, children's play area, gym, mini bar, Internet access, parking, bar, restaurant, BBQ area).
- In their groups, students make a list of useful / attractive facilities for their target groups and then choose the top four.

1c Where is it?
10+ mins

- Read out the instructions and questions to the class.
- In their groups, students talk about a location for their accommodation and make notes.

Part 2:
If short of time

If you notice you're getting short of time,
- just do the first part of the listening task in ***Exercise 2a***.

2a An exclusive hotel
1/21–22
10 mins

- Read out the instructions.
- Play ▶ 1/21. Students listen and tick the correct option.

✓ 1

- Say: *Listen again and make notes about the hotel's location and facilities.* Play ▶ 1/22.
  Location: in the south of England, a few minutes from the beach, the nearest town is Exeter
  Facilities: a talking lift, a library of Braille books and audio materials, voice-controlled electronic equipment like television, Internet access, etc., large gardens – including a sculpture garden, facilities for guests with guide dogs

> (HM = hotel manager)
> HM: Ladies and gentlemen. I'm from the Torrington Hotel in the south of England and I'd like to tell you about our wonderful hotel.
> The Torrington Hotel is a lovely old house in beautiful gardens, and it is also only a few minutes from the beach.
> We are a relatively small hotel, with rooms for 20 guests, which means we can offer a more personalised service in a friendly and relaxed atmosphere.
> The hotel is only five minutes' walk from the sea and there is a very nice, clean beach.
> The nearest city is Exeter. Exeter is famous for its cathedral and its university and it has a lot of good shops. There is also a small airport there.
> But the most important thing about our hotel is that it is a very exclusive hotel. It is exclusively for people who are blind, or partially sighted, and their partners, too, of course.
> We have special facilities for blind and partially sighted visitors, including a talking lift, a library of Braille books and audio materials, and voice-controlled electronic equipment like televisions, Internet access, etc. There are large gardens, including a sculpture garden, where visitors can touch and feel the sculptures. And of course we have facilities for guests with guide dogs.
> So, to finish, this is a beautiful hotel which gives blind and partially sighted people a safe, comfortable and stress-free holiday in a beautiful location. So, do you have any questions?

2b We'd like to tell you about our ...
10+ mins

Tip: Error correction When the aim of a speaking task is for students to speak fluently, it's not a good idea to stop them and correct them, as this will stop the flow of the conversation / presentation. However, many students appreciate being corrected. One way around this is to listen to their conversation / presentation and make some notes on the most important mistakes. When the task has finished, either correct these key mistakes or write one or two gap-fill sentences on the board linked to these mistakes and ask the students to put in the correct phrase.

- Read out the instructions.
- Emphasise that each member of the group should contribute something to the presentation.
- While the other class members are listening, they should think of questions to ask the group about their holiday accommodation, its guests, its facilities and its location.

Part 3:
I'd like to book
10+ mins

- First ask students to write down four questions. Give students about five minutes to do this. Then ask four volunteers to read out one question each. This will enable the less able students to finish their questions or to 'borrow' one that they hear.
- Ask students to work with a partner from another group and role play the phone call.
- If you have enough time, ask one or two pairs to act out their phone call. If you don't have enough time, ask one or two students to report back on the information they found out about their partners' accommodation.

4 Now you choose
15 mins

Tip: Task complexity (3) At the end of each *Now I can* section there is a choice of three tasks for students to do. These could be writing or speaking tasks. The tasks are graded using a star system: * easy, ** standard, *** challenging. This is a decision each student can make for him- / herself. Explain this to the students saying they can choose the level of difficulty.

→

- Board: * easy, ** standard, *** challenging
  Explain the star system in the *Now I can* section to the class.
- Tell students they should choose one of these tasks.
- Allow time for students to read the tasks and choose one.
- Tell students how long they have to complete the task (depending on how much time is left in the lesson).
- Monitor and help with any vocabulary / useful phrases needed.
- When students are finished, ask them to form a group with other students who completed the same task.
- Students read each other's work and decide on one to read out to the whole class.
- One student then reads out the text to the class.

And finally ...
5 mins

Look back at *In this unit, you will learn to: ...* (p. 9) to show your students how much they have learnt in this unit, to say how well they've done and to let them reflect on where they need more practice.

Point out the following features of the coursebook and give a short explanation:

- **Test yourself** (p. 24): Students can do this progress test and check their answers (p. 129).
- **Language and culture** (p. 25): Refer your students to any L&C texts and tasks that weren't done in class.
- **Now me** (p. 26): Students can do some free writing, using the vocabulary and structures they've learned in Unit 1. Introduce the idea of writing a blog by asking if any of the students write or read blogs. Read the information box: ***Now blog*** to the students. Students then read *Kathy's blog* and use this as a model for their own. The *Now explore the Internet* section encourages students to use the Internet to read about unusual hotels. Finally, refer students to the *Portfolio* section at the end and encourage them to photocopy the *Now me* pages for their personal dossier.

Your notes

Unit 2 Step 1 Learning

Contents

Text topic	An article about Bholaram Das, the oldest student in India
Functions	Talking about education and skills; Defining things, people and places
Vocabulary	Education and learning
Grammar	Relative pronouns *(that / which, who, where)*

Lesson notes

Additional material

For optional and additional material for Unit 2, Step 1, see pages 85/86.
Refer to this section before your lesson as some of the materials require preparation.

Optional stages

Optional stages of the lesson are written in grey in these notes.

Photo page
5 mins

- Hold up your open book at page 27 and introduce the topic of the unit by looking at the pictures with the class. Ask the questions to individual students.
- Refer students to *In this unit, you will learn to: ...* . Give them a minute to read the learning aims.

Starter:
Life-long learning
5 mins

- With closed books, ask individual students the *Starter* questions.

1a Comprehension
10 mins

- Still with closed books, students speculate about the text.
- Board: 100-year-old, university, India Students predict what they think the text is about.
- Students turn to page 28 to read the text and check their ideas.
- Read out the comprehension instructions.
- Board: * Students can refer to the text and underline the answers.
  ** As in the coursebook.
  *** Do ** and then make sentences about Bholaram with: *hundred-year-old, hundredth, a hundred.*

  (Hundred-year-old Bholaram Das has become the oldest student in India. On his hundredth birthday, he spoke to reporters. Bholaram Das decides to learn something new at the age of a hundred.)
- Ask volunteers to tell the class what they remember about the numbers.
- Students then read the text again and underline any information they couldn't remember.
- Ask individual students to read out any information they couldn't remember to the class.
  55 – His son got a doctorate. | 19 – He went to prison. | two – He was in prison for two months. | the 1930s – He trained and worked as a teacher. | 1971 – He retired. | 98 – He worked as a lawyer from home until he was 98.

Language and culture

Students can read the text *Schooldays* (p. 43) and do the related task at home – or you can use this as a 'filler' if you have time at the end of the lesson. For more information on this, look at page 86 of this TRB.

1b Vocabulary: Education and learning
5+ mins

! Check the meaning of *apprenticeship* (a training programme where people learn a job).
- Read out the instructions to the class.
- Students work individually and cross out the words that don't fit.
- Students check with a partner, then check in class.
  1 learn | study | ~~work~~, 2 ~~apprenticeship~~ | college | university, 3 course | ~~homework~~ | lesson, 4 ~~apprentice~~ | doctorate | student (both are related to university) / apprentice | ~~doctorate~~ | student (both are people), 5 certificate | diploma | ~~subject~~

NB: Refer students to the Unit vocabulary (pages 152–176) and to the Dictionary (pages 177–196). Please see *And point out ...* at the end of these notes.

2 Grammar
5 mins

Relative pronouns *(that / which, who, where)*
- Read out the sentences from the Grammar box. Have students repeat them in chorus.

→

- Board:

1 that / which	2 who	3 where
a) a person	b) a place	c) a thing

  Ask students to match the items. Say: *We use 'that' or 'which' for …* (a thing). *We use 'who' for …* (a person). *We use 'where' for …* (a place). Draw lines to match the items. (1c), 2a), 3b))

2a About Bholaram
10– mins

- Demonstrate the task by completing the first sentence.
- ↓ Read out the sentences. After each sentence ask: *(University): thing, place or person?*
- Students then read the sentences and add *that / which, who* or *where.*
- ↓ Check the answers to this section before students do the matching.
- Then students match the beginnings of the sentences to the endings.
- ↑ Students who finish quickly can be asked to write one extra sentence about something in the article, using *who, that / which* or *where.*
- Check answers in class.
  1 where b), 2 who e), 3 that / which f), 4 where a), 5 that / which d), 6 who c)

2b What's the word?
10 mins

Tip: Exchange information When doing a task where students do an A / B activity at the back of the book, clarity is the key word. Put all the A Students on one side of the room and all the B Students on the other. Write 'A:' and 'B:' on the board and note down the page number. Ask each group to read their task together before pairing up with students from the other group.

- Divide the class into two groups, A / B.
- Say: *A students, turn to page 123. B students, turn to page 125.*
- Read out the instructions on p. 123.
- Students work in A / B pairs and take it in turns to describe the words in their crossword.
- When they have finished, they can work out the keyword.
  Keyword: apprentice

3 How to say it: Talking about education and skills
1/24
5 mins

- Play ▶ 1/24. Students listen and repeat the sentences.

4a An interview
1/25–26
10 mins

- Read out the first part of the instructions and the gist question.
- Play ▶ 1/25. Students listen and write down the answer.
- Check answer in class.
  He's helping her to find the right job because he works at the job centre.
- Read out the second part of the instructions. Give students time to read the form.
- Play ▶ 1/26. Students listen and complete the form.
- ↓ Play ▶ 1/26 and stop the CD after each piece of key information to allow students time to write down the answers.
- Students compare answers in pairs. If necessary, play ▶ 1/26 again.
- Check answers in class.
  (1) 2002, (2) Training, (3) assistant, (4) diploma, (5) office, (6) beginner

(S1 = job centre employee, S2 = job-seeker)
S1: So, in this first meeting, we need to get some basic information about your education and skills so that we can try and find the right thing for you.
S2: All right.
S1: OK. Let's look at your education first. Where did you go to school?
S2: I went to Liphook Secondary School in Brighton.
S1: And when did you start and finish school?
S2: Oh, let me think … er … I started in 2002 and finished in … er … 2007.
S1: 2002 … to 2007 … . OK. Right, now, what did you do after you left school?
S2: I went to Richmond Training College to do a one-year apprenticeship to become an office assistant.
S1: So you're a qualified office assistant?
S2: That's right. I have a diploma from the college.
S1: Apprenticeship … diploma … as an office … assistant … . All right. Have you done any other courses?
S2: Er …, well, I did a Spanish course at an evening school last year.

S1: Oh, languages are always a good thing to have when you're looking for a job. Did you do an exam at the end?
S2: Yes, I did and I passed!
S1: So you have a certificate?
S2: Oh, yes, from the Cervantes Institute.
S1: Intermediate ... Spanish ... certificate ... . Great, that's another useful qualification. Any other courses?
S2: I did a short course in advanced office communication last month – you know, how to give a presentation, deal with customers, organise events, that kind of thing. But there was no certificate for that.
S1: Well, that's OK, it's still another course that we can write down. Advanced ... office ... communication. OK, now what other skills do you have? Obviously languages with the Spanish –
S2: ... – and Japanese. I've started learning Japanese, but I'm only a beginner.
S1: Wow, Japanese, how exotic! That's another good thing for a job application – Japanese is an important business language. Anything else?
S2: Well, I can use all the usual computer programs that you need in an office, like Word, Excel, PowerPoint ... . But that's everything, I think.
S1: That's good! Computer skills are really important for a job. Right, well, we'll use this information to make a profile and then see what jobs there are at the moment which fit your education and skills. That'll take a couple of days, so can you come to another meeting at the end of the week? On Friday?

If short of time

If you notice you're getting short of time,
- do ***Exercise 4b*** as a class activity.
- do just one of the ***Round up*** activities.
- do only one or two questions of ***Exercise 5b*** as a class discussion.

4b Now you: Your education and skills
10 mins

- Demonstrate this task by asking one or two students one of the questions.
- Students work in pairs and ask / answer the questions.
- Ask individual students to tell you two pieces of information about their partner.

Round up
5a Quiz time
5– mins

- Volunteers read out the sentences. The class say who / what / where the sentences are about.
- Students work in small groups to make similar sentences. They then read their sentences out to the class. The class guess who / what / where they are about.
  Dinner for One, Clint Eastwood, Madrid

5b Talk about it
5+ mins

Tip: Learner autonomy (2) – independent learners It's important that students start to become more independent learners. The *Talk about it* exercises are a good possibility to introduce student choice to the lesson. Remind students that they can choose which questions to 'chat' about.

- Students work in small groups or in pairs, and choose one or more of the questions to chat freely about. They can just talk about one, or two, or all of the questions.
- If communication seems to have come to a standstill, ask additional questions.

And finally ...
5+ mins

Remind students of the following:
- **Language study** (p. 30): An overview of the grammar of the step with exercises. Students can do this in their books or online.
- **Selfstudy** (p. 31): Students can do this in their books or online.
- **Keys** (p. 129 f.) to the Language study and Selfstudy exercises.
- **Language and culture** (p. 43), Step 1: *Schooldays* and the corresponding task.

And point out ...
- the **Unit vocabulary** (pp. 152–176), a chronological list of words in the coursebook. Students can use it to study specific vocabulary from each step – it's also useful if a student has missed a lesson and wants to catch up on the missed vocabulary.
  There are also lists of word groups and phrases from each step. They can be listened to on the Internet to help students with pronunciation and word stress – a code is provided (see 'Tipp' on page 152).
- the **Dictionary** (pp. 177–196), an alphabetical list of all the words in the coursebook so students can easily look up unknown vocabulary from texts and exercises. These words can also be listened to on the Internet – a code is provided on page 177.

Unit 2 Step 2 Working

Contents

Text topic An interview about Hiro Yamamoto an *oshiya* (a 'pusher')
Functions Talking about different ways of working; Describing jobs and responsibilities
Vocabulary The world of work
Grammar Question tags (*to be*, present simple)

Lesson notes

Additional material
For optional and additional material for Unit 2, Step 2, see pages 86/87.
Refer to this section before your lesson as some of the materials require preparation.

Optional stages
Optional stages of the lesson are written in grey in these notes.

Starter: Jobs
5 mins

- Ask students to work in two groups, A / B. Ask for a volunteer in each group to be the 'secretary' for the group. This person will write the list.
- Say: *Group A, you have two minutes to think of and write down as many outside jobs as you can; Group B, you have two minutes to think of and write down as many inside jobs as you can.*
- After two minutes, stop the activity and ask the 'secretary' from each group to read out their list. Write the words on the board.
  Possible answers: **outside jobs: fisherman, gardener, farmer, window cleaner, police officer, tennis trainer, dog walker, zookeeper, binman;**
  inside jobs: nurse, air steward, secretary, teacher, optician, doctor, receptionist, cook, plumber

1a Comprehension
10 mins

Tip: Using the pictures You can use the pictures linked to the reading texts to introduce the topic and provide a lead-in to the texts. By doing this, students will be encouraged to think about what the text might be about before they start to read. It provides students with a starting point to read the text and generates interest in what they are about to read.

- Point to the picture on page 32 and ask the class: *Where do you think this is? What are they doing? Why are they doing this?*
- Ask students to read the text and find out the name of the job and where the picture was taken. (oshiya; Japan)
- Tell students to close their books and to write down four things they can remember about Hiro and his job.
- ↓ Board:
  He's ______________ (nationality). He's a ______________ (job). He's responsible for ______________. He works ______________-time.
  (Japenese, pusher / an oshiya, passenger safety, full)
  Possible answers: **He's Japanese. He's an oshiya / a pusher. He pushes people onto the underground trains. He's responsible for passenger safety. He works full-time. He signals to the driver when it's safe to close the doors. He sometimes has to pull passengers off the train.**

Language and culture
Students can read the text *Problematic words* (p. 43) and do the related task at home – or you can use this as a 'filler' if you have time at the end of the lesson. For more information on this, look at page 86 of this TRB.

1b Vocabulary: The world of work
5+ mins

! Check the pronunciation of *colleague* ['kɒli:g], *retired* [rɪ'taɪəd], *employee* [ɪm'plɔɪi:] and *unemployed* [ˌʌnɪm'plɔɪd] by saying the words and having students repeat them in chorus.

- Demonstrate the task using one of the words, e.g. *colleague: You work with this person.*
- Students work in pairs and describe the people / things to each other.
- Board:
  * Choose four words to describe.
  ** As in the coursebook.
  *** Choose one word without telling your partner which one. Describe the word and your partner guesses which one it is.

Possible answers: **a colleague – you work with this person, an employee – they have a job in a company, a retired person – this person doesn't need to work anymore because he / she is old, an unemployed person – this person doesn't have a job, a full-time job – a job with 30 – 35 hours a week or more, a part-time job – a job with fewer than 30–35 hours a week**

1c Checking the facts
1/31
5 mins

- Read out the instructions. Allow students time to read the sentences.
- Play ▶ 1/31.
- Students listen and underline the correct information.
- If necessary, students listen a second time. Play ▶ 1/31 again.
  1 34, 2 different, 3 six, 4 a shared, 5 Five

(M = Margaret, H = Hiro)
M: So, Mr Yamamoto, I'd like to check a few bits of information to make sure I've got everything right. You're 34 years old, aren't you?
H: Yes, I am.
M: And you work full-time here, don't you?
H: That's right.
M: You work eight hours a day, don't you?
H: Yes, that's it. Three days a week I start work at four o'clock and finish at midday, and on the other three days I start at five o'clock in the afternoon and finish at one o'clock the next morning.
M: OK. Your office is on the platform, isn't it?
H: That's right. There's a small office for all the oshiyas at the end of the platform.
M: And four oshiyas work at your station, don't they?
H: No, actually, five altogether. Four colleagues and me.
M: Oh, right. OK. Well, I think that's everything I need. The article will come out ...

2 Grammar
10+ mins

Question tags (*to be*, present simple)
- Read out the first sentence from the Grammar box.
- Say: *We can use question tags to check information. If we have a positive sentence, we need a negative tag.*
- Read out the second sentence from the Grammar box.
- Say: *If we have a negative sentence, we need a positive tag.*
- Board:
  Grammar is interesting, _________?
  It isn't boring, _________?
  Elicit the question tags. (isn't it? / is it?)
- Read out the sentences with the question tags *doesn't he? / does he?* (sentences 5 and 6). Again, point out that if the sentence is positive, we need a negative question tag; if the sentence is negative, we need a positive question tag.
- Board:
  Hiro works eight hours a day, _________?
  He doesn't work part-time, _________?
  Elicit the question tags. (doesn't he? / does he?)
- Read the remaining sentences in the Grammar box, stressing the verb in the statement and the auxiliary in the question tag, and have students repeat them.

! Make sure your voice goes down at the end of the tag as you are checking information, not asking a question.

2a Say it like this
1/32–33
5 mins

- Read out the instructions.
- Say: *Listen to Margaret again.* Play ▶ 1/32.
- Say: *Listen again and repeat.* Play ▶ 1/33.

You're 34 years old, aren't you?
And you work full-time here, don't you?
Your office is on the platform, isn't it?

2b Hiro's an oshiya, isn't he?
5+ mins

- Read out the instructions.
- Students work in pairs and cross out the wrong question tags.
- Check answers in class.
  1 doesn't he? | ~~don't they?~~, 2 does it? | ~~is it?~~, 3 ~~aren't they?~~ | don't they?, 4 ~~is he?~~ | is it?, 5 aren't they? | ~~don't they?~~, 6 ~~are they?~~ | do they?

If short of time

If you notice you're getting short of time,
- ask students to choose only two sentences to add question tags to in ***Exercise 2c***.
- do ***Exercise 3b*** as a class activity.
- do just one of the ***Round up*** activities.
- do only one or two questions of ***Exercise 4b*** as a class discussion.

2c Hiro and his job
5+ mins

- Read out the instructions.
- Students look back at their sentences from *Exercise 1a* and add question tags.
- Ask students to work in pairs and read their sentences out to their partner to check the information.

3a How to say it: Describing jobs and responsibilities
1/34
5 mins

- Say: *Listen and repeat.* Play ▶ 1/34.
- Students listen to the phrases and repeat them in chorus.

! Refer students to the *Info box*. Remind them that they need to say *a* or *an* before a job. Also remind them about *a* + consonant / *an* + vowel.

3b Now you: Your job and responsibilities
10 mins

- Read out the instructions.
- ↓ Allow students time to complete the sentences in *Exercise 3a* about their job to prepare them for the speaking task.
- Students work in pairs to complete the task.

Round up

4a You work in an office, don't you?
10 mins

- Demonstrate the task by checking information that you know about individual students using question tags.
- Ask students to stand up and walk around the class and do the same.
- Ask individuals if they found out any new (unexpected) information.

4b Talk about it
10 mins

- Students work in small groups or in pairs, and choose one or more of the questions to chat freely about. They can just talk about one, or two, or all of the questions.
- If communication seems to have come to a standstill, join the group / pair and ask additional questions.

And finally ...
5+ mins

Remind students of the following:
- **Language study** (p. 34): An overview of the grammar of the step with exercises. Students can do this in their books or online.
- **Selfstudy** (p. 35): Students can do this in their books or online.
- **Keys** (p. 130) to the Language study and Selfstudy exercises.
- **Language and culture** (p. 43), Step 2: *Problematic words* and the corresponding tasks.

And point out ...
- The **FAQ** *How can I learn more English for my job?* at the end of the Selfstudy page (p. 35). FAQ reflects the kind of questions that more advanced learners may ask in order to improve their independent learning. Students can find more questions with more detailed answers on pages 198/199.

Unit 2 Step 3 Going to the library

Contents

Realia	A local library website
Functions	Understanding regulations; Talking about books and reading
Vocabulary	Types of books
Reading	Facts for Bookworms
Grammar	**You already know:** *must / have to* **And now:** *had to / didn't have to;*
Write it right	Apostrophes (1)

Lesson notes

Additional material

For optional and additional material for Unit 2, Step 3, see page 87.
Refer to this section before your lesson as some of the materials require preparation.

Optional stages

Optional stages of the lesson are written in grey in these notes.

Starter: Everyday reading
5 mins

- Start by briefly telling the class about something you have read today.
- Then ask individual students the question in the *Starter* task.

Joining a library

1a How to join the library
10 mins

- Tell students that they are going to read part of a library's website.
  ! Assure them that, although there may be unknown words in the text, they shouldn't panic. They will be able to understand and cope with the task. Remind them that it's good practice for coping with real-life situations.
- Say: *This is the library website. You want to join the library and you have some questions.*
- Point to the list of questions and ask students to read them.
- Board: * Do numbers 1, 2 and 5.
  ** As in the coursebook.
  *** Do **. Then write another question about the information on the website. Ask your question to the class.
- Students then read the website to find the answers to the questions. Check answers in class.
  1 Yes, you do. 2 A utility bill (such as your gas, electricity or water bill) or your driving licence. 3 A copy of your signature. 4 No, they don't. (They only need to produce proof of their name.) 5 Online. 6 You can collect your library card on the spot or they'll post it to your home address.

1b A study project
1/39–40
5+ mins

- Read out the first part of the instructions. Play ▶ 1/39.
- Students listen to find out what Erich's suggestion is.
- Check answer in class.

  Erich suggests joining the library.
- Read out the second part of the instructions. Play ▶ 1/40.
- Students listen and tick the true sentences.
- Ask students to check in pairs, before checking answers in class.
  ✓ 2, 4

(M = Marcel, E = Erich)
M: Erich, I don't know what I'm going to do about our homework project – we have to finish it for next week ...
E: What's the problem, Marcel?
M: Well, you know we have to find out information about this town – but our teacher says we mustn't use the Internet ...
E: That's not a problem – do what I did and join the library! They've got lots of books all about the town and this region. I found a really interesting one with all the information I needed.

→

M: I thought about joining the library, but don't you have to live in the town permanently? We're only here for two months.
E: No, not at all, everyone can join the library, it's really easy.
M: How much does it cost?
E: Nothing! It's free.
M: Really? So what do you have to do?
E: Well, I had to show them something "official" with my name and address on it. But I didn't have to take my passport or anything.
M: So what did you show them?
E: I just showed them a letter from my bank in Germany. It had my address on it, so the librarian said that was fine.
M: Did you have to fill in a form?
E: Yes, but I think you can download the form and fill it in at home.
M: That sounds easy. OK, I'll join tomorrow. Do you want another beer?
E: Yes, please!

2 Grammar
5+ mins

NB: There's only a minor grammar element in Step 3 – the main focus is on the realia tasks and reading.

You already know: *must / have to*
- Say: *What rules are there in a library?* and elicit some ideas. (You must be quiet. / You have to be a member. / You have to bring books back.)
- Read out the sentences from the *You already know* Grammar box. Have students repeat them in chorus.
- Ask: *Are the sentences about the past or present?* (present)

! Refer students to the *Info box* on *mustn't / don't have to.*

And now: *had to / didn't have to*
- Refer students to the sentences in the *And now* Grammar box. Read out the sentences. Have students repeat them in chorus.
- Ask: *Are these sentences about the past or present?* (past) *What phrase do we use to make the past of 'have to' and 'must'?* (had to)

2a Who can join?
5+ mins

- Read out the instructions.
- Students complete the sentences using *had to / didn't have to.*
- ↓ Students work in pairs to complete the sentences.
  Possible answers: **1 ... only had to bring proof of my name / didn't have to bring proof of my address. 2 ... had to have proof of address. 3 ... had to bring proof of address, with my name, and the form to the library. 4 ... had to bring proof of name / signature and they posted my library card to my home address.**

2b Now you: What did you have to do?
5+ mins

- Ask students to work in groups.
- Read out the instructions.
- Students talk together and discuss what they had to do in the situations.
- ↑ After the discussion, ask more able students to tell the class about what they had to do in one of the situations.

Books
3a Reading: Facts for Bookworms
10 mins

Tip: Gist reading Remind students that it's not essential to know every word in order to complete reading tasks and that it's important to develop gist reading skills. However, if there is a specific word which they didn't need for the overall understanding of the text, but they feel they'd like to know the meaning of, they can look it up later in the Dictionary section at the back of the book. Emphasise the fact that they shouldn't try to look up every unknown word.

- Allow students time to read the text silently.
- Ask students the following questions:
  How big is the largest book in the world? (It's 1.78 metres tall and one metre wide.)
  How long did Stanley Dudek have his library book? (He had it for 99 years.)
  How long are the shelves in the Library of Congress? (They're 850 kilometres long.)
  Where is Britain's smallest library? (It's in an old phone box in Westbury-sub-Mendip.)
- Ask individuals which facts they found most interesting / unusual.

Language and culture

Students can read the text *ISBNs* (p. 43) and do the related tasks at home – or you can use this as a 'filler' if you have time at the end of the lesson. For more information on this, look at page 87 of this TRB.

3b What's the title?
5 mins

- Follow coursebook instructions.
- Check answers in class.
  a) Fact 1, b) Fact 3, c) Fact 4, d) Fact 2

3c Now you: Your library
5 mins

- Students work in groups and discuss the questions.

If short of time

If you notice you're getting short of time,
- do ***Exercise 3d*** as a class activity.
- do only parts 1 and 2 in ***Exercise 4a***.
- do only one of the messages in ***Exercise 4b*** as a class activity.

3d What's that book?
5 mins

- Follow coursebook instructions.
- Check answers in class.
  1e), 2g), 3f), 4a), 5d), 6c), 7b)

3e Now you: Your favourite books
5 mins

- Demonstrate this task by briefly telling the class about the kind of books you like / dislike and who your favourite author is.
- Students work in groups and discuss the questions.

4a Write it right: Apostrophes (1)
10 mins

- Read out the use of an apostrophe.
- Read out question 1.
- Students say the long forms.
  1 He is | He has | They can not (cannot) | Let us
- Read out instruction 2.
- Students rewrite the sentences using apostrophes.
  2 We're going to visit our friends next week – they've got a house near the beach. You're welcome to come.
- ↑ Students write a sentence without apostrophes. They hand it to the teacher who writes it on the board. The class then tells the teacher where the apostrophes should go.
- Read out instruction 3.
- Students work in pairs and write down other words with apostrophes.
  3 Possible answers: **I've (I have), I'm (I am), isn't (is not), mustn't (must not), they're (they are)**

4b A hidden message
10 mins

- Divide the class into two groups, A / B.
- Tell the A Students to look at page 123; tell the B Students to look at page 125.
- Read out the instructions on page 123.
- Students write the message and add capital letters, apostrophes and full-stops.
- When students have finished, ask them to work in A / B pairs. They swap their message with their partner, who checks it for correct use of capital letters, apostrophes, full-stops.
- ↓ Students work in groups to write the message and then check the other group's message.
- Check answers in class.
  Partner A: If you visit Shanghai, don't miss the highest library in the world. You'll need to get the lift because it's on the sixtieth floor of a hotel. Partner B: Where's the world's most unusual library? Maybe it's the Camel Library in Kenya's desert. Twelve camels bring people's books.

And finally ...
5+ mins

Remind students of the following:
- **Language study** (p. 38): An overview of the grammar of the step (both *You already know* and *And now*) with exercises. Students can do this in their books or online.
- **Selfstudy** (p. 38): Students can do this in their books or online.
- **Keys** (p. 130) to the Language study and Selfstudy exercises.
- **Language and culture** (p. 43), Step 3: *ISBNs* and the corresponding tasks. Refer students to the *Listen in* task. (For more information on this, look at page 87 of this TRB.)

And point out ...
- **Reading: Languages of the world** (p. 39): A text and quiz 'just for interest'. If you want to use this text / quiz in class, there are some ideas on how to exploit it on page 120.

Unit 2 Now I can

Contents

Contents Review of vocabulary, functions and structures in Unit 2

Starter	Talking about education and skills; Defining things, people and places
Part 1	Defining things, people and places; Talking about different ways of working; Describing jobs and responsibilities; Understanding regulations
Part 2	Talking about education and skills; Describing jobs and responsibilities
Part 3	Understanding regulations; Talking about books and reading

Lesson notes

Additional material

For optional and additional material for Unit 2, *Now I can*, see pages 87/88.
Refer to this section before your lesson as some of the materials require preparation.

Optional stages

Optional stages of the lesson are written in grey in these notes.

Now I can: ...
5 mins

- Ask students to look at *Now I can: ...* at the top of page 40. Remind them that the symbols refer to different skills or vocabulary items which they learnt in Unit 2 and were listed in the unit aims on the photo page (p. 27).

Starter: Look back
5 mins

- Ask the class to tell you what they remember about Bholaram Das.

  Possible answers: **He's 100 years old. He's the oldest student in India. He is starting to study for his doctorate. As a teenager, he became interested in politics. He went to prison. He trained and worked as a teacher. He studied for a degree in law. He retired in 1971. He worked as a lawyer until he was 98.**

Starter: Now look forward
5 mins

- Read out the *Now look forward* information.
- Check that the class know what a 'gap year' is. (It normally refers to a year between school and university when students decide to travel or do voluntary work abroad before they begin their studies.)
  ! The words *sabbatical* and *career break* are also used to talk about taking time out of your working life to try something new.
- Ask the class: *Do you think that gap years are a good idea? Are they only for 18-year-olds or can anyone do them?* Encourage individual students to respond.

Part 1:
1a Gap Years For All
10 mins

- Tell students they're going to read some information about gap years.
- Read out the instructions.
- Students read the text, then work in pairs to tick the correct statements.
- Check answers in class.
  ✓ 1, 4, 6
- Students correct the false statements with their partners.
  Corrected statements: **2 You can't / don't earn money in these jobs. (The jobs are for volunteers.) 3 You don't have to be over 30 to apply. Adults of all ages can apply. 5 You don't need relevant qualifications to apply. (Full training is provided.)**

1b What does that mean?
10 mins

- Read out the instructions, then demonstrate the task by defining *assistant teacher.*
- Students work in pairs and explain the meaning of the highlighted words.
  ! Refer students to the sentence starters on the right of the text.
  Possible answers: Assistant teacher: **It's a person who helps a teacher in the classroom.** Primary school: **It's a place where young children go to school.** Geography: **It's a subject that / which teaches people about countries and places.** Wildlife conservation centre: **It's a place where people look after wild animals.** Child health clinic: **It's a place where you can take children who are ill.** Street children: **They're children who don't have a home and have to live on the streets.** Orang utan: **It's a type of monkey that / which lives in Sumatra and Borneo.** Marine wildlife: **It's a project that / which protects things that / which live in the sea.**

Part 2:
2a A job for Adele
1/43–44
10 mins

- Read out the instructions and the two questions.
- Play ▶ 1/43.
- Check the answers to the two questions in class.

1 Support worker for street children in Bolivia. 2 Assistant teacher at a primary school in Ecuador.

- Students listen again and decide whether Adele is a good candidate for either of the jobs and give a short reason why / why not. Play ▶ 1/44.
  Possible answers: **She's a good candidate for the assistant teacher job because she loves children, she has a little brother and she wants to start a training for working at preschool. She's not such a good candidate for the support worker for street children because she has never worked with children.**

(A = Adele, I = interviewer)
A: Hello?
I: Hello Adele. It's Peter Marcham here, from Gap Years For All.
A: Oh yes, hello.
I: I've got your online application here. I see you're interested in one of our projects in South America, in Bolivia.
A: Yes, I am. The support worker for street children.
I: OK, so let's talk a bit about it. What do you think a support worker for street children has to do? What do you think might be the responsibilities of the job?
A: Well, I think you have to listen to the children, to understand them, to give them the love that they need.
I: And, in a more practical way, what help do you think they might need?
A: Well, I don't know really. New clothes, maybe? Oh, and food, too, of course. Hot soup and that sort of thing.
I: OK ... now what skills or experience could you bring to this role? Have you ever worked with children?
A: Well, I've done some babysitting and I have a little brother, and I really love children. I want to work in a preschool. But before I start my training for that, I'd really like to travel a bit and do something useful in the world.
I: Ah, now that's interesting that you're going to train to work in a preschool. Did you see on our website? There's a primary school in Ecuador that's looking for an assistant teacher for its first year class, for the youngest children. I wonder if maybe that might be more interesting for you? Let me tell you a bit about it.

2b A job for you
10 mins

- Read out the first part of the instructions (to ... *on the form below*).
- Students work alone to choose a job and make some notes.
- ↓ Remind students about some of the structures for talking about education and skills / jobs and responsibilities.
  Board:

I t____________ as a teacher.	(trained)
I have a c____________ in business studies.	(certificate)
I'm a q____________ electrician.	(qualified)
I have a lot of e____________ with computers.	(experience)
I'm r____________ for dealing with customers.	(responsible)
I have to d____________ w________ people every day.	(deal with)

- Then ask students to work in A / B pairs and take it in turns to interview each other.
- When students have finished, ask individual students to say if they would give the job to their partner, and why (not).

If short of time

If you notice you're getting short of time,
- do ***Exercise 3a*** as a class activity.

Part 3:
3a What do you need?
5+ mins

- Read out the instructions.
- Students work in pairs to discuss the questions.

NB: *Proof* can be countable or uncountable, i.e. used with or without *a*: *I needed **a** proof of identity. / I needed proof of identity.*

3b A gift
10 mins

- Ask students to close their books (or cover the page).
- Recap the types of books covered in Step 3 by asking the students to work in groups of three or four and write down as many book types as they can think of.
- Make a list on the board.
- Read out the instructions and ask students to check that all the types of books listed in *Exercise 3b* are on the list on the board.
- In their groups, students discuss their book choice.
- Encourage students to provide a reason for their choice.

  ↓ Board: I'd choose a ________ because ...
  I think the best book to take is a ________ because ...

  You could also elicit some key adjectives to describe the books and make a list on the board, e.g. *useful, informative, long, factual.*

3b Now you choose
15+ mins

- Board: * easy, ** standard, *** challenging
  Remind students about the star system and tell them they need to choose one of these tasks.
- Allow time for students to read the tasks and choose one.
- Tell students they have ten minutes to complete the task.
- Monitor and help with any vocabulary / phrases they may need.
- When students are finished, ask them to form a group with other students who completed the same task.
- They read each other's work and decide on one to read out to the whole class.
- One student then reads out the chosen text to the class.

Tip: Correcting students' work It's important to give students feedback and correction on their written work. You can collect their work at the end of the lesson and 'mark' it at home. Remember to not only correct errors, but also to comment on the content of their writing. Also, it's a good idea not to mark every error, but focus on those related to the grammar, vocabulary etc. which were covered in the units and steps you have taught so far.

And finally ...
5 mins

Look back at *In this unit, you will learn to: ...* (p. 27) to show your students how much they have learnt in this unit, to say how well they've done and to let them reflect on where they need more practice.

Remind students of the following:

- **Test yourself** (p. 42): Students can do this progress test and check their answers (p. 130).
- **Language and culture** (p. 43): Refer your students to any L&C texts and tasks that weren't done in class.
- **Now me** (p. 44): Students can do some free writing, using the vocabulary and structures they've learned in Unit 2. Ask students to read the *Now blog* section. They can use this as a model for writing their own blog. Finally, refer students to the *Now explore the Internet* section to consider which clothes would be suitable for a job interview. Remind students that they can copy the *Now me* page for their portfolio.

If your course has more than 24 lessons, you'll find extra lessons after Units 2, 4 and 6: **Globetrotter.**
Globetrotter Work – one page (45 minutes) of material with the focus on English for work.
Globetrotter Travel – one page (45 minutes) of material with the focus on English for travel.
A further 45 minutes of material is provided on the Internet for each of these lessons.
Teaching notes on **Globetrotter A** can be found on pages 122/123.

Your notes

Unit 3 Step 1 Travel

Contents

Text topic	A website competition page about happiest holiday moments
Functions	Talking about holidays and travel; Describing past holidays; Describing a scene
Vocabulary	Holidays and travel; Adjective intensifiers
Grammar	**You already know:** Present progressive **And now:** Past progressive

Lesson notes

Additional material

For optional and additional material for Unit 3, Step 1, see page 88.
Refer to this section before your lesson as some of the materials require preparation.

Optional stages

Optional stages of the lesson are written in grey in these notes.

Photo page
5 mins

- Hold up your open book at page 47 and introduce the topic of the unit by looking at the pictures with the class. Ask the questions to individual students.
- Refer students to *In this unit, you will learn to: ...* . Give them a minute to read the learning aims.

Starter: Your first holiday memory
5 mins

- With closed books, ask individual students the *Starter* questions.

1a Competition entry titles
10+ mins

- Ask the class to read through the competition entries quickly (skimming) and find out what kind of holiday each of the competitors had. (Samira – backpacking in Jordan; Karl – camping in Brazil; Pippa – a self-catering holiday in Switzerland; Bruce – a Caribbean cruise)
  ! Skimming a text for specific information is a skill needed for some exam tasks.
- Read out the instructions and the titles. Tell the students they only need four titles.
- Students then read the competition entries in detail and match a title to each one.
  5 Samira, 6 Karl, 2 Pippa, 3 Bruce

1b Comprehension
5+ mins

Students read the text again to find the answers to the comprehension questions.

1 Because she felt totally alone in the universe. It was completely dark. The stars were shining and the wind was blowing. 2 Because the animals were very loud and were making a lot of strange noises. 3 They were listening to music and drinking a good bottle of red wine. 4 Because dolphins were following the ship.

- ↑ Students write one more comprehension question to ask the class.

Language and culture

Students can read the text *Holidays* (p. 63) and do the related task at home – or you can use this as a 'filler' if you have time at the end of the lesson. For more information on this, look at page 88 of this TRB.

2 Grammar
10 mins

You already know: Present progressive

- Read out the sentences from the *You already know* Grammar box. Have students repeat them in chorus.
- Board: at the moment – next week – two days ago
  Ask: *Which phrase can we put on the end of the sentence?* (at the moment)
- Say: *We use the **present** progressive to talk about something happening now.*

And now: Past progressive

- Read out the sentences from the *And now* Grammar box. Have students repeat them in chorus.
- Say: *We can use the **past** progressive to describe a scene – something which was happening at a specific moment in the past.*
- Say: *To form the past progressive we use 'was' / 'were' + the '-ing form' of the verb.*
- Ask students to look at the photos on page 27 for half a minute and then close their books.

→

- Ask what the people in the photos were doing. (The young woman was reading a book in the library. The child was swimming and his mother was helping / teaching her. The older people were working with / using computers. The four people were talking about / looking at plans.
- Board He was ...ing – They were ...ing

NB: If you have time, and if you feel your students need more consolidation of these grammar points, there's an explanation in German and some example sentences in the *Language study* (p. 50).

2a On a cruise ship
5+ mins

- Read out the instructions.
- ↓ Board: take a photo, read, lie, listen, stand, hold, eat, cook, play, sleep
  Tell students they can use these verbs in the *-ing* form to describe the picture.
- In class the students say what is happening.
  A woman is taking a photo of the dolphins. A man is reading a book. Two women are lying in the sun, one of them is listening to music. A man is standing near the rails holding a cocktail. Two people are eating. The cook is cooking (making / flipping pancakes). Two people are playing table tennis. A man is sleeping.

Tip: On the spot correction As the aim of this task is accuracy (producing correct present progressive sentences), it's important to correct errors immediately. If students make a mistake, encourage them to correct themselves. Repeat the sentence up to the mistake, e.g. *A man is ...* and get the student to repeat the phrase and add the correct ending. If a student can't correct him- / herself, provide the correction yourself and ask the student to repeat it.

! Point out to students that when describing a picture they should use the present progressive.

2b Memory game
5 mins

- Tell students to turn back to page 49.
- Read out the instructions and ask the example questions to individual students. (No, he wasn't. He was drinking a cocktail. Two women were sunbathing. The old man was reading a book.)
- Students work in pairs to ask and answer past progressive questions about the picture.

3a Vocabulary: Types of holiday
5+ mins

- Read out the instructions.
- Students work in pairs. Together they find the matching words.
- Board: * Student A does 1, 3 and 5. Student B does 2, 4 and 5.
  ** As in the coursebook.
  *** Read the descriptions and try to guess / remember the words first, then find them in the text.

1 cruise, 2 camping, 3 self-catering, 4 backpacking, 5 city break
! Check the pronunciation of *cruise* [kru:z]. Say the word and have students repeat it in chorus.

3b The best holiday I've ever had
2/2–3
10 mins

! As the first task is a gist listening task, remind students that it's not important to understand every word. They need to listen for the overall meaning of what each of the four people is saying.

- Read out the first part of the instructions and the types of holiday, making sure students are clear there are only four speakers, so not every type of holiday will be mentioned.
- Play ▶ 2/2. Students listen and number the boxes. Check answers in class.
  1c), 2e), 3d), 4f)
- Read out the second part or the instructions.
- Allow students time to read the sentences. Play ▶ 2/3.
- Check answers in class.
  1 (unbelievably) | very, 2 really | (truly), 3 (absolutely) | totally, 4 (completely) | so

S1: The best holiday I've ever had? I went with five friends to the Austrian Alps for a week in January last year. We were staying in a chalet up in the mountains. There was a lot of snow and the weather was perfect for skiing. I even tried snowboarding for the first time. It was unbelievably cold, but we drank a lot of schnapps to keep us warm and we had a really good time!

S2: I love walking, so two years ago I went on holiday to Indonesia to do a walking tour of the temples there. It was a really special experience. I did the tour with a group of other tourists and a local guide, and we trekked about four hundred kilometres in ten days! The countryside that we walked through was really amazing and the temples were so beautiful. The atmosphere there was truly magical. It's an experience I'll never forget.

S3: The best holiday I've ever had was after my exams about ten years ago. I went with a couple of friends to Mallorca. We didn't have a lot of money because we were students, but we found a special deal at the travel agent's – two hundred pounds for two weeks, all-inclusive – the flight, hotel, food, everything! It was absolutely brilliant! We spent all our time sunbathing during the day and getting very drunk in the nightclubs in the evenings.

S4: I have a really stressful job, so when I have a holiday, I like to relax and do something good for my body. My favourite holiday was in a really lovely hotel in the country. I booked it on the Internet because they were offering a really attractive programme of sauna, massage, acupuncture and sport. And the food was, of course, very healthy! Everything was specially chosen for me by a doctor in the hotel. At the end of it, I was completely relaxed and I felt really healthy!

4a How to say it: Making descriptions stronger
2/4
5 mins

- Direct attention to the *How to say it* box and explain that the phrases in the blue boxes go together and the phrases in the green boxes go together.
- Play ▶ 2/4. Students listen and repeat the sentences.

I was so relaxed.
I was very happy.
I felt really healthy.
I felt totally peaceful.
It was truly magical.
It was completely brilliant.
It was absolutely amazing.
It was unbelievably relaxing.

If short of time

If you notice you're getting short of time,
- do ***Exercise 4b*** as a class activity.
- do just one of the ***Round up*** activities.
- do ***Exercise 5b*** as a class discussion.

4b Now you: Your holiday memories
10 mins

- Demonstrate this task by briefly telling the class about your holiday memories.
- Students work in small groups and ask / answer the questions.
  ! Encourage students to use the phrases from *Exercise 4a*.
- Ask individual students to tell you one interesting piece of information about the holiday of someone in their group.

Round up

5a Guess what I was doing
5– mins

- Board: coursebook, pens, computer, paper
  Say: *What do you think I was doing yesterday at … in the morning / evening?* Encourage students to ask questions to guess the answer *(Were you teaching? Were you watching TV? etc.)*.
- Read out the instructions. In pairs, students complete the task.

5b Talk about it
5+ mins

- Students work in small groups or in pairs, and choose one or more of the topics to chat freely about. They can just talk about one, two, or three, or all of the topics.
- If communication seems to have come to a standstill, join the group / pair and ask additional questions. (e.g. *Have you ever been abroad? Have you ever been camping? What's the most exotic place you've been to?*)

And finally …
5+ mins

Remind students of the following:
- **Language study** (p. 50): An overview of the grammar of the step (both *You already know* and *And now*) with exercises. Students can do this in their books or online.
- **Selfstudy** (p. 51): Students can do this in their books or online.
- **Keys** (p. 130) to the Language study and Selfstudy exercises.
- **Language and culture** (p. 63), Step 1: *Holidays* and the corresponding task. Encourage students to do the Internet task at home.

And point out …
- The **FAQ** *How can I get more practice writing English?* at the end of the Selfstudy page (p. 51). FAQ reflects the kind of questions that more advanced learners may ask in order to improve their independent learning. Students can find more questions with more detailed answers on pages 198/199.

Unit 3 Step 2 Transport

Contents

Text topic	An article about Macavity, a cat who likes travelling on buses
Functions	Telling a story
Vocabulary	Public transport
Grammar	**You already know:** Past simple; Past progressive **And now:** Past simple and Past progressive (interrupted activities)

Lesson notes

Additional material

For optional and additional material for Unit 3, Step 2, see pages 88/89.
Refer to this section before your lesson as some of the materials require preparation.

Optional stages

Optional stages of the lesson are written in grey in these notes.

Starter: What were you doing at quarter to two?
5 mins

- Ask students to stand up and come to the middle of the room (if possible).
- Demonstrate the task by asking one or two students the example question.
- Students walk around asking each other questions about what they were doing yesterday. When they find someone who was doing the same at that time, they sit down together.
- Once half of the class is sitting down, ask pairs to tell the class what they were both doing.

Tip: Bringing an activity to a close For walk and talk activities, it's a good idea to give students a specific time frame to complete the task. You can use an egg timer or the stop watch alarm on your mobile phone to do this and say: *You've got three minutes to find someone who was doing the same thing as you.* Then set the timer. When it rings, this signals the end of the task and makes a potentially noisy activity easy to bring to an end.

1a Vocabulary: Travelling by bus
5+ mins

- Point to the picture on page 52 and introduce Macavity (the cat). Say: *This is Macavity. Where do you think he is in the top picture?* (on a bus) *What's he doing in the bottom picture?* (getting off the bus) *Do you think he's alone or with someone?* (alone)
- Ask students to read the text to check their answers.
- They then read the text again and tick the things that Macavity does. Check answers in class.
  ✓ 2, 4, 5, 7, 8

! Refer students to the *Info box*. Remind them that different forms of transport use different prepositions. A guide to knowing whether to say *get into* or *get on*, *get out of* or *get off* which is easy is this: if you have to bend down or crouch, the phrase is *get into / get out of* (a car, a taxi); if you can remain upright while boarding, the phrase to use is *get on / get off* (a plane, a bus).

1b Comprehension
10 mins

- Ask students to read the false sentences and use the information in the text to correct them.
- Board: * Work in pairs.
  ** As in the coursebook.
  *** As in the coursebook. Then write another false sentence. Read this out to the other students for them to correct.

  1 ... at the same bus stop. 2 ... the cat was alone. 3 ... was getting on the bus ..., 4 ... outside the post office. 5 ... don't have to buy a ticket for a cat.

Language and culture

Students can read the text *Queues* (p. 63) and do the related task at home – or you can use this as a 'filler' if you have time at the end of the lesson. For more information on this, look at page 89 of this TRB.

2 Grammar
10 mins

You already know: Past simple, Past progressive
- Direct the students' attention to the *You already know* Grammar box and say: *The past simple tells us about an action or a series of actions. What did the cat do?* Get students to answer the questions to get across the idea of chronological events (e.g. The cat got on the bus.). *And then?* (The cat sat down on the nearest free seat.) *And then?* (The cat jumped down from the seat.) *And then?* (It got off the bus.) *And then?* (It walked to the fish and chip shop.)

And now: Past simple and Past progressive (interrupted activities)

- Read out the first sentence from the *And now* Grammar box, and have students repeat it in chorus.
- Board: We were getting on the bus when a cat ran past us.
  Underline were getting. Ask: *Which tense is this?* (past progressive) Underline ran. Say: *Which tense is this?* (past simple) *The past simple interrupts the past progressive.*
  ! You can indicate the idea of the progressive by inserting a whispered *'in the middle of'* when you read progressive verbs, e.g. We were *in the middle of getting on the bus when a cat ran past us.*
- Read out the remaining sentences from the *And now* Grammar box.

2a What were they doing?

2/9
5 mins

- Read out the instructions. Play ▶ 2/9.
- Check answers in class.

1 walking; 2 eating; 3 listening to music; 4 watching football; 5 opening a bottle of wine; drinking wine; 6 having a shower

1 Someone walking outside – mobile phone RING tone – phone drawn out of pocket – beep of button to answer – answering: S1: Hi Toby! 2 Someone munching on crisps or something equally loud – landline RING – picks up phone – answering: S2: Hello? 3 Someone listening to music on the radio and humming along – mobile phone RING tone – radio turned down – answering: S2: Hello Steve! 4 Someone watching a football match on TV – landline RING – person stands up from	couch – picks up receiver – answering: S1: Yeah? 5 Someone opening a bottle of wine – guggling of wine being poured into a glass – sound of drinking – mobile phone RING tone – putting down glass on table – answering: S2: Jenny! Hi! 6 Someone under the shower – landline RING – annoyed groan – shower switched off – shower curtain being opened – fumbling with towel – rushed, heavy steps to phone – answering: S1: Yes, hello?

2b Now you: When you arrived
5 mins

- Students say what they think other students were doing when they came into the classroom.
- Then students tell the class what they were doing when you came into the classroom.

3 Can I have your autograph?

2/10–11
10 mins

- Use the photo in the book to introduce the topic of the listening. Ask: *Who's this?* (Brad Pitt)
- Read out the instructions for the gist task. Play ▶ 2/10.

The woman met | didn't meet Brad Pitt.

- Read out the instructions for the specific detail listening task.
- ↓ Students do only questions 2, 3 and 6.
- Allow students time to read the questions. Play ▶ 2/11.
- Play ▶ 2/11 again if necessary. Check answers in class.
  1 She was visiting her girlfriend. 2 She was sitting in the train (chatting to her friend). 3 He was standing at the doors (alone) reading the newspaper. 4 He wrote his name on the postcard. 5 He wrote his name and his phone number. 6 She felt confused (and then embarrassed).

S1: It happened last month when I was on holiday in New York. I was visiting my girlfriend, Melanie. She moved there last year. Anyway, one evening, we went to a bar for happy-hour cocktails. It was a great evening and we drank quite a lot! When we left the bar, it was raining, so we caught the underground home. We were sitting in the train and I was chatting to Melanie when a man got on. I couldn't believe my eyes! It was Brad Pitt!
S2: Brad Pitt! Wow, I love him!
S1: Me, too! He's *so* good-looking – oh, and a really great actor, of course.
S2: Of course! So what did you do?
S1: Well, he was standing at the doors alone, reading a newspaper. No-one in the train seemed to notice him, only me. I stood up and went over to him and asked him for his autograph. I gave him a postcard to write it on.

→

S2: What happened then?
S1: Well, he looked at me surprised, then he smiled and wrote his name on the postcard. He said something to me, but I didn't really understand him because he spoke so fast and the train was really loud. So I just smiled at him and I thanked him and went back to Melanie. I didn't even look at the autograph because I was so excited to meet a big Hollywood star!
S2: I know what you mean! I'd love to meet Brad Pitt! So what happened after that?
S1: Well, he got off at the next stop and I showed Melanie the autograph. I was so happy! Melanie looked at the postcard and read the name to me. It said: "Frank Williams" and there was a phone number.
S2: Oh, no! Really?
S1: Yes! First I was confused. Then I realised – the man wasn't Brad Pitt! But he looked exactly like him!
S2: Hmm, maybe because you were a bit drunk from all the cocktails.
S1: Probably! That really was the most embarrassing moment of my life!
S2: I believe you! So, did you call the number he gave you? I mean, if he looked like Brad Pitt ...

4a How to say it: Telling a story
2/12
5 mins

- Say: *You're going to listen and repeat some phrases which are useful when you're telling a story.* Play ▶ 2/12. Students listen to the phrases and repeat them in chorus.

It happened when I was in New York.
I was visiting my friend.
I was sitting on the train when a man got on.
First, I gave him a postcard.
Then, he wrote his name.
After that, I sat down again.
Later, I looked at the postcard.
I was really embarrassed.

4b A funny thing happened to me
10+ mins

- Students work in groups of three. Write an example for number 1 on the board and ask for other possible beginnings: Board: It happened three weeks ago on a dark, stormy night.
- In their groups, the students create the story using the prompts.
- When they've finished, they open their pieces of paper. Each member of each group reads out the story on the piece of paper he / she has.
- The group chooses which one story should be read out to the class.

If short of time

If you notice you're getting short of time,
- do ***Exercise 4c*** in pairs and set a time limit of 5 minutes.
- do just one of the ***Round up*** activities.
- do only one, two, or three questions of ***Exercise 5b*** as a class discussion.

4c Now you: A story from your life
10 mins

- Read out the instructions. Allow students a minute to think of a story from their lives.
- Volunteers tell the class their story – remind them to use the phrases from *Exercise 4a.*

Round up
5a A journey on public transport
5+ mins

- Follow coursebook instructions.

5b Talk about it
5+ mins

- Students work in small groups or in pairs, and choose one or more of the questions to chat freely about. They can just talk about one, two, or three, or all of the questions.
- If communication seems to have come to a standstill, join the group / pair and ask additional questions (e.g. *How did you meet your partner / best friend?*).

And finally ...
5+ mins

Remind students of the following:
- **Language study** (p. 54): An overview of the grammar of the step (both *You already know* and *And now*) with exercises. Students can do this in their books or online.
- **Selfstudy** (p. 55): Students can do this in their books or online.
- **Keys** (p. 131) to the Language study and Selfstudy exercises.
- **Language and culture** (p. 63), Step 2: *Queues* and the corresponding task.

Unit 3 Step 3 Travelling by train

Contents

Realia	National Rail website to help you choose and buy tickets
Functions	Buying tickets for public transport; Asking for travel information; Understanding train announcements
Vocabulary	Travelling by train
Reading	Animal station masters
Grammar	**You already know:** Present simple (routines) **And now:** Present simple (timetabled events in the future)
Write it right	Apostrophes (2)

Lesson notes

Additional material

For optional and additional material for Unit 3, Step 3, see pages 89/90.
Refer to this section before your lesson as some of the materials require preparation.

Optional stages

Optional stages of the lesson are written in grey in these notes.

Starter: Tickets
5 mins

- Ask the *Starter* questions in class.

Train tickets
1a Choosing a train ticket
10 mins

- Tell students that they are going to read part of the National Rail website.
  ! Assure them that, although there may be unknown words in the text, they shouldn't panic. They will be able to understand and cope with the task. Remind them that it's good practice for coping with real-life situations.

! Refer students to the *Info box* to help clarify the use of *any* on the website.

- Students read the website silently and use the information to match the types of train tickets to their descriptions. Check answers in class.
  1b), 2c), 3e), 4a), 5d)

1b Now you: Your train ticket
5 mins

- Students work in small groups. Read out the instructions.
- Ask individual students to tell the class who bought the most expensive ticket / had the longest journey in their group.

Buying a ticket
2 How to ask for train information
2/18–19
10 mins

- Read out the first part of the instructions. Play ▶ 2/18.
- Students listen and tick the questions they hear. Check answers in class.

  Passenger 1: ✓ a), b); Passenger 2: ✓ a), b), c)
- Read out the second part of the instructions. Play ▶ 2/19. Students answer the ticked questions.
  Passenger 1: a) The next train leaves at 11.20. b) It arrives at eleven forty.
  Passenger 2: a) It goes / leaves from platform 3. b) No, you don't have to change. (It's a direct train.) c) Yes, there is (a buffet car).

(P1 = passenger 1, P2 = passenger 2, T = ticket seller)
P1: Morning! What time's the next train to Bath, please?
T: Bath? Let's see ... the next train to Bath leaves at 11.20.
P1: And what time does it arrive?
T: Eleven forty.
P1: Oh, OK. I'd like a single, please.
T: Certainly. That'll be £9.40.
P1: £9.40 – it gets more expensive every month! Here you are.

→

T: £10. Thank you, and that's 60p change.
P1: Thanks. Bye.

P2: Hello, could I have a return to Leeds, please?
T: Certainly. Would you like a period return or a day return?
P2: A day return, please.
T: OK, that's £34.30.
P2: Right. Er ... which platform does the train go from?
T: It leaves from platform 3.
P2: And do I have to change?
T: No, you don't have to change, it's a direct train.
P2: Excellent. And is there a buffet car on the train?
T: Let me check, yes, there's a buffet car next to the first class coaches on that train. You need to hurry – that train leaves in six minutes.
P2: OK. Thanks very much.
T: Thank you.

3 Grammar
10 mins

NB: There's only a minor grammar element in Step 3 – the main focus is on the realia tasks and reading.

You already know: Present simple (routines)
- Read out the sentences from the *You already know* Grammar box. Have students repeat them in chorus.
- Say: *We can use the Present simple to talk about routines.*
- Ask a few volunteers to make sentences about their routines (e.g. *I get up at ... / I come to this English class once a week. / I practise the guitar every evening.*).

And now: Present simple (timetabled events in the future)
- Refer students to the sentence in the *And now* Grammar box.
- Say: *Here we use the Present simple to talk about timetabled events in the future.*
- Use the blue bus timetable in *Exercise 3a* to provide examples. Point to the timetable and say: *When does the train to Manchester leave?* Ask for full sentences. (It leaves at 11.27.) *When does it depart from Stoke on Trent?* (It departs at 12.07.)

3a How long does it take?
5+ mins

- Read out the instructions.
- Students work in pairs to ask / answer questions about the journey times.

4 Buying a ticket
10 mins

- Ask students to work in pairs, A and B.
- Ask the A Students to read the information at the top of the right column on page 123. B Students read the timetable at the top of the right column on page 125.
- Once they have read the information / timetable, students role-play buying a ticket.
- Board:
  - * Just do one of the role plays.
  - ** As in the coursebook.
  - *** Do **, then tell the class about the ticket your partner bought.
- Then students change roles, and use the second part of the information on their page.

At the station
5a Announcements
2/20
5 mins

- Read out the instructions. Play ▶ 2/20.
- Students listen and choose the correct information.
- Check answers in class.

1 6; 2 cancelled; 3 first; 4 trolley service; 5 late

(SA = station announcer)
1 SA1: The train now standing at platform 6 is the 6:10 service for Buxton, calling at Stockport, Hazel Grove, Disley and Buxton. That's the 6:10 train for Buxton, now standing at platform 6.
2 SA2: This is an announcement for passengers on platform 12. We're sorry to announce that the 9:30 train service from Manchester to Leeds has been cancelled.
3 SA1: The train now approaching platform 5 is the 10.15 Intercity Express to London. First class seats are in the first three coaches at the front of the train.

4 SA2: There is a trolley service on this train serving tea, coffee and snacks.
5 SA1: City Rail would like to apologise that the 12.30 airport service will be delayed by approximately 12 minutes. That's the 12:30 airport service delayed by 12 minutes. Thank you.

5b Reading: Animal station masters
5+ mins

Tip: Prediction tasks Before students read a text, it's useful to get them thinking about what the text might be about. This is a natural process which we all do in our own language. We read a title or we look at a picture and begin to think about what we are going to read.
Here are two types of prediction task: 1 Ask students to close their books. Write the title of the text on the board. In pairs, students predict what the text is about. They then read the text and check if they were right. 2 Choose some key words from the text. Put these on the board. Students predict the text content from these words. Then they read the text and check if they were right.

- Let's try the second prediction task with this text (see Tip above).
- Ask students to close their books.
- Board: railway, Japan, staff, monkeys, uniform
- In pairs, students discuss what the text could be about.
- Students then read the text silently and check if their predictions were correct.

Language and culture

Students can read the text *Uniforms* (p. 63) and do the related task at home – or you can use this as a 'filler' if you have time at the end of the lesson. For more information on this, look at page 90 of this TRB.

5c Talk about it
5 mins

- In groups, students discuss the two questions.

1 Because they want to publicise the company's new bio-diesel trains, which run through the forests where the monkeys live.
2 They could bite passengers. They could make a mess on the platform. They could escape and get into the trains.

- ↑ Ask pairs of students to write a third question to ask the class.

If short of time

If you notice you're getting short of time,
- do ***Exercise 6a*** in class.
- students write only one name and city in ***Exercise 7***.

6a Write it right: Apostrophes (2)
5+ mins

- Read out the instructions.
- Students cross out the wrong words. Check answers in class.

1 one | ~~more than one~~, before | ~~after~~; 2 ~~one~~ | more than one, ~~before~~ | after; 3 before | ~~after~~

6b Where's the apostrophe?
5+ mins

- Read out the instructions.
- Students complete the task and then check with a partner.
- Check answers in class by asking volunteers to write the words + apostrophes on the board.
1 Peter's, 2 passengers', 3 children's, 4 men's, 5 boss's

7b Fifteen minutes later
5+ mins

- Read out the instructions and use the example to demonstrate the task.
- Allow students time to write down three names and cities.
- ↓ First brainstorm a few cities and names and write them on the board.
- Complete the task in class.

And finally ...
5+ mins

Remind students of the following:
- **Language study** (p. 58): An overview of the grammar of the step (both You *already know* and *And now*) with exercises. Students can do this in their books or online.
- **Selfstudy** (p. 58): Students can do this in their books or online.
- **Keys** (p. 131) to the Language study and Selfstudy exercises.
- **Language and culture** (p. 63), Step 3: *Uniforms* and the corresponding task. Refer students to the *Listen in* task. (For more information on this, look at page 90 of this TRB.)

And point out ...
- **Reading: I want to complain about our holiday** (p. 59): Holiday complaints 'just for fun' with a glossary of unkown words. If you want to use these texts in class, there are some ideas on how to exploit them on pages 120/121.

Unit 3 Now I can

Contents

Review of vocabulary, functions and structures in Unit 3

Starter	Talking about travel and transport; Telling a story
Part 1	Talking about travel and transport; Getting travel information; Buying tickets for public transport; Understanding train announcements
Part 2	Describing past holidays; Describing a scene; Telling a story
Part 3	Describing past holidays; Describing a scene; Telling a story

Lesson notes

Additional material

For optional and additional material for Unit 3, *Now I can*, see pages 90/91.
Refer to this section before your lesson as some of the materials require preparation.

Optional stages

Optional stages of the lesson are written in grey in these notes.

Now I can: ...
5 mins

- Ask students to look at *Now I can: ...* at the top of page 60. Remind them that the symbols refer to different skills or vocabulary items which they learnt in Unit 3 and were listed in the unit aims on the photo page (p. 47).

Starter: Look back
5 mins

- Point to the pictures and ask the class to tell you what they remember about the animals.

Possible answers: **Monkeys: They're baby monkeys. They're station masters. They wear miniature railwaymen's uniforms. They're publicising the new bio-diesel trains.**
Cat: His name's Macavity. He gets on the (number 331) bus. He always gets on at the same stop. He catches the bus two or three times a week.

Starter: Now look forward
5 mins

- Read out the *Now look forward* information.
- Ask who has been to Britain and which area(s) he / she visited.

NB: If you have registered as a *Network* teacher, you will have been sent a map of Britain with the names of the places which appear in *Network Now* so you can point out where Swanage is.

Part 1:
1a The Swanage Railway
10 mins

- Tell students they're going to read some information about the Swanage Railway.
- Read out the instructions. Students read the text silently and ask and answer the questions in class.
1 No, it doesn't. (It has steam and diesel trains.) 2 It's six miles long. 3 You can see beautiful scenery and the ruins of Corfe Castle. 4 No, it isn't. (It's a ruin.) 5 No, it doesn't. (There's a separate entry charge.) 6 There are Steam Galas, Family Events, Evening Dining, Sunday Lunch services and Santa Special trains at Christmas.

1b We'd like to go to Corfe Castle
10 mins

- Read out the instructions.
- ↓ Board: How much ...? How long ...? What time ...? When ...?
Students use these prompts to form their questions.
- ↑ Students write as many questions as they can think of in the allocated time.
- While students are writing their questions, monitor and help them correct any mistakes.
- Students read out their questions for you to write on the board.
Possible questions: **How much are the tickets? How long is the journey? What time is Sunday lunch? What are the family events? When is the next Steam Gala?**

1c What time's the train?
10 mins

- Ask students to work in pairs, A and B.
- Ask the A Students to look at page 123 and read the information and the timetable. Ask the B Students to read the *What time's the train?* section on page 125.
- The B Students then ask the A Students about the trains and the A Students use the information they have to answer the questions.
- Then students change roles.
- Monitor the activity, checking that the students are managing the task.

1d At the ticket office
5 mins

- Ask students to work in pairs, A and B. Partner A is the passenger and Partner B is the employee at the ticket office.
- Students now know the time of the train they want (from *Exercise 1c*) and now they decide what kind of ticket they want by using the ticket information in the orange *Tickets* box.
- Partner A buys a ticket from Partner B.

1e Three announcements
2/23
5 mins

- Read out the instructions. Remind students that this task refers to the journeys they chose in *Exercise 1c*.
- Play ▶ 2/23.
- Ask students to tell the class which announcements are relevant to them and why.

(SA = station announcer, TG = train guard)
1 SA: The next train from platform one will be the steam service to Norden, calling at Harman's Cross, Corfe Castle and Norden. Platform one for the steam service to Norden.
2 TG: The train will shortly be passing through Herston Halt. This is a request stop only, so passengers wishing to get off here should inform the guard. Passengers for Herston Halt, please make yourselves known to the guard.
3 TG: We will soon be arriving at Corfe Castle. Next stop, Corfe Castle. Please ensure you take all your belongings with you and thank you for travelling with us today.

Part 2:
2a A special moment
2/24–25
10 mins

Tip: Reading / Listening for gist and specific information Remind your class regularly that when they're reading or listening to English, they don't have to understand every word that is written or spoken. It's often sufficient to understand the general topic of a text or conversation (Reading / Listening for gist). And sometimes it's enough to pick out one or two details (Reading / Listening for specific information). When students are in an English-speaking country, they won't understand every single word they hear – but they will probably be able to cope with most situations as long as they are used to concentrating on what they can understand rather than what they can't understand.

- Read out the instructions and the gist listening question.
- Play ▶ 2/24. Students listen and answer the question.
  He decided he wanted to spend the rest of his life with / marry Mary and asked her to marry him.
- Read out the instructions for the specific listening task and the four categories.
- Suggest that students make notes about each category to help them remember the information.
- ↓ Students make notes for categories 2 and 4 only.
- Play ▶ 2/25.
  1 The trains weren't running. 2 They were sitting on his jacket. 3 The sun was coming up. 4 He felt so happy and peaceful.

(P = passenger)
P: Oh, I love Corfe Castle. My wife Mary came from a little village near here and so I used to come here to visit her before we were married. She died three years ago. But I have very happy memories of this part of the world. In fact, it was at Corfe Castle that I had one of the happiest moments of my life. If you've got time, I'll tell you the story. It was a long time ago, when I first met my wife and we started going out together. One evening we were at her parents' house and we started talking, and we talked and we talked. We didn't want to say goodnight, so we talked all night. At about four o'clock in the morning, we thought, well, it's too late to go to bed now, so let's go for a walk. So we walked from her village, all the way to Corfe Castle. We climbed the hill and sat down. It was a very special moment. Everything was quiet. It was too early for tourists and the trains weren't running. It was just us two together, alone in the world. We were sitting there on my jacket, just enjoying the scenery. The sun was coming up. The sky was beautiful – pink and orange – and I felt so happy and peaceful. And I knew at that moment that I wanted to spend the rest of my life with Mary, so I asked her to marry me. And that was that. We were married for forty years. And we often used to come back to Corfe Castle, to our special place, and remember that morning.

2b The end of the story
2/26
5 mins

- Read out the instructions and the three possible endings of the man's story.
- Play ▶ 2/26. Students listen and tick the right sentence.

✓ 3

(P = passenger)
P: And I'll tell you a funny thing. You won't believe this, but it's true. A couple of years ago, not long after Mary died, one of my grandchildren gave me a present. It was a jigsaw puzzle of Corfe Castle. The little boy knew it was a special place for his granddad, so when he saw it in a shop, he bought it for me with his own money. Anyway, I was doing this puzzle when I found us in the picture. Yes, I found me and my family in the photo. It was Mary and me with two of our grandchildren. We were walking around the castle ruins. We were only very small, but there we were, I can't tell you how I felt. It was unbelievable. Totally unbelievable.

If short of time

If you notice you're getting short of time,
- do ***Exercise 3*** as a class activity.
  Begin with: *It was* (course day) *and it was time to go to the English lesson ...*
  Invite volunteers to contribute and be ready to add your own ideas if there's a shortage of ideas.

Part 3: What happened?
5+ mins

- Read out the instructions.
- Students work in pairs to discuss what happened and make some notes, using the question prompts.
  ! If necessary, point out to less confident pairs of students that there are some ideas to help them on page 127.
- Students then tell their stories to another pair.

4 Now you choose
10+ mins

- Remind students about the star system and tell them they need to choose one of these tasks.
- Allow time for students to read the tasks and choose one.
- Ask students to sit together with students who want to do the same task.
- Students complete the task in their groups.
- Monitor and help with any vocabulary / phrases they may need.

And finally ...
5 mins

Look back at *In this unit, you will learn to: ...* (p. 47) to show your students how much they have learnt in this unit, to say how well they've done and to let them reflect on where they need more practice.

Point out the following features of the coursebook and give a short explanation:
- **Test yourself** (p. 62): Students can do this progress test and check their answers (p. 131).
- **Language and culture** (p. 63): Refer your students to any L&C texts and tasks that weren't done in class.
- **Now me** (p. 64): Students can do some free writing, using the vocabulary and structures they've learned in Unit 3. Ask students to read the *Now blog* section. They can use this as a model for writing their own blog. Finally, refer students to the *Now explore the Internet* section to consider which holiday they would like to go on. Remind students that they can copy the *Now me* page for their portfolio.

Your notes

Unit 4 Step 1 Going out

Contents

Text topic	A *What's on* guide with information about places to eat and things to do
Functions	Finding information about leisure events; Making arrangements
Vocabulary	Event guides; Arrangements to go out
Grammar	**You already know:** Present progressive *(now)* **And now:** Present progressive (future arrangements)

Lesson notes

Additional material
For optional and additional material for Unit 4, Step 1, see pages 91/92.
Refer to this section before your lesson as some of the materials require preparation.

Optional stages
Optional stages of the lesson are written in grey in these notes.

Photo page
5– mins
- Hold up your open book at page 65 and introduce the topic of the unit by looking at the pictures with the class. Then ask the questions to individual students.
- Refer students to *In this unit, you will learn to: ...* . Give them a minute to read the learning aims.

Starter: What's on?
5– mins
- Ask the first *Starter* question to the class. Make a list of the students' responses on the board.
- Then ask individual students the following two *Starter* questions.

1a Comprehension
10 mins
- Tell students they are going to read a *What's on Guide*. Read out the instructions.
- Students then read the text silently and write a number / the numbers next to each sentence.
- Board: * Work in pairs.
  ** As in the coursebook.
  *** As in the coursebook. Then write one question to ask the class about an event (e.g. *Which event ...?*)

a) 2, 5; b) 4; c) 1, 3; d) 1; e) 3, 5; f) 3; g) 1, 5

Language and culture
Students can read the text *Mealtimes* (p. 81) and do the related task at home – or you can use this as a 'filler' if you have time at the end of the lesson. For more information on this, look at pages 91/92 of this TRB.

1b Vocabulary: Event guides
5+ mins
- Read out the instructions to the class. Students look back through the text to find the words.
- ↓ Do this exercise as a class activity and give the class the number of the event. Say: *For number 1 look at '1 Dinner in the air'.*

1 a head, 2 booking essential, 3 in advance, 4 box office, 5 concession, 6 free admission

1c Arranging to go out
2/28
5+ mins
- Read out the instructions. Play ▶ 2/28. Students answer the questions.
- ↑ Tell the class one other piece of information you heard.

1 He's waiting for the bus back home. 2 His parents are visiting him. / He's having dinner with his parents. 3 He's going to a friend's wedding. 4 On Friday at quarter to eleven outside the club / Huxley's club.

(M = Mark, E = Ed)
M: Yeah, hello?
E: Hi Mark! It's Ed. Oh, er, is it a good time to call? It sounds like you're outside.
M: Hi Ed. No problem. I'm in town, and I'm waiting for the bus back home at the moment, so it's OK.
E: Oh, right. Well, listen, I'm calling about going out next weekend. There's an alternative disco at Huxley's club. It's called a 'silent disco', where they give you headphones when you go in and you listen to the music through them so no one else can hear it.
M: That sounds cool. When is it?

→

E: Well, it's on Friday, Saturday and Sunday. Next Saturday's best for me. Are you free then?
M: Let me think ... next Saturday, that's the fifteenth, isn't it? ... Oh no, sorry, I can't. My parents are visiting me then and I'm having dinner with them on Saturday evening. But Sunday would be OK. How about Sunday?
E: No, Sunday's no good for me. I'm going to a friend's wedding in Liverpool. So Friday's the only possibility. I'm going to a party at eight, but I could leave early and meet you at the club. What about you?
M: Yeah, I'm not doing anything on Friday, so let's go then. What time do you want to meet?
E: Well, the disco's from 11 pm, so let's meet outside the club at quarter to eleven.
M: Quarter to eleven outside Huxley's club. Great. I'll write it on the calendar as soon as I get home so I don't forget.
E: Great. Well, see you then.
M: OK, Ed, bye!

2 Grammar
10 mins

You already know: Present progressive *(now / at the moment)*
- Read out the sentence from the *You already know* Grammar box. Have students repeat it in chorus.

And now: Present progressive (future arrangements)
- Read out the sentence from the *And now* Grammar box. Have students repeat it in chorus.
- Point out that we are using the Present progressive to talk about a future arrangement. Ask concept-checking questions: *Is the cinema here now?* (No.) *When is it coming?* (Next Monday.) *Are we talking about the present or the future?* (About the future.)

! When the Present progressive refers to the future, it's sometimes known as the 'diary future' because it's used to talk about arrangements you've made.

NB: If you have time, and if you feel your students need more consolidation of this grammar point, there's an explanation in German and some example sentences in the *Language Study* (p. 68).

2a A busy social life
10– mins

- ↓ Board: Helen's having dinner at Susie's on Monday.
  Ask the class: *What's Helen doing on Monday?* (She's having dinner at Susie's.), *When is she having dinner at Susie's?* (She's having dinner at Susie's on Monday.), *Where's Helen having dinner on Monday?* (She's having dinner at Susie's.)
  Then ask individual students to ask a question to the class. Give the prompts: *What's Helen ...? When is she ...? Where's Helen ...?*
- Ask students to work in A / B pairs.
- Read out the instructions. Partner As look at page 124, Partner Bs look at page 126.
- Say: *Partner A, ask Partner B questions about Mark and fill in the missing information. Partner B, use the information in your calendar to answer your partner's questions. When you have finished, swap roles, Partner Bs ask about Katya, and Partner As use the calendar to answer.*

2b Changes to the calendar
2/29
5+ mins

- Read out the instructions. Play ▶ 2/29.
- Check answers in class. Encourage students to use the structure: *Mark / Katja isn't + ...-ing. He's / She's + ...-ing.*

Mark isn't going to the Rock the Park concert with Andy. Maybe they're doing something else.
Katja isn't meeting Fatima at the bus stop at 9 pm. She's meeting her at Dave's party.
Mark's (Mark is) meeting Ed outside the club at 10.30 pm, not at 10.45.
Katja's (Katja is) having dinner with Ben at 9 pm, not at 8 pm.
Mark's (Mark is) going to the Star Wars night on Thursday, not on Wednesday. He's only going with Jeff and not with Jeff and Tim.

Andy: Mark. Andy here. It's about the Rock the Park concert. I tried to buy the tickets online today, but they've sold out, so I'm afraid we can't go. I'm really annoyed – I really wanted to be there. Anyway, I'll call you later. Maybe we can do something else. Bye for now.
Fatima: Katya, hi! It's Fatima. I'm calling about Dave's party on Friday. I'm going to Dave's a bit earlier to help him to tidy the flat and prepare some food, so I won't be able to meet you at the bus stop as we arranged. I hope that's OK. But I'll see you at the party anyway. Bye!

Ed:	Hi Mark, Ed here. This silent disco on Friday looks like it's going to be really popular, so we need to get there early if we want to get in. Let's meet at ten-thirty outside the club, not ten forty-five. OK, see you then!
Ben:	Hi Katya, it's Ben here. I phoned the restaurant today to book a table, but they're really busy on Tuesday night. We can still go, but I could only book a table for nine o'clock, not eight as we arranged. I hope that's OK. Can't wait to see you on Tuesday!
Jeff:	Hi Mark, it's Jeff. The Star Wars night is on Thursday, not Wednesday like I said, so we'll have to go then. I know you're free on Thursday, so I've bought the tickets. Oh, and Tim isn't coming – he isn't free on Thursday because he's going out with his new girlfriend. Speak to you soon. Bye.

2c Now you: Your arrangements for next week
5+ mins

- Read out the instructions. Students work in small groups to complete the task.
- Ask one volunteer from each group to tell the class about some of their group's arrangements.

Tip: Real life To give students opportunity to practise this tense out of the classroom, tell them to look at their diaries or at their phone calendars for the week ahead and talk themselves through their arrangements in English, e.g.: *So, on Monday I'm (meeting Kim for coffee) and on Tuesday I'm ...*

3a How to say it: Making arrangements to go out
2/30
5 mins

- Say: *Listen and repeat.* Play ▶ 2/30.

Are you free on Monday evening? I'm afraid I'm busy on Monday. Shall we go to the cinema? Good idea! Let's meet at six-thirty. Yes, OK.	How about going for a drink? I'd love to. Why don't we go to a museum? Sorry, I can't. I'm working. I'd prefer to go shopping.

! Refer students to the *Info box* and have them repeat: *Let's meet at 8 o'clock.*

If short of time

If you notice you're getting short of time,
- students only arrange to do two things with two different people in ***Exercise 3b***.
- do just one of the ***Round up*** activities.
- do only one of the questions of ***Exercise 4b*** as a class discussion.

3b Are you free on Monday?
10 mins

- Read out the instructions.
- ↓ Elicit ideas from students for things they can arrange to do before starting the activity.
- Students first write one prior arrangement they have in their diary. Then they stand up and walk and talk to make four more arrangements with four other students.
- Ask individual students to tell the class about two things they are doing next week.

Round up

4a What are you doing then?
5– mins

- Ask students to work with a partner.
- Read out the instructions. Students work together and tell each other about their arrangements.

4b Talk about it
5+ mins

- Students work in small groups or in pairs, and choose one or more of the questions to chat freely about. They can just talk about one, or two, or all of the questions.
- If communication seems to have come to a standstill, join the group / pair and ask additional questions, e.g. *Where can you find out about events in your area? Do you know of any events?*

And finally ...
5+ mins

Remind students of the following:
- **Language study** (p. 68): An overview of the grammar of the step (both *You already know* and *And now*) with exercises. Students can do this in their books or online.
- **Selfstudy** (p. 69): Students can do this in their books or online.
- **Keys** (p. 131) to the Language study and Selfstudy exercises.
- **Language and culture** (p. 81), Step 1: *Mealtimes* and the corresponding task.

And point out ...
- The **FAQ** *How can I improve my vocabulary?* at the end of the Selfstudy page (p.69). FAQ reflects the kind of questions that learners may ask in order to improve their independent learning. Students can find more questions with more detailed answers on pages 198/199.

Unit 4 Step 2 Staying in

Contents

Text topic	An invitation to a birthday party and two emails linked to this invitation
Functions	Making, accepting and refusing written invitations; Writing a thank-you note
Vocabulary	Types of party; Invitations
Grammar	**You already know:** Present perfect + *ever / never* **And now:** Present perfect + *already / (not) yet*

Lesson notes

Additional material

For optional and additional material for Unit 4, Step 2, see page 92.
Refer to this section before your lesson as some of the materials require preparation.

Optional stages

Optional stages of the lesson are written in grey in these notes.

Starter: Birthday parties
5 mins

- Ask individual students the *Starter* questions.

1a Comprehension
10 mins

- Tell the students that William and Rita are having a joint birthday party. Ask them to quickly look through the invitation and find the following information: *Who is having a party?* (William and Rita.), *Where is the party?* (In their garden.), *When is the party?* (On 19th June.)
- Ask students what they need to do if they see 'RSVP' on an invitation. (Say they can / can't come.) **!** R.S.V.P. stands for the French phrase, 'Répondez, s'il vous plait'. This translates to 'Respond if you please.', and means: 'Please reply to the invitation to let us know if you are coming or not.'
- Ask students to read the invitation and the emails silently. Then ask them to work in pairs. Students ask and answer the questions with their partner.
- Check answers in class.

1 ... because it's William's 55th and Rita's 45th birthday. 2 Costumes from 100 years ago. 3 To say they are coming to the party. 4 No, they don't. 5 They want the address of a costume shop because they haven't found their costumes yet. 6 No, he hasn't (, but he is going to).

Language and culture

Students can read the text *Party gifts* (p. 81) and do the related task at home – or you can use this as a 'filler' if you have time at the end of the lesson. For more information on this, look at page 92 of this TRB.

1b Vocabulary: Types of party
5 mins

- Read out the instructions.
- Students match the type of party to its description and write the numbers in the boxes.
- Check answers in class.
- ↑ Work with a partner. Test him / her. Cover the types of parties 1–6 and, in turn, read out the definition sentences a) – f). Your partner has to remember the word for the type of party.

1e), 2a), 3b), 4c), 5d), 6f)

2a How to say it: Making, accepting and refusing written invitations
2/36
5 mins

- Play ▶ 2/36 and have the class repeat the phrases in chorus.

> I'd like to invite you to my birthday party.
> We'd like you to join us on 19th June at 7 pm.
> Please come in fancy dress.
> We hope you can come.
> Thanks for the invitation.
> We'd love to come.
> I'm afraid I can't come.
> I'm really sorry, but I'm busy.
> It's very nice of you to invite us, but we're on holiday then.

2b We'd like to invite you to our party
15 mins

- Ask students to work in pairs. For this activity it would be useful to pair mixed ability students to ensure that pairs are working at similar speeds.

Tip: Getting mixed ability pairs You can do this by handing out pieces of coloured card, e.g. blue to the higher level students, green to the lower level students. There is no need to tell students what the colours represent, as this may be demotivating. Simply say you would like the students to make blue / green pairs.

- Read out the first part of the instructions.
- Students decide which type of party to have and write their invitations.

Tip: Correction When students are writing in class, walk around the room and either correct, or help students self-correct, the mistakes so that when they display their work, or 'send' it to another pair, there aren't too many mistakes in it.

- Monitor and help students correct any mistakes.
- Once students have written their invitations collect them.
- Read out the second part of the instructions and 'deliver' the invitations.
- Students read the invitations they've got and decide if they can / can't go. They write their thank-you notes and 'send' them to the party hosts.

3 Organising a party
10 mins

- Read out the instructions.
- Students work in small groups to discuss what they have to do when organising a party.
- Ask individual students to make sentences with each of the verbs.

4 Grammar
5+ mins

You already know: Present perfect + *ever / never*
- Read out the sentences from the *You already know* Grammar box. Have students repeat them in chorus.
- Ask individual students the question *Have you ever organised a big party?* and encourage them to answer using only the short answers: *Yes, I have.* or *No, I haven't.* You can extend this and ask further party related questions beginning with *Have you ever ...?*, e.g. *Have you ever been to a fancy dress party? Have you ever been to a 100th birthday party? Have you ever had a party in your garden?*

And now: Present perfect + *already / yet*
- Read out the sentences from the *And now* Grammar box. Have students repeat them in chorus.
- Ask students to choose the correct endings to these sentences:

Board:

They've already ordered the food, so ...	a) they can cross that off their to-do list. b) they have to order the food next week.	(a))
They haven't got the drinks yet, so ...	a) they can cross that off their to-do list. b) they have to buy the drinks next week.	(b))

4a They've already done that
2/37
10 mins

- Hold up your open book, point to the 'to-do' list and say: *This is William and Rita's 'to-do' list.*
- Read out the first part of the instructions (up to *the things they've already done*).
- Allow time for students to read the 'to-do' list.
- Play ▶ 2/37. Students listen and tick the things William and Rita have already done.

Rita ✓ order the food, hire the costumes, write the guest list
William ✓ hire the tent, invite the neighbours
- Students then compare their answers in class using *already / (not) yet.*

(R = Rita, W = William)
R: Right, William, I've got our to-do list here and I want to check with you that we haven't forgotten anything for the party on Saturday.
W: Oh, right, OK.
R: Now, everyone we sent an invitation to has answered, so I've written the guest list. Here, have a look. Of the thirty people we invited, twenty-six are coming altogether!
W: Oh, that's good. Oh yes, I forgot to tell you – I saw June and Glyn from next door this morning and invited them. They're coming, too.
R: Oh, well, that makes twenty-eight, then. I hope I've ordered enough food ...
W: You're joking, aren't you? You've ordered enough food for fifty!
R: Yes, that's true. And you're going to get the drinks on Friday, aren't you?

→

W: Yes, that's right. I'll drive to the supermarket and make sure we have enough drinks for fifty people as well!
R: Good. Now, then. You hired the tent last week, so when are you going to get it?
W: On Saturday morning. Then I'll put it up in the garden. I hope it's easy to do ...
R: Saturday morning? Oh, well, you can get the costumes I hired last week from the shop at the same time as the tent. I'll give you the address.
W: What? Why only me? Why can't you come with me?
R: Because I'll have to clean and tidy the whole house before the guests arrive – and that'll probably take all day!
W: Oh, right, I see.
R: Good. Well, we've already done most of the things on the list, which is good. Right, I have to go out now to buy the party decorations. Do you want to come with me?
W: To buy party decorations? Er, well, I have a few things to do around the house, so I don't think I can ...

If short of time

If you notice you're getting short of time,
- do ***Exercise 4b*** as a class activity.
- do ***Exercise 4c*** as a class activity.
- do just one of the ***Round up*** activities.
- do only one or two questions of ***Exercise 5b*** as a class discussion.

4b Has he ordered the food yet?
5+ mins

- Ask students to work in A / B pairs.
- Read out the instructions.
- ↓ Board:
  buy – ____________, put – ____________, get – ____________, write – ____________
  Elicit the irregular past participles. (bought, put, got, written)
- Students work in pairs to ask and answer questions about the 'to-do' list.

4c Now you: Have you done it yet?
5+ mins

- Ask students to work in small groups.
- Read out the instructions.
- Individually students tick the things they've already done.
- When students have completed this, they ask the other members of their group.
- Board:
  * Ask about the first three points.
  ** As in the coursebook.
  *** Do ** and then ask your group members two other questions about what they've already done in their coursebook using *Have you ... yet?*

Round up
5a Can I help you?
5– mins

- Read out the instructions.
- Students work in pairs and offer help with the party organisation.

5b Talk about it
5 mins

- Students work in small groups or in pairs, and choose one or more of the questions to chat freely about. They can just talk about one, or two, or all of questions.
- Monitor the activity and help with any vocabulary.
- If communication seems to have come to a standstill, join the group / pair and ask additional questions, e.g. *What was the last party you went to? Did you ever have a party as a child without your parent's permission?*

And finally ...
5+ mins

Remind students of the following:
- **Language study** (p. 72): An overview of the grammar of the step (both *You already know* and *And now*) with exercises. Students can do this in their books or online.
- **Selfstudy** (p. 73): Students can do this in their books or online.
- **Keys** (p. 131/132) to the Language study and Selfstudy exercises.
- **Language and culture** (p. 81), Step 2: *Party gifts* and the corresponding task.

Unit 4 Step 3 Look in the newspaper

Contents

Realia	Small ads in a local newspaper
Functions	Finding information in small ads; Talking about things that have just happened
Vocabulary	Small ads
Reading	San Francisco or Glasgow?
Grammar	**You already know:** Present perfect + *already / (not) yet* **And now:** Present perfect + *just*
Write it right	Capital letters

Lesson notes

Additional material

For optional and additional material for Unit 4, Step 3, see pages 92/93.
Refer to this section before your lesson as some of the materials require preparation.

Optional stages

Optional stages of the lesson are written in grey in these notes.

Starter: Small ads
5 mins

- Ask individual students the *Starter* questions.

In the paper
1a Headings
10 mins

- Hold up your open book and point to the small ads 1–5. Say: *Here are some small ads from a local newspaper.* Read out the instructions.
- ↓ Students only do a), c) and e).
- Students read the small ads silently and match the headings with the ads.
- Check answers in class.
  4a), 1b), 5c), 2d), 3e)

1b True or false?
5 mins

- Read out the instructions.
- Students refer back to the small ads, and tick the true sentences.
- Check in class which statements are true.
  ✓ 1, 3, 5
- Students correct the false statements.
- Board:

*	Students work in pairs to correct the statements.
**	As in the coursebook.
***	As in the coursebook. Then write an extra false statement about the ads for the students to correct.

Corrected statements: **2 Eye-tech isn't an optician's / is an IT service. 4 Cilladrive has got a lady instructor.**

1c Who can help?
2/42–43
10 mins

Tip: Gist listening and listening for detail Many of the listening tasks will have an initial gist question or task to encourage the students to listen for the overall meaning of the text. It's a good idea to play the CD once for the gist task, then check the answer(s) in class. The gist question will often be followed by a task which requires them to listen for more detail. For this second task, play the CD once, let students compare their answers in pairs and then, if necessary, play the CD again before checking the answers in class.

- Read out the instructions for the gist task. Play ▶ 2/42.
- Students listen and say which service the man needs. Check answers in class.
  eye-tech computer (IT services)
- Students listen again and tick the correct sentences. Play ▶ 2/43. If necessary, play ▶ 2/43 a second time. Check answers in class.
  ✓ 1 The computer has just broken down. 2 He's already tried turning the computer on and off. 3 He hasn't started writing the report yet. 4 He's just bought his computer. 5 He's just finished putting the software on the computer.

→

Man: Oh hello. Can you help me? I saw your ad in the paper, in the 'IT Services' column.
I've got a problem with my computer. ...
Yes, it's broken down – I can't do anything. ...
That's right, it's just happened. About five minutes ago. I was using the Internet. ...
No, I can't read my emails or do anything. ...
Yes, I've already tried turning it on and off. How long will it take to repair it? ...
A week? Oh, that's difficult – you see I've got a big report to write this week and I haven't started it yet. ...
No, it's a brand new computer – I've just bought it. In fact, I've only had it a week, and I've only just finished installing the software. ...
OK, I'll bring it in to your shop tomorrow – can you tell me where it is, please?
39 East Street. That's fine. ...
Thanks, see you tomorrow.

2 Grammar
10 mins

NB: There's only a minor grammar element in Step 3 – the main focus is on the realia tasks and reading.

You already know: Present perfect + *already / yet*
- Read out the sentences from the *You already know* Grammar box. Have students repeat them in chorus.
- Ask a few volunteers to make sentences about what they have already done / haven't done yet today (e.g. *I've already done my shopping. I haven't done my housework yet.*).

And now: Present prefect + *just*
- Refer students to the sentence in the *And now* Grammar box. Read out the sentence.
- Say: *When did the computer break down? A long time ago or a short time ago?* (A short time ago.)
- Open your book. Ask students: *What have I just done?* (You've just opened your book.) Repeat this process with the door and the window. Then close your book, the door, the window and elicit: You've just closed ...

2a Do you want to go to the cinema?
2/44–45
10 mins

- Read out the instructions for the gist task. Play ▶ 2/44. Check the answer in class.

They decide to stay in.
- Read out the instructions for the specific listening task. Play ▶ 2/45.
- Students listen and complete the sentences. Let students listen again if necessary. Play ▶ 2/45 again. Check answers in class.
1 has just put, 2 has already seen it, 3 has already started, 4 hasn't seen ... yet

(S = Steve, T = Tracey)
S: So what do you want to do this evening? Do you want to go to the cinema?
T: Maybe. What's on?
S: Um ... I'm not sure. There are cinema listings in the free newspaper. Do you know where it is?
T: I've just put it in the recycling bin.
S: Oh, OK – here it is. Let's see, Cinemas ... right. There are three new films on at the Odeon.
T: What are they?
S: There's '*Vampire Sunset*'.
T: Oh yes – they filmed that in my home city, Glasgow.
S: In Glasgow? That can't be right – *Vampire Sunset* is set in San Francisco.
T: Yes, but they made it in Glasgow – a lot of films set in San Francisco are made in Glasgow. I think it's cheaper or something. Anyway, I've already seen it – I went with Katya last week.
S: OK. Well, there's '*Captain Fantastic*' ...
T: I don't really want to see that. Is '*His and Hers*' on? We haven't seen that yet.
S: Yes, but it's already started – it started at 6 o'clock.
T: Hmm, so it's too late for '*His and Hers*', and that's the only film we both want to see. Why don't we stay home, get a take-away pizza and watch a DVD?
I've just bought a new romantic comedy we can watch – '*301 Wedding Dresses*'! It's got Hugh James in it – he's my favourite actor!

S: '*301 Wedding Dresses*'? I'm not watching that! And I think Hugh James is a terrible actor! Let's watch that action movie you gave me for Christmas, I haven't seen that yet.
T: I *like* Hugh James, and I don't want to watch your stupid action film!
S: I know – you watch your film on the TV, and I'll watch mine on my laptop, with headphones. But we can still share the pizza!
T: That sounds great! Now we need a number for the pizza company ... Where's that newspaper?
S: Um ... I've just put it back in the recycling bin ...

On location
3a Reading: San Francisco or Glasgow?
10 mins

- Ask students to read the text and write one question about it to ask the class.
- Once students have finished reading and writing their questions, ask individual students to read out their question for the class to answer.

Language and culture

Students can read the text *American place names* (p. 81) and do the related tasks at home – or you can use this as a 'filler' if you have time at the end of the lesson. For more information on this, look at page 93 of this TRB.

3b Comprehension
5 mins

- In class, students answer the comprehension questions. Check answers in class.

1 Film companies can use its wonderful buildings as locations. Glasgow City Council are really helpful. The city centre streets can be closed off for filming. 2 The art gallery has been used as New York's Grand Central Station. The City Hall has been the Kremlin and the Vatican. 3 The film industry puts a lot of money into Glasgow's economy. 4 ... because the closed streets mean it takes longer to get to work.

If short of time

If you notice you're getting short of time,
- do ***Exercise 3c*** in class.
- do only sentences 1 and 2 in ***Exercise 4***.

3c Now you: A film in your town
5 mins

- In small groups, students discuss the questions.
- Ask individuals from each group to report back on what their group decided for the first two questions.

4 Write it right – Capital letters
10 mins

- Read out the instructions.
- Students work together to translate the sentences and write them using capital letters where appropriate. Check answers in class.
1 The streets in the city centre are closed for filming every Sunday. 2 Filmmakers have used Glasgow's City Hall as the Kremlin and the Vatican. 3 The work on the new James Bond film will start next July. 4 Would you like to be an extra in an American film?

5 Movie mistakes
5+ mins

- Read out the instructions.
- Students read the titles and try to spot the correct one. Check answer in class.
***Star Wars* is correct.**
- In pairs, students correct the other titles. Check answers in class.
Corrected film titles: ***Singing in the Rain, Saturday Night Fever, Pirates of the Caribbean, When Harry met Sally, Sleepless in Seattle***

And finally ...
5+ mins

Remind students of the following:
- **Language study** (p. 76): An overview of the grammar of the step (both *You already know* and *And now*) with exercises. Students can do this in their books or online.
- **Selfstudy** (p. 76): Students can do this in their books or online.
- **Keys** (p. 132) to the Language study and Selfstudy exercises.
- **Language and culture** (p. 81), Step 3: *American place names* and the corresponding tasks. Encourage students to do the Internet task at home. Refer them to the *Listen in* task. (For more information on this, look at page 93 of this TRB.)

And point out ...
- **Reading: Where shall we meet?** (p. 77): Short texts about the changing style of meetings, depending on people's age, with a glossary of unknown words. If you want to use these texts in class, there are some ideas on how to exploit them on page 121.

Unit 4 Now I can

Contents

Review of vocabulary, functions and structures in Unit 4

Starter	Making arrangements
Part 1	Finding information about leisure events; Making arrangements
Part 2	Making, accepting and refusing written invitations; Writing a thank-you note
Part 3	Finding information in small ads
Part 4	Talking about things that have just happened

Lesson notes

Additional material

For optional and additional material for Unit 4, *Now I can*, see pages 93/94.
Refer to this section before your lesson as some of the materials require preparation.

Optional stages

Optional stages of the lesson are written in grey in these notes.

Now I can: ...
5 mins

- Ask students to look at *Now I can: ...* at the top of page 78. Remind them that the symbols refer to different skills or vocabulary items which they learnt in Unit 4 and were listed in the unit aims on the photo page (p. 65).

Starter: Look back
5 mins

- Point to the pictures and ask the class to tell you what they remember about the events.

  Possible answers:
  Dinner in the air: It's at a table hanging from a crane. It's 50 metres up in the air. There is a chef and a waiter. Places are limited to 22 people. It's on Wednesday – Friday at 8pm and 10.30 pm. It costs £95 a head. You must book online.
  Car parts in the park: It's at Queen's Park. It's on Thursday at 3.30 pm. It's an orchestra. The musicians play instruments made from car parts. It's free.
  100th Birthday Party: It's William and Rita's birthday party. William's going to be 55 and Rita's going to be 45 years old. It's in their garden. It's a fancy dress party. You need to wear a costume from 100 years ago.
- Students then work in pairs to arrange to go to one of these events.
- ↓ Refer students back to the phrases for making arrangements in *Exercise 3a*, p. 67.

Starter: Now look forward
5 mins

- Read out the *Now look forward* information.

Part 1:
1a What's on?
10 mins

- Hold up your open book and point to the leaflet. Read out the title: *Death comes to town on Saturday 21st!* and the four headings.

Tip: Scanning With some text types we would naturally scan through the text quickly to find key information without taking in the details. We might be looking for a date, a price or a time. With this leaflet, you could practice this skill.
Scan questions: *Which event costs £8?* (Who killed Miss Mullins?), *Which event lasts 45 minutes?* (Deadly plants), *How much is the Detective quiz?* (£3), *Which event has a 10pm start?* (1930s detective night at the Picture House)

- Ask students to read the information in the leaflet and answer the scan questions in class.
  1 The 1930 detective night at the Picture House and the play *Who killed Miss Mullins?* at the Arts Centre. 2 The guided tours of the poison garden at the botanic gardens. 3 The detective quiz. 4 The guided tours of the poison garden. 5 The play *Who killed Miss Mullins?*. 6 The guided tours of the poison garden and the 1930 detective night.

1b What shall we do?
10 mins

- Read out the instructions.
- Students work in pairs to choose an event and make arrangements.
- ↑ Students act out their conversations for the class.

Part 2:
2a We'd like to invite you ...
10 mins

- Ask students to work in small groups.
- Read out the instructions.
- ↓ Refer students to *Exercise 2a*, p. 71 for the phrases for making written invitations.
- Students write their invitations.
- Monitor the activity while the students are writing and correct any mistakes.
- Students then 'send' their invitations to another group.

2b Thank you for your invitation
5 mins

- Allow time for the groups to read their invitations.
- Read out the instructions.
- ↓ Refer students to *Exercise 2a*, p. 71 for the phrases for accepting and refusing written invitations.
- Students write their replies.
- Monitor the activity while the students are writing and correct any mistakes.
- Students then 'send back' their replies.
- Allow time for the groups to read their replies, then ask them to tell the class if their invitations were accepted or refused.

Part 3:
We need help
5 mins

- Students work in the same groups.
- Read out the instructions.
- Students talk together and complete the task.
- Ask individual students from each group to tell the class which ads they thought were useful for their group and why.
  Possible answers: **Cleaning – to clean your house before / after the party. DJs / Disco hire – to provide music for the party. Take-away food – to provide the food for the party.**

Part 4:
4a What's just happened?
2/48–49
10 mins

- Read out the first part of the instructions.
- Allow time for the students to read the list of characters.
- Play ▶ 2/48. Students listen and tick the characters which are mentioned.
- Check answers in class.

  ✓ a private detective, the cook, the owner of the house, a police inspector, an assistant detective, the gardener
- Read out the second part of the instructions.
- Allow time for the students to read the sentences.
- Play ▶ 2/49. Play ▶ 2/49 a second time if necessary.
- Check in class which sentences are true.
  ✓ 2, 4
- Students correct the false sentences.
  Corrected sentences: **1 There's a body in the garden (not in the kitchen). 3 The detective has found a man's body (not a gun). 5 The police inspector hasn't arrived yet / is on his way to the house. 6 The gardener has just left by car (not by bike).**

(PD = private detective, AD = assistant detective)
PD: Good evening, ladies and gentlemen. I'm sorry to interrupt your dinner, but I have an announcement to make. I am a private detective. I'm sorry to tell you that there has been a death here this evening. There's a body in the garden. A dead body. About twenty minutes ago, the cook went out into the garden and she found a man's body. It was lying under an apple tree. I can tell you that the dead gentleman is Sir Roderick Buxton, the owner of this house. It is most probable that this death was not a natural death. I believe that it was murder. I have informed the local police and a police inspector is on his way to the house now. He will be here very soon. Until then, I would like to ask you to stay in this room. We will need to speak to each of you separately.
AD: Excuse me, sir.
PD: Excuse me, ladies and gentlemen. I need to speak to my assistant for a moment. Yes, what is it?
AD: It's the gardener.

→

PD: What about the gardener?
AD: He's just left.
PD: Left the house?
AD: Yes. I've just seen his car.
PD: Right. I want you to stay here with these people and I'll go and see what's happening.

If short of time

If you notice you're getting short of time,

- do *Exercise 4b* as a class activity.

4b You're the detective
10– mins

- Read out the instructions.
- Students work in pairs to speculate about the crime, using the clues and the pictures to make sentences.
- Ask individual students to tell the class one of their sentences.
  Possible answers: **Someone has just / Some people have just ... eaten an apple, drunk a beer, fired a gun, spilled some red wine, smoked a cigarette / some cigarettes.**

5 Now you choose
10 mins

- Remind students about the star system and tell them they need to choose one of these tasks.
- Allow time for the students to read the tasks and choose one.
- Ask students to sit together with a student who wants to do the same task.
- Students complete the task with their partners.
- Monitor and help with any vocabulary / phrases they may need.

And finally ...
5 mins

Look back at the *In this unit, you will learn to: ...* (p. 65) to show your students how much they have learnt in this unit, to say how well they've done and to let them reflect on where they need more practice.

Remind students of the following:

- **Test yourself** (p. 80): Students can do this progress test and check their answers (p. 132).
- **Language and culture** (p. 81): Refer your students to any L&C texts and tasks that weren't done in class.
- **Now me** (p. 82): Students can do some free writing, using the vocabulary and structures they've learned in Unit 4. Ask students to read the *Now blog* section. They can use this as a model for writing their own blog. Finally, refer students to the *Now explore the Internet* section to choose an English speaking film to see this week. Remind students that they can copy the *Now me* page for their portfolio.

If your course has more than 24 lessons, you'll find an extra lesson after Unit 4: **Globetrotter.**
Globetrotter Work – one page (45 minutes) of material with the focus on English for work.
Globetrotter Travel – one page (45 minutes) of material with the focus on English for travel.
A further 45 minutes of material is provided on the Internet for each of these lessons. Teaching notes on **Globetrotter B** can be found on pages 124/125.

Your notes

Unit 5 Step 1 Sickness

Contents

Text topic	An article about the worst excuses people have made for being off work
Functions	Identifying parts of the body; Saying what's wrong with you
Vocabulary	Parts of the body; Health problems
Grammar	Reflexive pronouns

Lesson notes

Additional material

For optional and additional material for Unit 5, Step 1, see pages 94/95.
Refer to this section before your lesson as some of the materials require preparation.

Optional stages

Optional stages of the lesson are written in grey in these notes.

Photo page
5– mins

- Hold up your open book at page 85 and introduce the topic of the unit by looking at the pictures with the class.
- Read out the first question and ask students to tick the relevant boxes.
- Compare the number of ticked boxes in class by asking individual students to say how many boxes they ticked and find out who ticked the most boxes (this person is the healthiest).
- Refer students to *In this unit, you will learn to: ...* . Give them a minute to read the learning aims.

Starter: I can't come to work today
5– mins

Ask individual students the *Starter* question.

1a Comprehension
10 mins

Tip: Personal response to a text It's a natural response to want to comment on a text you've read, so offer students the chance to do this in class. When they read a text, you can briefly ask for a general response, e.g. whether they agree with what the writer says or what they found most interesting. Or you can ask for a more specific response, e.g. with this text, ask which excuse they find the funniest or the most unlikely.

- Ask students to read the text and tell the class which excuse they like best.
- Read out the instructions for the comprehension task.
- Students read the sentences and tick the true ones. They can refer back to the text.
- Check answers in class.
  ✓ 2, 3, 5, 7
- Students then correct the false sentences.
- Check answers in class.
  Corrected sentences: **1 The article isn't about accidents at work. (It's about people taking time off work when they are well). 4 An employee fell over his cat. 6 An employee's wife cut herself when she was making sandwiches. 8 An employee hurt his foot when a beer can fell out of the refrigerator.**

Language and culture

Students can read the text *Thanksgiving in America* (p. 101) and do the related tasks at home – or you can use this as a 'filler' if you have time at the end of the lesson. For more information on this, look at page 95 of this TRB.

1b Vocabulary: Parts of the body
5+ mins

- Ask students to read the article again and underline all of the words for parts of the body.
- Once they've done this, ask them to check their answers with a partner.
- Check answers in class.
  nose, back(ache), fingers, head, neck, mouth, legs, foot
- Then, one student reads out a sentence containing one of the words, and another student points to that part of his / her body.

2 Grammar
10 mins

Reflexive pronouns

- Read out the sentences from the Grammar box. Have students repeat them in chorus.
- Say: *We use reflexive pronouns with certain verbs, for example: hurt, injured, cut.*
- Elicit the reflexive pronouns from students by saying: *I hurt …* (students provide *myself*). *Did you hurt …? (yourself)., My son didn't hurt … (himself)., My sister cut … (herself)., The children hurt … (themselves). Etc.* Write the pronouns into the correct columns on the board:

Singular	Plural
myself yourself himself / herself / itself	ourselves yourselves themselves

! Refer students to the *Info box*. Point out that, unlike in German, we don't need a reflexive pronoun in these sentences.

NB: If you have time, and if you feel your students need more consolidation of this grammar point, there's an explanation in German and some example sentences in the *Language study* (p. 88).

2a I hurt myself!
5 mins

- Read out the instructions.
- Students work individually to complete the sentences.
- ↓ Students work in pairs to complete the sentences.

2 myself, 3 herself, 4 themselves, 5 yourself

- ↑ Students write two more sentences using a reflexive pronoun. They then read out their sentences to the class but don't say the pronoun (they could say *dot dot dot* to indicate where it is). Volunteers repeat the sentence with the pronoun inserted.

2b Now you: An accident you had
10 mins

- Read out the instructions. Students work in small groups to complete the task.
- Ask one volunteer from each group to tell the class about the accidents their group had.

3a How to say it: Saying what's wrong with you
3/2
5 mins

- Say: *Listen and repeat.* Play ▶ 3/2.

I've got backache. I've got a cold. I've got a temperature. I've got a pain in my leg.	My neck hurts. I burnt myself. I cut myself. I injured my hand.

! Refer students to the *Info box*. Read out the *Ache rhymes with 'make'* section. Have students repeat the sentence in chorus. Read out the remainder of the *Info box*. Students then cover the *Info box* and tell you what the five aches are.

3b Health problems
5+ mins

- Read out the instructions.
- Students use the phrases in *Exercise 3a* to tell the class what's wrong.

(a) **I've got toothache.** (b) **I cut my finger / myself.** (c) **I've got a cold.** (d) **I've got backache.** (e) **My neck hurts.** (f) **I hurt my head.**

3c I don't feel well
3/3
5+ mins

- Read out the instructions. Tell students they won't hear the word they have to write, they need to listen to the symptoms and guess the health problem. Play ▶ 3/3.
- Students listen and write the word. If necessary, play the CD again. Play ▶ 3/3.

1 neck pain, 2 toothache, 3 a cold, 4 backache

1
S1: I think it's because I sit in the same position at my computer all day at work and don't move my head very much. It really hurts when I try to look left or right. I hope it gets better soon.
2
S2: It started aching in the night and I couldn't sleep. It feels like my whole head is aching! And I can't eat anything because it hurts so much! I'm going to the dentist's later, so I hope he can do something about it.

3
S3: I don't feel well. As you can hear, my nose is really full, and I can't stop ... a-a-atchoo!
4
S4: It started hurting last week after I helped John to move house and it's got worse. I can't walk very fast and it's really painful to stand up or sit down! Maybe I injured it when I was lifting all that heavy furniture.

If short of time

If you notice you're getting short of time,
- do ***Exercise 4*** as a class activity, with individual students asking each other.
- do just one of the ***Round up*** activities.
- do only one or two questions of ***Exercise 5b*** as a class discussion.

4 What's wrong?
10 mins

- Read out the instructions.

Tip: Demonstrations It's advisable to demonstrate activities so that students have a pattern to base their answers / conversations on.

- Demonstrate the task with one student, using some of the example phrases.
- Board: * Underline the phrases in the A: / B: dialogue which you want to use before you start.
  ** As in the coursebook.
  *** As in the coursebook and then ask additional questions, e.g. When did it start? Have you had this problem long? Have you already been to the doctor's?
- Students to stand up and walk and talk.

Round up
5a It hurts!
5 mins

- Read out the instructions and demonstrate the task.
- Students work in small groups. They think of a health problem and mime it for the other students in their group, who then guess the problem.
- ↓ If students are struggling to think of ailments, refer them to the Unit vocabulary on p. 170 where there are two lists of health problems they could use.

5b Talk about it
5+ mins

- Students work in small groups or in pairs, and choose one or more of the questions to chat freely about. They can just talk about one, or two, or all of the questions.
- If communication seems to have come to a standstill, ask additional questions, e.g. *Do you think people should stay at home when they've got a cold or go to work? Why?*

And finally ...
5+ mins

Remind students of the following:
- **Language study** (p. 88): An overview of the grammar of the step with exercises. Students can do this in their books or online.
- **Selfstudy** (p. 89): Students can do this in their books or online.
- **Keys** (p. 132) to the Language study and Selfstudy exercises.
- **Language and culture** (p. 101), Step 1: *Thanksgiving in America* and the corresponding tasks. Encourage students to do the Internet task at home.

And point out ...
- The **FAQ** *What's the difference between British English and American English?* at the end of the Selfstudy page (p. 89). FAQ reflects the kind of questions that more advanced learners may ask in order to improve their independent learning. Students can find more questions with more detailed answers on pages 198/199.

Unit 5 Step 2 Health

Contents

Text topic	An online health advice page called 'Dot.Com Doctor'
Functions	Giving advice
Vocabulary	Health advice
Grammar	**You already know:** Adjectives **And now:** Adverbs

Lesson notes

Additional material

For optional and additional material for Unit 5, Step 2, see pages 95/96.
Refer to this section before your lesson as some of the materials require preparation.

Optional stages

Optional stages of the lesson are written in grey in these notes.

Starter: The last time I was ill
5 mins

- Before students open their books, ask volunteers the *Starter* question.

Tip: Sensitive topics There are some topics which have the potential to cause distress and must therefore be treated carefully in class. When dealing with these, be aware that some students may not want to re-tell an experience or voice an opinion. Here, for example, only ask volunteers questions related to their own health experiences.

1a Comprehension
10 mins

- Board: Dot.com doctor Ask the class what they think a website called 'Dot.com doctor' does. (It offers general advice to health questions.)
- Ask students to open their books and look at the website. Say: *There are three health questions and three answers from Dr Gillespie.*
- Split the class into groups of three and allocate one text to each student in the group.
- Students read their text silently and then tell their group about it.
- In their groups, they read and answer the comprehension questions.
  1 No, they don't. (Jogging or swimming a couple of times a week is enough.) 2 Eat healthily / fruit. 3 It gives you important vitamins and minerals (that can stop a cold). 4 Dress warmly, drink a lot of water and rest. 5 They should be able to walk and talk comfortably at the same time. 6 Swimming exercises the whole body gently.

Language and culture

Students can read the text *Active or not?* (p. 101) and do the related task at home – or you can use this as a 'filler' if you have time at the end of the lesson. For more information on this, look at pages 95/96 of this TRB.

1b The doctor's advice
5 mins

- Read out the instructions.
- Allow students time to read all of the texts and underline the matching sentences.
  1 Do you exercise regularly? 2 You don't have to train hard – ... 3 ... eat healthily ... 4 ... dress warmly, ... 5 ... don't try to walk too fast – ... 6 ... you should be able to ... talk comfortably ... 7 ... you can't walk well, ... 8 ... it exercises your whole body gently.

2 Grammar
10 mins

! Students may have problems with this area of grammar because in German adjectives and adverbs have the same form.

You already know: Adjectives
- Read out the sentences from the *You already know* Grammar box. Have students repeat them in chorus.
- Ask students to finish this sentence with one word: *The weather today is ...*
- Do the same with: *This town is ...; My best friend is ...; This classroom is ...*
- Board: An adjective (e.g. warm) describes a p__________ or a th__________.
  Elicit *person* or *thing* and write this in the board.

And now: Adverbs
- Read out the regular adverb sentences from the *And now* Grammar box. Have students repeat them in chorus.

- Board: An adverb (e.g. warmly) describes how somebody *does* something.
- Say: *Most adverbs end in -ly.*
- Ask (whisper): *How am I speaking?* (quietly) Ask (shout): *How am I speaking now?* (loudly)
- Say: *Some adverbs don't end in -ly.* Read out the irregular adverb sentences from the *And now* Grammar box. Have students repeat them in chorus.

2a Fit at work
10 mins

- Students read the tips and cross out the wrong words. Check answers in class.
- ↓ Ask students to check answers in pairs before checking in class.
- Ask students which of these fitness tips they would do at work.

1 ~~regular~~ | regularly, 2 ~~correct~~ | correctly, 3 ~~quick~~ | quickly, 4 slow | ~~slowly~~, 5 ~~good~~ | well, 6 quick | ~~quickly~~, 7 ~~healthy~~ | healthily, 8 good | ~~well~~

2b Eat healthily
5+ mins

- Read out the instructions.
- Students work individually to write the adverbs for the given adjectives. Check answers in class.
- **badly, carefully, fast, well, hard, healthily, quickly, regularly, slowly, unhealthily**

2c Now you: How do you do it?
5+ mins

- Board: drive

Ask the class how many adverbs they can think of which match *drive*. Make a spider diagram on the board:

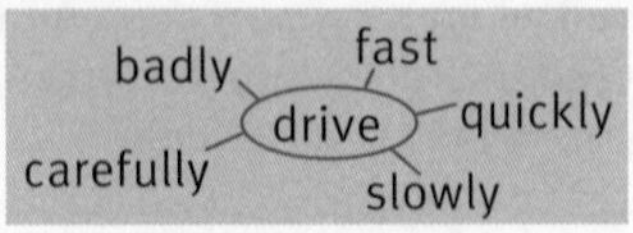

- Read out the instructions and use the spider diagram to demonstrate the task. Say: *I drive slowly and carefully. What about you?* Ask individual students to respond.
- Board:
  - * In small groups, choose four of the verbs and create spider diagrams for them before starting the task.
  - ** As in the coursebook.
  - *** As in the coursebook but keep a record of which students in your group do the same things in the same way. Report back to the class, e.g. All of us drive carefully, some of us exercise regularly, none of us sing well.
- Students work in small groups to complete the task.

3a Vocabulary: Health advice
5+ mins

- Read out the instructions.
- Students work individually to match the verbs. Check answers in class.

ask a pharmacist, eat a lot of fruit, exercise regularly in your free time, go on a diet, join a gym, stop smoking, take a paracetamol

- ↑ Think of two other pieces of health advice to tell the group.

3b Mum knows best!
3/8–9
10 mins

- Read out the first part of the instructions. Allow time for students to read the advice.
- Students listen and tick the good advice. Play ▶ 3/8. Check answers in class.

✓ 1, 4

- Read out the second part of the instructions.
- Play ▶ 3/9. Students listen and complete the sentences. Check answers in class.

1 hot; 2 out into the fresh air, exercise; 3 vitamin C; 4 fruit; 5 alcohol

(I = radio interviewer, G = Dr. Gillespie)
I: In this week's Health Watch, we're talking about colds and traditional ways to deal with them. We're asking the question "Did mum *really* know best?" With me in the studio is Dr. Gillespie, the well-known TV and Internet doctor. Welcome to the show.
G: Thank you.
I: Now, we asked you, the listener to email us and tell us what your mothers' advice was for getting better when you had a cold. Our first email comes from Barbara in Stockport. She says, "My mother always said that we had to keep warm. So she made me stay at home all day and I had to sit by the fire wearing three pullovers!" Dr Gillespie, did Barbara's mother do the right thing?
G: Well, it *is* important to keep warm when you have a cold. But only warm. If you're too *hot*, it can actually make you feel worse.

→

I: I didn't know that.
G: A lot of people don't! But, Barbara, I'm afraid your mother wasn't right about staying inside all day. You should go out into the fresh air at least once a day and do a little bit of exercise – nothing big, just a short walk is fine. That helps a lot more than staying at home all day.
I: I see. So your mother was only partly right, Barbara. Here's another email, this time from Keith in Trafford. He says, "My mum believed that eating a lot was bad for you when you had a cold, so she only ate a couple of pieces of toast a day." So, Dr Gillespie, is *not* eating good for a cold?
G: No, I'm afraid Keith's mum wasn't right. Your body needs food when you have a cold. You should always eat as normally as possible, and eating healthily means that the cold goes away more quickly.
I: What kind of food is best?
G: Well, you should eat food with lots of vitamin C in it, so fruit and vegetables like oranges, lemons, kiwi fruit, broccoli and tomatoes are best. And yes, as everyone knows, chicken soup really does help your body fight the cold and it keeps you warm and strong.
I: So *my* mum was right! She always gave me chicken soup! OK, there's just time for one last email, this time from Pat in Salford. She says, "My mother always drinks warm milk with a little bit of whisky in it when she has a cold. And it seems to work – she's ninety-five!"
G: Well, first of all, you need to drink a lot when you have a cold. And warm drinks help a lot – so Pat's mother's warm milk is a good idea. But the best warm drinks are *fruit* drinks because the fruit gives you vitamin C. It *is* true that a very *small* amount of whisky can also help to fight a cold, so Pat's mother is also right about that. It can help you to relax and sleep well. But, of course, generally, it's best *not* to drink *any* alcohol at all when you have a cold.
I: Right, well, thank you Dr Gillespie. It's good to know that our mothers were often right! And now we're going to play some relaxing music before we look at stress in the workplace ...

4a How to say it: Giving advice
3/10
5 mins

- Play ▶ 3/10 and have the class repeat the phrases in chorus.

You should drink warm milk. You shouldn't eat so much. I think you should go on a diet.	I don't think you should smoke. Why don't you go to bed? If I were you, I'd do some exercise.

If short of time

If you notice you're getting short of time,
- do ***Exercise 4b*** as a class activity.
- do just one of the ***Round up*** activities.

4b Your health advice
5 mins

- Read out the instructions. Students work in pairs to give the woman advice.

Possible answers: **I want to stop smoking: I think you should reduce the number of cigarettes slowly. You should get a nicotine plaster from the chemnist. I'm stressed at work: Why don't you talk to your boss? You should make a list of things to do. I think you should have a holiday. If I were you, I'd find a different job. I need to lose weight: You should eat less. Why don't you join a weight loss club? You should stop eating sweets. If I were you, I'd start eating more healthily.**

Round up

5a What's your advice?
5– mins

- Follow coursebook instructions. Monitor the activity, correcting any mistakes you see.

5b Talk about it
5 mins

- Students work in small groups or in pairs, and choose one or more of the questions to chat freely about. They can just talk about one, or two, or all of the questions.
- If communication seems to have come to a standstill, ask additional questions.

And finally ...
5+ mins

Remind students of the following:
- **Language study** (p. 92): An overview of the grammar of the step (both *You already know* and *And now*) with exercises. Students can do this in their books or online.
- **Selfstudy** (p. 93): Students can do this in their books or online.
- **Keys** (p. 132) to the Language study and Selfstudy exercises.
- **Language and culture** (p. 101), Step 2: *Active or not?* and the corresponding task.

Unit 5 Step 3 Stress and relaxation

Contents

Realia	Instructions on a bottle of tablets
Functions	Understanding instructions; Talking about quantity
Vocabulary	Sleep and relaxation
Reading	Relax!
Grammar	**You already know:** *a lot of / not many / not much* **And now:** *a few / a little / a bit of*
Write it right	Words that end in *-y*

Lesson notes

Additional material
For optional and additional material for Unit 5, Step 3, see pages 96/97. Refer to this section before your lesson as some of the materials require preparation.

Optional stages
Optional stages of the lesson are written in grey in these notes.

Starter: A good night's sleep
5 mins

- Ask individual students the *Starter* questions.

How to relax
1 Instructions
10 mins

- Tell students that they are going to read part of the instructions on a Calm Life tablets bottle.
- Students read the instructions and use the information to tick the correct statements.
  ✓ 2, 5, 6
- Then correct the false statements in class.
  Corrected statements: **1 You should take 2 tablets, 2 times a day plus 3 tablets at bedtime. 3 You should take the tablets after you eat (not before) / after meals. 4 Children can't take these tablets. / They are not recommended for anyone under 18 years old.**

2a All about sleep
3/16
10 mins

- Ask individual students how many hours of sleep they like to have each night. Ask whether they dream regularly and if they remember their dreams or not.
- Tell the class they are going to listen to part of a talk on sleep. Read out the instructions.
- Play ▶ 3/16. Students listen and tick the information they hear.
  ✓ 1a), 2b), 3a)

(C = Chair, W = Dr. West)

C: Good evening and welcome to the Community Education Centre. This evening's speaker is Dr David West, an expert on sleep. Dr West ...

W: Good evening, everybody. This evening I'm going to tell you a few surprising facts about sleep.
First, let's think about how much sleep people need. Well, it's different for everybody, but most people sleep for five to nine hours every night; six to seven hours is ideal. Some people only need a little sleep. This is true of certain famous people in history, for example, Leonardo Da Vinci only slept about three hours a day – he took little ten-minute naps during the day and night. Michelangelo and Napoleon didn't need much sleep – only about four hours a night. Britain's ex-prime minister, Margaret Thatcher, also only slept for about four hours a night – and this once saved her life! In 1984, she was staying in a hotel when a terrorist bomb exploded in the middle of the night. She wasn't killed because she wasn't in bed – she was working in her office.
A lot of people have problems sleeping at night. If you've slept badly, you can catch up on sleep with a quick nap during the day. If you sleep for half an hour, you'll wake up refreshed. A lot of busy business people have a power nap – a short sleep in the afternoon to give them more energy for the rest of the day. In the USA, a few companies provide special rooms so that staff members can go to sleep for half an hour during the day. But to help get a good night's sleep, do a bit of exercise before you go to bed – →

nothing extreme, just a bit of yoga or a short walk. And having a little food or a milky drink can also help to relax you.
Who can remember his or her dream last night? Hmmm – not many of you. But, you know, you *did* dream – in fact, everyone dreams, but not many people remember their dreams. We think that dreaming helps the brain to sort out the events of the day. Do you know that nowadays most of us dream in colour – not many people dream in black and white. And it's an interesting fact that about 40 years ago, more people dreamed in black and white. Some experts think this is connected to watching TV. Forty years ago, television was black and white, but in the early 1970s, people started to watch colour TV – and they started to dream in colour! I'm not sure that's true but experiments suggest that ...

2b A talk on sleep
3/17
5+ mins

- Ask students to work in groups of three, A, B and C.
- Tell the students to read the instructions for their part (e.g. A, B or C).
- Play ▶ 3/17. Students listen and make notes. If necessary, play the CD again. Play ▶ 3/17.
- In their groups, students then tell each other about their topic using the notes they have made.
  Student A – How much sleep people need: Most people sleep for five to nine hours every night; six to seven hours is ideal.
  Students B – Power naps: This is a short sleep in the afternoon to give you more energy for the rest of the day. In the USA, a few companies provide special rooms so that staff members can go to sleep for half an hour during the day.
  Student C – Dreaming: Dreaming helps the brain to sort out the events of the day. Nowadays most of us dream in colour – not many people dream in black and white. About 40 years ago more people dreamed in black and white.

Audio script: see above in *Exercise 2a.*

3 Grammar
10 mins

You already know: *a lot of / not many / not much*
- Say: *Some things we can count – for example, tablets. (There are some tablets).*
- Say: *Some things we can't count – for example, medicine. (There is some medicine).*
  Board:

Countable	Uncountable
There are some ...	There is some ...

- Ask students to read the *You already know* Grammar box. Say: *Read out the sentence that shows us we can use a lot of with countable nouns.* (sentence 1) Write *There are a lot of ...* under the Countable heading on the board.
- Say: *Read out the sentence that shows us we can use a lot of with uncountable nouns.* (sentence 2) Write *There is a lot of ...* under the Uncountable heading on the board.
- Say: *Do we use not much with countable or uncountable nouns?* (uncountable) Read out the fourth sentence from the Grammar box and add *not much ...* under the Uncountable heading on the board.
- Say: *Do we use not many with countable or uncountable nouns?* (countable) Read out the third sentence from the Grammar box and add *not many ...* under the Countable heading on the board.

And now: *a few / a little / a bit of*
- Refer students to the sentences in the *And now* Grammar box. Have students repeat them in chorus.
- Ask: *Do we use a few with countable or uncountable nouns?* (countable) Add this to the Countable list on the board.
- Ask the same for *a little* (uncountable) and then *a bit* (uncountable) and add these to the Uncountable list on the board.
- Point out the *NB* in the *And now* Grammar box on page 96.

3a What helps you to sleep?
5+ mins

- Read out the instructions. Students work individually to complete the sentences.
- ↓ Go through the sentences as a class. Underline the nouns and get the class to identify them as *countable* or *uncountable* and encourage students to write *c* or *u* above each noun.
- Check answers in class.
  1 a little, 2 a little, 3 a few, 4 a little, 5 a few, 6 a little
- Read out the second part of the instructions and allow students time to complete the task.
- Ask individual students to read out their sentences.
  1 a bit of, 2 a bit of, 4 a bit of, 6 a bit of

3b Now you: Your bedtime
10 mins

- Read out the first question. Ask the class: *Do we say: How much or How many hours?* (How many?). *Why?* (Because 'hours' is a countable noun.) Do the same with question 2. *Do we say: How much or How many food?* (How much?). *Why?* (Because 'food' is an uncountable noun.)
- Then ask students to complete the remaining questions with *many* or *much.*
  1 many, 2 much, 3 much, 4 many, 5 much
- Demonstrate the speaking task by asking the first question to individual students.
- Ask students to work in pairs and ask and answer the questions.

Reducing stress
4a Reading: Relax!
10+ mins

- Ask students to read the text silently and, with a partner, write four questions about it.
- When the students have written their questions they give them to another pair to answer.
- To check the answers, the pairs swap the papers back and 'mark' them.
  Possible questions: **How can you deal with stress? (go for a walk, have a meal with friends, choose a hobby), What do some young people enjoy? (extreme sports), Which game can help you forget your worries? (chess), How do people in China relax? (practising tai chi), What can you do in a 'cat café'? (enjoy a coffee and stroke a cat)**

Language and culture

Students can read the text *Therapies* (p. 101) and do the related task at home – or you can use this as a 'filler' if you have time at the end of the lesson. For more information on this, look at pages 96/97 of this TRB.

If short of time

If you notice you're getting short of time,
- ask students to choose one question to discuss in ***Exercise 4b***.
- do ***Exercise 6*** in class.

4b Talk about it
5 mins

- Students work in small groups and talk about the questions.

5 Write it right: Words that end in -*y*
10 mins

A Verbs
- Students work in pairs or small groups and write the past tenses. Check answers in class.

  hurried, studied, enjoyed, played, stayed
- Students then work together to complete the sentences. Check answers in class.
  enjoy, play and stay: add -ed; hurry and study: delete the -y and add -ied
- Then students work out the spelling rule. **!** Refer them to page 128 if needed.
- Ask students how to spell the present simple form for *hurry – he / she / it* (hurries). Write this on the board. Do the same for *stay* (stays). Remind them of the rule – if there's *a, e, i, o, u* before the *y*, just add *s*. Otherwise, change the *y* to *ies*. Students then write the present simple forms.
  hurries, studies, enjoys, plays, stays

B Nouns
- Students underline six nouns ending in *y* in the text. (way, day, hobby, activity, body, city)
- Ask students what the plural of *family* and *way* is and write this on the board.
- Say: *Are the spelling rules the same for nouns and verbs?* (Yes.)
- Students then write the plural forms for all of the nouns.
  1 way – ways, 2 day – days, 3 hobby – hobbies, 4 activity – activities, 5 body – bodies, 6 city – cities

6 A strange dream
5+ mins

- Read out the beginning of the story and ask a volunteer to continue it.
- Ask students to work in small groups and complete the task.

And finally ...
5+ mins

Remind students of the following:
- **Language study** (p. 96): An overview of the grammar of the step (both *You already know* and *And now*) with exercises. Students can do this in their books or online.
- **Selfstudy** (p. 96): Students can do this in their books or online.
- **Keys** (p. 133) to the Language study and Selfstudy exercises.
- **Language and culture** (p. 101), Step 3: *Therapies* and the corresponding task. Refer students to the *Listen in* task. (For more information on this, look at page 97 of this TRB.)

And point out ...
- **Reading: A body of stories** (p. 97): A text 'just for interest' about body stories with glossaries of unknown words. If you want to use this text in class, there are some ideas on how to exploit it on page 121 of this TRB.

Unit 5 Now I can

Contents — **Review of vocabulary, functions and structures in Unit 5**

Starter	Identifying parts of the body
Part 1	Identifying parts of the body; Explaining health problems; Giving advice; Talking about quantity
Part 2	Identifying parts of the body; Giving advice
Part 3	Explaining health problems; Giving advice
Part 4	Understanding instructions

Lesson notes

Additional material

For optional and additional material for Unit 5, *Now I can*, see page 97.
Refer to this section before your lesson as some of the materials require preparation.

Optional stages

Optional stages of the lesson are written in grey in these notes.

Now I can: ...
5 mins

- Ask students to look at *Now I can: ...* at the top of page 98. Remind them that the symbols refer to different skills or vocabulary items which they learnt in Unit 5 and were listed in the unit aims on the photo page (p. 85).

Starter: Look back
5 mins

- Hold up your open book and point to the picture of Dr Gillespie.
- Ask the class the questions.
  He's called Dr Gillespie. He answers your health questions online.
  Tips: Jog or swim a couple of times a week, eat healthily.

Starter: Now look forward
5 mins

- Read out the *Now look forward* information.

Part 1:
1a The parts of the body
10 mins

Tip: Recycling vocabulary It's important to recycle vocabulary on a regular basis to help students remember and use the words they have come across. There are several ways you can do this. You can start the lesson by playing hangman for five minutes, or give a definition of the words students learnt last lesson and ask them to tell you the word. You could also use anagrams, as in the example below.

- Board: cbak, tomuh, eteht
  Say: *Which parts of the body are these?* (back, mouth, teeth)
- Ask students to work in pairs.
- Give them two minutes to write down the parts of the body they can remember from Unit 5 and any other body parts they know.
- Ask individual students to read out the items from their list, and write them on the board until you have all of the words from Unit 5.
  head, nose, mouth, neck, arm, finger, back, legs, foot

1b My body
10 mins

- Demonstrate the task by briefly telling the class about any aches and pains you have.
- Students work in pairs and use the prompts to tell each other about any health issues they have.

1c A healthy lifestyle?
10 mins

- Ask individual students one or two of the questions in the apple. Encourage them to answer using a response from the pear.
- Ask students to work in pairs and ask and answer the lifestyle questions.
- ↑ Ask students to report back to the class two points about their partner.
- They each decide on one lifestyle aspect they could change to become healthier.

Part 2:
2a How can we get more exercise?
3/20–21
10 mins

- Read out the first part of the instructions and the gist listening task.
- ↓ Board: balance t____________, g__________ gyms, circus s__________.
- Play ▶ 3/20. Students listen and complete the names of the three activities.

balance training, green gyms, circus skills

- Read out the instructions for the specific listening task. Play ▶ 3/21. Students listen and make notes. They tell the class about the three activities.
balance training: gentle exercise, do it very slowly, good for your whole body, one element is to stand on one leg, think and move carefully;
green gyms: group of people, meet outside and work, cut wood or plant trees, start with warm-up exercises, good for all ages, hard work, not for people with back or neck problems;
circus skills: learn some clown skills, how to fall without hurting yourself, practises balance, active, juggle, a lot of fun, great for families

(DJ = Glen, a radio DJ, D = Dayna Duchene, a film expert)
DJ: Hi and welcome back to the show. Our guest here in the studio this morning is Dayna Duchene. She's a very fit lady, in fact she's a personal trainer and a fitness expert. And she's here with some ideas to get us all up and active – right, Dayna?
DD: That's right, Glen.
DJ: So, how can we get more exercise? What suggestions do you have for us today?
DD: Well, you'll be pleased to hear that I'm not going to say that you should go to the gym.
DJ: Well, that's good news!
DD: Yes, a lot of people don't feel comfortable in a gym. They want to do something different, less stressful maybe, so I have three alternative suggestions for you.
DJ: Great.
DD: And the first suggestion is balance training.
DJ: Balance training?
DD: Correct. It's a very gentle form of exercise and you do it very slowly, so it's great for older people, but it's good for your whole body – your legs, your arms, your back ...
DJ: What do you have to do? Stand on one leg?
DD: Well, there's a bit more to it than that, but, yes, standing on one leg is one element! You have to think carefully and move carefully, too.
DJ: It sounds very gentle. That's good!
DD: Yes, you should try it. Why not find a class near you?
DJ: Maybe I will. What's your next idea, Dayna?
DD: My next idea isn't so gentle. It's much harder exercise. Have you ever heard of 'green gyms'?
DJ: No, I haven't. But it sounds like a sort of gym to me – and you said no gyms today!
DD: Well, this is no ordinary gym. When you go to a normal gym, it's good for *you*, but if you go to a green gym, it's good for you and for the local area. A green gym is a group of people who meet outside – in a park, in a forest or at a lake, for example – and they work. They might cut wood, maybe, or plant trees. They help the local area and they get some exercise in the fresh air at the same time. There are warm-up exercises to start, and then everyone works together. It's great for all ages and it's a good way to meet new friends. But it's hard work, so it's not a good choice for people with back or neck problems.
DJ: Right. And what's your last idea for us?
DD: Well, this is the idea I like the best. It's circus skills.
DJ: Circus skills? You mean, like, clowns and elephants?
DD: Well, maybe not the elephants, but, yes, you can learn some clown skills – how to move like a clown and of course how to fall without hurting yourself. Like the balance training, it practises balance, but it's more active. And you can learn how to juggle – you know, with balls or rings. Circus skills classes are a lot of fun. It's great for families – you can have fun and be active with your kids or your grandkids. They'll love it.
DJ: What a fantastic idea. Thanks for that, Dayna.

2b I'd like to try ...
5 mins

- Students work in pairs using the questions to talk about the activities.
- Ask individual students to report back on their partner's answers.

If short of time

If you notice you're getting short of time,
- do ***Exercise 3*** in class: one person says a health problem and members of the class offer advice.
- put the class into two groups for ***Exercise 4***. After reading the text, one group prepares answers 1, 3 and 5, the other group prepares answers 2, 4 and 6. In turn, a member of one group asks the other group a question. Check answers in class.

Part 3:
Are you OK?
10– mins

- Read out the instructions and demonstrate the role play with a more able member of the class.
- ↓ Refer students to the *Phrases to learn* from Step 1, p. 170 and to the *Phrases to learn* from Step 2, p. 171 to read before the role play.
- In pairs, students complete the task.
- If time permits, ask individual pairs to role play their conversation to the class.

4 Always read the instructions
10+ mins

- Ask the class if anyone has had acupuncture or acupressure. If yes, ask them about their experience of it.
- Tell the class they are going to read a text about acupressure balls.
- Read out the instructions.
- Ask students to read the text and answer questions 1–6.
- Check answers in class.
  1 Yes, it is., 2 Gently., 3 Regularly during the day (e.g. every hour) for 15–30 seconds., 4 For a maximum of 3 days., 5 No, you don't need to take them off., 6 Pain, swelling, redness or heat.

5 Now you choose
10 mins

- Remind students about the star system and tell them they need to choose one of these tasks.
- Allow time for students to read the tasks and choose one.
- Students complete their tasks.
- Monitor and help with any vocabulary / phrases they may need.
- Ask students to sit together with students who did the same task. They then read each other's work and choose one to read to the class.

And finally ...
5 mins

Look back at the *In this unit, you will learn to: ...* (p. 85) to show your students how much they have learnt in this unit and say how well they've done.

Remind students of ...
- **Test yourself** (p. 100): Students can do this progress test and check their answers (p. 133).
- **Language and culture** (p. 101): Refer your students to any L&C texts and tasks that weren't done in class.
- **Now me** (p. 102): Students can do some free writing, using the vocabulary and structures they've learned in Unit 5. Ask students to read the *Now blog* section. They can use this as a model for writing their own blog. Finally, refer students to the *Now explore the Internet* section to choose a spa which they would like to visit. Remind students that they can copy the *Now me* page for their portfolio.

Your notes

Unit 6 Step 1 Saving

Contents

Text topic	A web article about the Freegans, people who live off recycled waste
Functions	Talking about waste and recycling; Agreeing and disagreeing
Vocabulary	Materials
Grammar	**You already know:** First conditional **And now:** Second conditional

Lesson notes

Additional material
For optional and additional material for Unit 6, Step 1, see pages 97–99.
Refer to this section before your lesson as some of the materials require preparation.

Optional stages
Optional stages of the lesson are written in grey in these notes.

Photo page
5– mins
- Hold up your open book at page 103 and introduce the topic of the unit by looking at the photos with the class. You can ask students to say what the people are doing in the photos and why they feel it is linked to saving or spending. Give students time to read the questions in the box. Then ask the class if they identify more with a 'spender' or a 'saver'. Ask why.
- Refer students to *In this unit, you will learn to:* … . Give them a minute to read the learning aims.

Starter: Recycling
5– mins
- Ask students which of the things they recycle. Then ask volunteers to answer the second *Starter* question.

1a Comprehension
10 mins
- Hold up your open book and point to the photo. Ask the class what they think the man is doing and why? (He's looking in a rubbish bin for things to recycle.) Tell the class that he's a Freegan and that they are going to read about a group of people called Freegans.
- Students read the FAQs and their answers silently and answer the comprehension questions.
1 … because they think that our society consumes and wastes too much and will ruin our planet. / … because they get most of the things they need by recycling things that other people have thrown away. 2 They share with other Freegans, grow their own food, repair things that they can still use and go 'bin diving'. 3 … because it's one day past its use-by date or the packaging is a bit damaged. 4 They don't take anything they can't repair or that's dangerous, food that's bad or in open packaging or used underwear.

Language and culture
Students can read the text *Too much bread* (p. 119) and do the related tasks at home – or you can use this as a 'filler' if you have time at the end of the lesson. For more information on this, look at pages 98/99 of this TRB.

1b Vocabulary: Materials
5+ mins
Tip: Use items in your classroom If students don't know the vocabulary, you can use items in the classroom to explain and practise the words. Point to an item and say the material – or elicit the word from a more able student e.g. a desk is made of … (wood), this page is made of … (paper).
- Choose an object in the classroom to demonstrate the task e.g. Say: *What's a desk usually made of?* (A desk is usually made of wood or plastic and metal.)
- Read out the instructions and the example.
- Board: * Do the task in class.
  ** As in the coursebook. Students work in small groups or pairs.
  *** Do ** and then write two descriptions of items in the classroom: *This is made of* … . Read your descriptions out to the class for them to guess the item.

  Possible answers: **A bed's usually made of fabric, wood or metal. A book's usually made of cardboard and paper. Boxer shorts are usually made of fabric. A can is usually made of metal. A TV is usually made of glass, plastic and metal.**

1c It's rubbish!
5 mins
- Read out the instructions. Students use one word to complete the sentences.
- Check answers in class.
1 boxer shorts, 2 TV, 3 can, 4 bag, 5 bed, 6 book

→

- In pairs, students discuss what the Freegans would / wouldn't take and say why.
  They wouldn't take the boxer shorts because they don't take underwear. They wouldn't take the TV because it isn't in its original packing. They would take the can of soup because it's still good to eat. They would take the bread because it's in a plastic bag. They wouldn't take the bed and mattress because they're in someone's garden. They would take the book.

2 Grammar
10 mins

You already know: First conditional
- Read out the sentence from the *You already know* Grammar box. Students repeat it in chorus.
- Say: *A conditional sentence is an 'if'-sentence. This is the first conditional. We use this kind of sentence for things which could easily happen. Which tense do we use in the 'if'-part of the sentence?* (present simple) *Which tense do we use in the other part of the sentence?* ('will' future)

! Many German students will say *If I will ...*, as this is possible in German. Watch out for this error and encourage students to self-correct when you hear it.
- Say: *'Will' does not go in the 'if'-part of the sentence. Remember:*
  Board: 'If' plus 'will' makes teachers ill!
  First conditional = 'If' + present simple, 'will' future

And now: Second conditional
- Read out the sentences from the *And now* Grammar box. Have students repeat them in chorus.
- Say: *This is the second conditional. We use this for unrealistic situations. For example: If a fire started in the classroom, what would you do?* (I'd ... run outside / phone 112 / jump out of the window, etc.) *Do you really think a fire is going to start here? No, it's unlikely.*
  Look at the tenses. Which tense do we use in the 'if'-part of the sentence? (past simple) *Which tense do we use in the other part of the sentence?* (would)
- Say: *If I had more time, I would ...*(e.g. go running every day). Ask individual students to say what they would do if they had more time.

NB: If you have time, and if you feel your students need more consolidation of this grammar point, there's an explanation in German and some example sentences in the *Language study* (p. 106).

2a If ...
5+ mins

- Read out the instructions.
  ! Point out to students that *I would = I'd.*
- Students read sentences a)–c) and then complete the sentences which demonstrate the use of the first and second conditional (first conditional is for likely / probable situations; second conditional is for unrealistic or impossible situations).
  1a); 2b), c)

2b Saving the planet
5 mins

- Read out the instructions.
- Students match the sentence halves and write the numbers in the boxes.
  1d), 2e), 3a), 4c), 5b)
- ↑ Students choose two or three sentence starters and write an alternative ending for them.

2c Now you: Your daydreams
5 mins

- Demonstrate this activity by briefly telling the class about your daydreams, using the phrases in the coursebook.
- In small groups, students talk about their daydreams using the four prompts.

3 An interview with a Freegan
3/24–25
10 mins

- Ask students what they can remember about the Freegans, and what 'bin diving' is. (Looking through bins and containers outside of shops and offices.)

Tip: Setting up listening activities It's important to set up listening activities well by taking time to tell students who they are going to listen to, how many people will be talking and what type of conversation it is, e.g. an interview. They also need time to read the questions / statements which they will have to answer. This helps students prepare for the listening before you press 'Play'.

- Tell them they are going to listen to an interview with Alex, a Freegan, talking about bin diving.
- Allow time for students to read sentences 1–5. Say: *Listen and cross out the wrong information.* Play ▶ 3/24.
- If necessary, play the CD a second time. Play ▶ 3/24. Check answers in class.
- ↓ When you play the CD a second time, pause it just after they hear the relevant information.
  1 the same as | ~~different from~~, 2 ~~clothes~~ | food, 3 took | ~~didn't take~~, 4 cardboard box | ~~plastic bag~~, 5 ~~broken~~ | too big
- Read out the second part of the instructions. Play ▶ 3/25. Students listen and mark the answers.
  + 1, ✓ 2, ✗ 3

(I = radio interviewer, A = Alex)

I: Today I'm talking to Alex, a Freegan, about bin diving. Now, Alex, a lot of people think that taking things out of bins is a strange thing to do.

A: Well, yes, maybe it is a bit strange, but I think it's stranger that people are happy to throw things away that are still OK. I'm a normal person – I'm married, have a son and live in a nice house. All I'm doing is saving things that people shouldn't throw away.

I: You went out bin diving last night, didn't you? What did you bring home?

A: Oh, last night was really good. As well as getting all the food I need for this week, I found lots of other things for the house.

I: Tell us about the food first.

A: Well, that's mainly why I go bin diving. My family can live for a week on the food I find. Last night, I got some bread, a whole chicken, some fish, a lot of fruit and vegetables, meat and cheese and a box of chocolates – everything in its packaging and still good!

I: If you asked most people, they'd say that food from a bin isn't clean. Do you agree?

A: You're absolutely right! Food that's open and has been in a bin for a long time is dangerous! So you have to be careful what you take. That's why I only take food that's still fresh and in unopened packaging. Yesterday, for example, I found some apples in their plastic packaging. They were a little bit damaged, but I checked them carefully and washed them well and they're completely OK to eat.

I: Now, you said that you got some other things last night. What were they?

A: Well, an office block closed recently and they've put a lot of stuff in big containers round the back. So I went round to have a look. It was great! I found an office chair, a cardboard box full of CDs and some printer paper – just thrown away! There was also a lovely coffee table made of wood, but it was too big for my living room, so I left it for someone else.

I: I think a lot of people would say that bin diving is stealing.

A: No, I'm sorry, I don't agree. If you throw something away, it doesn't belong to you anymore, so anyone can take it. If people really wanted the things, they wouldn't throw them away.

4a How to say it: Agreeing and disagreeing
3/26
5 mins

- Say: *Listen and repeat.*
- Play ▶ 3/26.

If short of time

If you notice you're getting short of time,
- ask students to choose just one topic to discuss in ***Exercise 4b.***
- do just one of the ***Round up*** activities.
- do only one or two questions of ***Exercise 5b*** as a class discussion.

4b Opinions
5 mins

- Ask students to work in small groups.
- Refer students to the speech bubbles with the opinions in them. Say: *Do you agree with these opinions? Talk about it in your groups. Try to use some of the 'How to say it' phrases.*

Round up

5a Chain game
5+ mins

- Demonstrate the activity by starting the chain yourself and encouraging a student to then continue it. Continue around the class with each student saying one sentence.

5b Talk about it
5+ mins

- Students work in small groups or in pairs, and choose one or more of the questions to chat freely about. They can just talk about one, or two, or all of the questions.
- If communication seems to have come to a standstill, ask additional questions, e.g. *Would you ever go bin diving? Why? Why not? What do you do with your old clothes? Do you recycle them?*

And finally ...
5+ mins

Remind students of the following:
- **Language study** (p. 106): An overview of the grammar of the step (both *You already know* and *And now*) with exercises. Students can do this in their books or online.
- **Selfstudy** (p. 107): Students can do this in their books or online.
- **Keys** (p. 133) to the Language study and Selfstudy exercises.
- **Language and culture** (p. 119), Step 1: *Too much bread* and the corresponding tasks. Encourage students to do the Internet task at home.

Unit 6 Step 2 Spending

Contents

Text topic	The Millionaire's Menu – an article with excerpts from very expensive menus
Functions	Speculating; Asking for help with a menu
Vocabulary	Food on a menu
Grammar	**You already know:** *must be* **And now:** *could / might be, can't be*

Lesson notes

Additional material
For optional and additional material for Unit 6, Step 2, see page 99.
Refer to this section before your lesson as some of the materials require preparation.

Optional stages
Optional stages of the lesson are written in grey in these notes.

Starter: If I were rich, ...
5 mins
- Ask volunteers to answer the *Starter* questions.

1a Comprehension
10 mins
- Refer students to the main picture and read out the headline. Ask the class: *What's that man doing?* (Eating money.) *What do you think the article is about?* (It's about expensive meals.)
- As a gist task ask students to read the texts and choose a meal they would like to order. Ask students to tell the class which meal they have chosen.
- Read out the comprehension questions to the class. Then students read the text silently and write the numbers in the boxes. Check answers in class.
  5a), 1b), 2c), 4d), 3e)

! Refer students to the *Info box*. Read out the definitions and tell students words like these are called 'false friends' – they look and sound the same but have different meanings.

Language and culture
Students can read the text *Haute cuisine* (p. 119) and do the related task at home – or you can use this as a 'filler' if you have time at the end of the lesson. For more information on this, look at page 99 of this TRB.

1b Vocabulary: Food on a menu
10 mins
- Board: Meat | Fish & Seafood | Fruit & Vegetables
  Tell students to write this down on a piece of paper or in their notebooks.
- Ask students to read the text again, find the food words and write them in the correct columns.
- Check answers by asking students to call out the items they have in each column and writing the words on the board.
  Meat: sausage, pork, beef, duck, chicken, ham
  Fish & Seafood: caviar, lobster, prawns
  Fruit & Vegetables: potato, lemon, onions, side salad, tomato, truffles, mushrooms
- As a class, add one more word to each category then say what you can make with the different types of food.

1c It must be!
5 mins
- Students find and underline the sentences which match numbers 1–3.
  1 It might be the most expensive menu in the world! (paragraph 1) 2 There can't be a more expensive pizza. (paragraph 6) 3 It must be the most expensive fast food in the world! (paragraph 6)

2 Grammar
10 mins
You already know: *must be*
- Read out the sentence from the *You already know* Grammar box.
- Say: *How sure are we that this is the most expensive fast food? Very sure or not very sure?* (Very sure.)
  Board: ↑ certain
  possible
  ↓ impossible

Say: *Where does 'must be' go?* (Next to 'certain'.) Write this on the board.

And now: *could / might be, can't be*

- Read out the first sentence from the *And now* Grammar box. Have students repeat it in chorus.
- Point to the board and say: *Where does 'could / might be' go?* (Next to 'possible'.) Write this on the board.
- Read out the second sentence from the *And now* Grammar box. Have students repeat it in chorus.
- Say: *So, 'can't be' is ...?* and elicit 'impossible'. Write this on the board.

NB: If you have time, and if you feel your students need more consolidation of this grammar point, there's an explanation in German and some example sentences in the *Language study* (p. 110).

2a What could it be?
3/31
5+ mins

- Read out the instructions.
- Play the first sound. Play ▶ 3/31 and stop the CD so that students can guess what the first sound is, using *could / might be, must be* or *can't be*. Repeat this process for each sound.

1 someone cooking, 2 someone doing the dishes / washing up, 3 someone making coffee, 4 someone paying, 5 someone making a cocktail

> 1 ((Chef chopping vegetables quickly on a chopping board & plopping them into a pan of water.))
>
> 2 ((Water sloshing around, squeaking of plates being cleaned then put on draining board.))
>
> 3 ((Coffee being made with a professional coffee machine: coffee holder being placed in machine, steam for frothing milk, percolating, sound of machine pouring coffee into cup.))
>
> 4 ((Rustling of bill and notes, till being opened, money taken out, change being given, tip dropped into a jar.))
>
> 5 ((Barman mixing a cocktail: bottles being opened, pouring liquids into shaker, ice being dropped into shaker, top being put on shaker, shaking.))

2b Pub food
5+ mins

- Ask students to work in pairs. Read out the instructions and the names of the dishes.

Tip: Pronunciation To help students improve their pronunciation refer them to the recorded Dictionary online and encourage them to use it (see 'Tipp' on page 177.).

- Students match a name to each picture and use the phrases to talk about the dishes.
- When most people have finished, refer students to p. 128 to check their answers.
See coursebook page 128.

3 What's on the menu?
3/32
5 mins

- Read out the instructions. Play ▶ 3/32.
- ↓ Look at the pictures in *Exercise 2b* with the class and make a list of the food you can see in each one. ((a) meat, potatoes, carrots, peas, broccoli, Yorkshire pudding (b) bacon, eggs, tomato, sausage, mushrooms, potatoes (c) potatoes, carrots, meat (d) fish, chips, (mushy) peas (e) quiche, broccoli (f) sausage, mashed potatoes, peas)
- Students listen and write the correct letter in each box.
- Play the first conversation, then stop the CD and ask students which meal it was. Repeat for each conversation.
- Play the CD a second time if necessary. Play ▶ 3/32. Check answers in class.
1b, 2c, 3d, 4e

> 1
> S1: Excuse me, can I ask you about something before I order? What's this?
> S2: It's a cooked breakfast – bacon, eggs, sausages, baked beans, mushrooms and a grilled tomato.
> S1: Oh, no, that sounds too much for me. I think I'll just have ...
>
> 2
> S3: I'm from Germany and I've never heard of this meal before. What's in it?
> S4: It's pieces of lamb with carrots in gravy and potatoes on top. It's cooked in the oven in a pot.
> S3: Mmm, that sounds nice. I think I'll have that, please.

→

3
S5: I don't know this word so I'm not sure what this meal is. Has it got meat in it?
S6: Oh, no, it's a kind of fish – the traditional English fish and chips with peas.
S5: Oh, I don't eat meat or fish. Could you tell me what this is?

4
S7: I don't eat meat so I just want to check before I order. Is it vegetarian?
S8: Yes, it is. It's made with broccoli and Roquefort cheese.
S7: Oh, lovely! OK, well, I'd like that, please

If short of time

If you notice you're getting short of time,
- talk about the sentences in ***Exercise 4*** in pairs, not in groups.
- do just one of the ***Round up*** activities.
- do only one or two questions of ***Exercise 6b*** as a class discussion.

4 Now you: You and your food
5 mins

- Divide the class into small groups. See the *Getting ready for* section of this TRB p. 99 for a suggestion on how to do this.
- Demonstrate the task by completing relevant sentences about yourself.
- Once in their groups, students work individually to complete the sentences. Ensure the students realise they don't have to complete every sentence, only the relevant ones.
- Board: * Complete the first two sentences only.
  ** As in the coursebook.
  *** Do **. Then write two more sentences about you and your food.
- Students then tell the other members of the group about themselves and their food.

5a How to say it: Asking for help with a menu
3/33
5+ mins

- Say: *Listen and repeat.* Play ▶ 3/33.

What's 'hotpot'? What's it made with? What's in it?	Has it got meat in it? Is it vegetarian? Does it come with salad?

5b Checking the menu
10 mins

- Divide the class in half (left side of the room and right side of the room).
- Tell one half they are Group A, the other they are Group B.
  ! Check students know what *today's specials* means (meals only served on that day).
- Say: *Group A, you are the customers in a pub. Turn to page 124 and read the instructions and today's specials. Group B, you work in the pub. Turn to page 126 and read the instructions and the notes about the food on today's specials.*
- Monitor carefully while the students are looking at the information and answer any questions.
- Once students have read the information, say: *Find someone from the other group to work with.*
- Students role play the first conversation, then change roles for the second one.

Round up

6a What's my food?
5– mins

- Demonstrate the task by drawing a type of food and encourage students to guess what it is.
- Then encourage volunteers to come up to the board and do the same.

6b Talk about it
5 mins

- Students work in small groups or in pairs, and choose one or more of the questions to chat freely about. They can just talk about one, or two, or all of the questions.

And finally ...
5+ mins

Remind students of the following:
- **Language study** (p. 110): An overview of the grammar of the step (both *You already know* and *And now*) with exercises. Students can do this in their books or online.
- **Selfstudy** (p. 111): Students can do this in their books or online.
- **Keys** (p. 133) to the Language study and Selfstudy exercises.
- **Language and culture** (p. 119), Step 2: *Haute cuisine* and the corresponding task (p. 119).

And point out ...
- The **FAQ** *Why do some of the speaker on the CD have accents?* at the end of the Selfstudy page (p. 111). FAQ reflects the kind of questions that learners may ask in order to improve their independent learning. Students can find more questions with more detailed answers on pages 198/199.

Unit 6 Step 3 Save it or spend it

Contents

Realia	A cash machine screen
Functions	Making simple transactions at the bank
Vocabulary	Bank; Synonyms for *say*
Reading	A dream come true
Grammar	**You already know:** *too* **And now:** *not ... either*
Write it right	Direct speech

Lesson notes

Additional material

For optional and additional material for Unit 6, Step 3, see pages 99/100.
Refer to this section before your lesson as some of the materials require preparation.

Optional stages

Optional stages of the lesson are written in grey in these notes.

Starter: Receipts
5 mins

- Ask volunteers to look in their purse or wallet for any receipts they have got. Ask volunteers to say what the receipts are for.

A cash machine
1 Cash machine services
10 mins

- Ask: *How do you do your banking?* (online / in the bank / by phone / machines at the bank)
- Hold up your open book and point to the cash machine screen. Say: *You're in England and you want to get some money. Which button do you press?* (4 or 5)
- Read out the instructions. Students complete the task. Check answers in class.
  4a), 2b), 3c), 5d), 1e), 6f)

! Refer students to the *Info box* and read out the information. Remind them that sometimes British English (BE) and American English (AE) differs.

Tip: Storing vocabulary If your students have vocabulary notebooks, you could encourage them to start a section on the different BE / AE words / spellings.

Foreign currency
2a At the currency exchange counter
3/39–40
10 mins

- Tell students they are going to listen to a conversation between a bank cashier and a customer.
- Read out the instructions for the gist task.
- Play ▶ 3/39. Students listen and fill in the relevant currency. Check answers in class.

Canadian, American

- Read out the instructions for the specific listening task.
- Before listening again, students speculate and write (B) or (C) in the boxes.
- Say: *Listen and check your answers*. Play ▶ 3/40. Students listen and check.
  1C, 2B, 3B, 4C, 5C, 6C, 7C, 8B, 9B, 10B

(BC = bank cashier, C = customer)
BC: Good morning, Sir, can I help you?
C: Yes. I need to change some money because I'm going on a business trip next week.
BC: And which currency do you need?
C: Well, first I'm going to Canada, so I'll need some Canadian dollars.
BC: Right – Canadian dollars. I don't think we have any Canadian dollars but I can order some for you. How many do you need?
C: Well, I don't need many. I'm only there for three days – I just need some for taxi fares, tips and things – let's say 100 Canadian dollars.
BC: One hundred Canadian dollars. OK, we can order those for you and they'll be here on Friday. That will come to 77 euros, plus commission.
C: Er – how much commission do you charge?

→

BC: It's 2%.
C: OK. And then I'm going on to the US, so I need some American dollars, too. What's the exchange rate?
BC: It's one dollar thirty-one cents to the euro today. And how much money would you like to change?
C: I'd like $500.
BC: So ... $500 comes to ... let's see ... three hundred and eighty-two euros and sixty-eight cents. And then there's the commission, of course.
C: Right. I have an account here, so can I pay with my bank card?
BC: Yes, of course you can. Just put it in the machine and enter your PIN, please. Thanks very much. So, here's your money ... oh, I'm sorry – we don't have any ten-dollar notes. And we don't have any five-dollar notes, either. I'll have to give you big notes – is that OK?
C: Yes, that's fine.
BC: Right, that's one hundred, two hundred, three hundred, three fifty, four hundred, four fifty, five hundred. Five hundred US dollars.
C: Thank you.
BC: Can you sign here, please?
C: Yes, of course.
BC: Can I help you with anything else?
C: No, that's fine thanks – I'll be back on Thursday to pick up the Canadian money.
BC: Right – see you then. Goodbye.
C: Thank you. Bye.

2b What did she say?
5+ mins

- Read out the instructions and the verbs below.
- Do number 1 with the class as an example. (asked) Remind students that different answers are possible in some cases.
- Board: * Allow time for students to check the meaning of the verbs by looking them up in the Dictionary at the back of the book (p. 177–195) before starting the task.
  ** As in the coursebook.
  *** Do **. Then look at numbers 3 and 4 again and see if you can think of a second verb to use here.
- Check answers in class.
  1 asked, 2 offered, 3 explained / repeated, 4 answered / replied, 5 apologised, 6 added

3 Write it right: Direct speech
10 mins

- Read out the instructions and do sentence 1 in class.
- Allow time for students to rewrite the sentences. Monitor while they are working.
- Once students have finished the task, they compare their sentences with other students.
  Possible answers: **1 "I need to change some money because I'm going on a business trip next week," he said. 4 He asked, "How much commission do you charge?" 5 He asked, "What's the exchange rate?" 6 "I'd like $500," he answered. 7 He asked, "I have an account here, so can I pay with my bank card?"**

2 Grammar
10– mins

You already know: *too*

- Read out the sentence from the *You already know* Grammar box. Students repeat it in chorus.
- Ask: *Does he need Canadian dollars?* (Yes.), *Does he need US dollars?* (Yes.)
- Board: 'too' comes at the e______ of a sentence, it comes after a c___________.
  Elicit the gapped information from the students. (end, comma)
- You can provide further examples by holding up your coursebook and saying *I've got a coursebook* then holding up your teacher's book saying *and a teacher's book, too.*
- Board: 2 positive sentences – use 'too'.

And now: *not ... either*

- Read out the sentence from the *And now ...* Grammar box. Have students repeat it in chorus.
- Say: *Do they have $10 notes?* (No.), *Do they have $5 notes?* (No.). *They don't have any $10 notes and they don't have any $5 notes, either.*
- Board: 2 negative sentences – use 'either'.
- Then elicit sentences from them by making negative sentences they can agree with: *I don't wear a ring* and invite someone with no ring to respond: I don't wear a ring, either, etc.
  ! There are two ways of pronouncing the word *either*, in British English it's ['aɪðə] and in American English it's ['iːðə].

3a *Too* or *either*?
5+ mins

- Read out the instructions. Students read the sentences and cross out the wrong word.
- Check answers in class.
  1 too | ~~either~~, 2 ~~too~~ | either, 3 too | ~~either~~, 4 ~~too~~ | either

If short of time

If you notice you're getting short of time,
- instead of working in groups, ask students to read out one sentence each from their three in ***Exercise 3b*** to the class and ask another student to respond with a ..., *too* or ..., *either* sentence.
- read out the numbers in ***Exercise 4c*** and ask volunteers to say what they referred to.

3b Now you: Your money matters
5+ mins

- Demonstrate the task by completing three sentences about yourself.

! Money may be an issue that not all students want to talk about. When in doubt, ask only volunteers to answer, or tell students they don't need to answer if they don't want to.

- Ask students to choose three sentences to complete for themselves.
- ↑ Choose more sentences to complete.
- Ask students to work in small groups. See the *Getting ready for* section in this TRB (p. 100) for an idea about how to do this.
- Read out the second part of the instructions. Students work in groups comparing their sentences then telling the class.

Saving for something special

4a What's it about?
5 mins

- Hold up your open book, point to the picture of the ride-on lawnmower and read out the title.
- Ask students to predict what the text in *Exercise 4b* could be about.
- ↓ If students are struggling to predict the content of the text, write these words on the board, one by one:
  14 year-old, save, expensive item, fifteen years, $1053, owner, ride-on lawnmower
  ! You can encourage students to use the language from Step 2 here: *It could be about ... It might be about ... It can't be about ...* for their speculations.

4b Reading
5 mins

- Students read the article to find out if they were right.

Language and culture

Students can read the text *Coupons* (p. 119) and do the related task at home – or you can use this page as a 'filler' if you have time at the end of the lesson. For more information on this, look at page 100 of this TRB.

4c Numbers
5 mins

- Read out the instructions. Students try to remember what the numbers refer to.
- Once they have done this, they can read the article again to check. Check answers in class.
  14 – 14-year-old Brian McPherson | 1996 – He bought a hockey stick in 1996. | 10¢ – He got a savings coupon worth ten cents. | $30 – The store gave its customers ten-cent coupons for every thirty dollars they spent. | $1053 – Brian saved $1053 in coupons. | first – Brian's daughter's first birthday.

4d Now you: Your free gifts
5+ mins

- Demonstrate the task by briefly telling the class about a free gift you received.
- In small groups, students then do the same.

5 A money puzzle
5+ mins

- Ask students to work in pairs. Read out the instructions and monitor, helping if needed.
- Tell students they can check the answer on page 128.

And finally ...
5+ mins

Remind students of the following:
- **Language study** (p. 114): An overview of the grammar of the step (both *You already know* and *And now*) with exercises. Students can do this in their books or online.
- **Selfstudy** (p. 114): Students can do this in their books or online.
- **Keys** (p. 133) to the Language study and Selfstudy exercises.
- **Language and culture** (p. 119), Step 3: *Coupons* and the corresponding tasks. Refer students to the *Listen in* task. (For more information on this, look at page 100 of this TRB.)

And point out ...
- **Reading: I'm not selling anything!** (p. 115): A story with a glossary of unknown words. If you want to use this story in class, there are some ideas on how to exploit it on page 121 of this TRB.

Unit 6 Now I can

Contents — **Review of vocabulary, functions and structures in Unit 6**

Starter	Talking about waste and recycling
Part 1	Speculating; Making simple transactions at the bank
Part 2	Asking for help with a menu
Part 3	Talking about waste and recycling; Agreeing and disagreeing

Lesson notes

Additional material

For optional and additional material for Unit 6, *Now I can*, see pages 100/101.
Refer to this section before your lesson as some of the materials require preparation.

Optional stages

Optional stages of the lesson are written in grey in these notes.

Now I can: ...
5 mins

- Ask students to look at *Now I can: ...* at the top of page 116. Remind them that the symbols refer to different skills or vocabulary items they learnt in Unit 6 (see photo page 103).

Starter: Look back
5 mins

- Read out the *Starter* question and encourage individual students to answer.

  Possible answers: **Freegans recycle things they get from 'bin diving'.**

Starter:
Now look forward
5– mins

- Ask the class how many people have visited an English-speaking country. Find out where they went / what they did and whether they enjoyed it.
- Read out the *Now look forward* information.

Part 1:
1a At the bank
3/43–44
10 mins

- Read out the first part of the instructions and the beginnings of the sentences (1 and 2).
- Play ▶ 3/43. Students note down what each customer wants to do.

  1 ... change her pin. 2 ... order some US dollars.
- Read out the second part of the instructions. Play ▶ 3/44.
  Customer 1 should change her PIN at the cash machine. Customer 2 should take the money out of his account / should put his card in the machine and enter his number.

(BE = bank employee, C1/2 = customer 1/2)

1 BE: Good morning.
C1: Hello. I'd like to change my PIN, please.
BE: That's no problem. You can do it at the cash machine if you know your old PIN. That's the easiest way. It only takes a few seconds. Do you know your old number?
C1: Yes, I just want to change it because I think someone else might know it.
BE: Good idea. The cash machine is over there. Just let me know if you have any problems.
C1: OK. I'll do that. Thank you for your help.

2 BE: Good morning.
C2: Hello. I'd like to order some dollars, please.
BE: US dollars?
C2: Yes. About £500 in American dollars.
BE: Do you have an account here?
C2: Yes, I do.
BE: OK, then we can take the money out of your account. Have you got your bank card with you?
C2: Yes, I have.
BE: OK ... if you could just put your card in the machine and enter your number. Thank you. That's all done. Your dollars will be ready for you on Friday.
C2: That's great. I'll come and collect them on Friday afternoon. Thanks.

1b I'd like to change some money, please.
10 mins

- Tell the class they are in a bank in the UK. They want to change some money.
- Board: You say ... | The bank employee says ...
- Allow students time to think about which phrases could be used. Ask them for their ideas.
- Write the phrases onto the board in the correct column.
- Ask students to work in pairs and role play the conversation.

1c I need more money!
5 mins

- Read out the instructions and the example sentence.
- Students work in pairs and discuss the good and bad points of each job.
- ↑ Students then present the good and bad points of one job to the class.

Possible sentences: **If I worked behind a bar in a pub, I'd meet lots of people / I'd have to work late. – If I gave German lessons, I'd meet lots of people / I wouldn't speak a lot of English. – If I worked in a supermarket, I'd have to work late / I wouldn't have to advertise my own services. – If I worked as a waiter / waitress, I'd speak a lot of English / I'd have to work late. – If I delivered newspapers, I'd be able to study in the day / I wouldn't earn a lot of money. – If I did babysitting, I'd have a lot of flexibility / I'd have to work late. – If I did dog-walking, I wouldn't earn a lot of money / I'd have to advertise my own services.**

Part 2:

2a What's on the menu?
5 mins

- Ask the class if they have ever worked in a restaurant. If they have, find out where it was and whether they enjoyed it or not.
- Tell the class they've found a job as a waiter / waitress in the New Orleans Diner.
- Hold up your open book and point to the menu. Say: *This is the menu, but there is a small problem, you don't know what some of the dishes are.*
- Ask students to work individually and to look at the menu and write three different questions about the meals on it.
- ↓ Refer students back to the *How to say it: Asking for help with a menu* section on p. 109.
- Monitor and correct any mistakes you see / help with question formulation.
- Students then compare their questions with a partner.
- ↓ Write a selection of the suggested questions on the board. Students copy them if they wish.

Possible questions: **What's Crawfish Etouffee? Has it got meat in it? Could you tell me what Jambalya is? Is it vegetarian?**

2b Excuse me, what's on this menu?
45–46
10 mins

- Read out the instructions for the gist task. Play ▶ 3/45. Check answers in class.

Crawfish Etouffee, Salmon Creole, Chicken and Chorizo Jambalya

- Say: *Listen again and make some notes about these three dishes.* Play ▶ 3/46.
- Students listen and make notes. If necessary, play the CD again. Play ▶ 3/46.
- Ask students to compare their notes with a partner, then check the notes in class.

Crawfish Etouffee: Crawfish is seafood, like lobster. It has a spicy sauce and it's served with rice. Salmon Creole: It's a simple dish, the fish is cooked with spices. There isn't a sauce. It's very healthy. It's comes with vegetables. Chicken and Chorizo Jambalya: It's chicken and chorizo (which is a spicy sausage) cooked with vegetables, Cajun spices and rice in a big pot.

- Refer students to the German menu on p. 128, if necessary.

(W = waiter, C1 / C2 = customer 1 / 2)
W: Are you ready to order?
C1: Er, not yet, I'm afraid.
W: Do you need more time? Or can I help you?
C1: Well, we've never eaten this sort of food before, so I think we need some help.
W: Yes, of course. I'm here to help.
C1: I'd like to have fish. I can see catfish, crawfish and salmon here. What's Crawfish Etouffee?
W: Crawfish isn't really fish, it's seafood. It's like lobster. It's very good. And Crawfish Etouffee is with a spicy sauce. It's very good. And it's served with rice.
C1: Mm, I'm not so sure. What's the Salmon Creole made with? Fish, of course, because of the salmon, but what does 'Creole' mean here?
W1: It's a very simple dish. The fish is cooked with a mix of spices.

→

C1: Is it in a sauce?
W: No, it isn't in a sauce. It's very healthy and it comes with vegetables.
C1: I'll have that then, please.
W: With rice or potatoes?
C1: With rice, please. And what about you, Frank?
C2: I'd like chicken, I think. Or pork? Something meaty. What's in the Chicken and Chorizo Jambalaya? Chorizo is a sort of sausage, isn't it? A spicy sausage?
W: That's right. The chicken and sausage are cooked with a mix of vegetables and Cajun spices in a big pot with rice. So it's all cooked together – the meat, the vegetables, the sauce and the rice.
W: Or how about the Smothered Pork Chops? That's good. It's pork, served with a thick, spicy sauce. And it comes with rice or potatoes.
C2: I think I'd like the Fried Chicken, please. I know what that is! Does that come with vegetables?
W: Yes, sir. And would you like rice or potatoes with that?
C2: Potatoes, please.
W: OK. And what would you like to drink?
C2: I think I'll have a beer. What have you got?

If short of time

If you notice you're getting short of time,
- do ***Exercise 2c*** in pairs and each choose one dish.
- do ***Exercise 3a*** as a class activity.

2c Are you ready to order?
5 mins

- Students work in groups of three – one waiter and two customers.
- Read out the instructions.
- Students role play the scenario, then change roles and practise again.

Part 3:
3a Waste
5 mins

- Ask students to work in small groups. Read out the instructions.
- Students discuss the problem then report their ideas back to the group.

3c Which picture?
10 mins

- Hold up your open book and point to the pictures. Ask individual students which picture they think is best for a recycling poster.
- Read out the first part of the instructions (up to ... *make the best poster?*).
- Students then work in small groups and discuss which picture is best.
- Once students have decided on the picture they think will make the best poster, ask them to decide on a message to write on it.
- Students then tell the class which picture they have chosen and what their message is.

Part 4:
4 Now you choose
10 mins

- Allow time for the students to read the tasks and choose one.
- Ask students to find a partner who wants to do the same task.

And finally ...
5 mins

Look back at the *In this unit, you will learn to:* ... (p. 103) to show your students how much they have learnt in this unit and say how well they've done.

Remind students of ...
- **Test yourself** (p. 118): Students can do this progress test and check their answers (p. 133).
- **Language and culture** (p. 119): Refer your students to any L&C texts and tasks that weren't done in class.**Now me** (p. 120): Students can do some free writing, using the vocabulary and structures they've learned in Unit 6. Ask students to read the *Now blog* section. They can use this as a model for writing their own blog. Finally, refer students to the *Now explore the Internet* section to find out about more pub food and choose something they'd like to cook or eat. Remind students that they can copy the *Now me* page for their portfolio.

If your course has more than 24 lessons, you'll find an extra lesson after Unit 6: **Globetrotter.**
Globetrotter C Work – one page (45 minutes) of material with the focus on English for work.
Globetrotter C Travel – one page (45 minutes) of material with the focus on English for travel.
A further 45 minutes of material is provided on the Internet for each of these lessons.
Teaching notes on **Globetrotter C** can be found on pages 125/126.

Note: Getting ready for … is divided into two sections, **FYI** and **Preparing …**, for most of the steps in Units 1–6.

FYI: When you prepare your lessons, you might want to have some background knowledge of an aspect of the lesson – just for your own personal interest. Where it seems useful, the FYI provides links to relevant sites via the *Network Now* homepage.

Preparing …: If your lesson is longer than 90 minutes, or if you have a particularly quick class, this section offers some additional activities which you can use. **NB:** Some of the activities and materials require preparation before the lesson.

Getting ready for Unit 1

FYI Unit 1 Step 1

Find out more about **Swindon** by going to www.klett-langenscheidt.de/networknow/fyi.

Preparing Unit 1 Step 1

Starter:
Where are you from?

- Bring pictures or postcards from your hometown to class.

Getting to know your class
10 mins

- To be used after the *Starter*, coursebook p. 10.
- Write five names / places on the board, e.g. the name of the place you were born, the name of your child / partner / pet, your favourite holiday destination, etc. Students guess what these represent. Then on a piece of paper students write down five words (names / places) for themselves. They mingle and try to guess what the words which other students have written represent.

In and around town
10 mins

- To be used any time after *Exercise 1a*, coursebook p. 10.
  ! When you see the phrase *To be used any time after …* this simply tells you the earliest possible time in the lesson to do this activity. You may choose to do the activity at this point, or later in the lesson.
- **Photocopy *1 In and around town*** (p. 102) – one copy for each pair of students.
- Cut along the dotted line so that you have a sheet of paper for Partner A and a sheet of paper for Partner B.
- Students work in pairs to complete the puzzle. Partner A asks Partner B: *What's number …?* Partner B responds by giving him / her a definition of the word: *It's (a place with lots of trees).* (FOREST) Partner A then writes this word in his / her puzzle. Then Partner B asks Partner A for the next word and so on until they have all of the words.
- Once they have all of the words they can read the mystery word (SWINDON) and write this on their sheets.

		1 L	A	K	E	S					
						2 W	O	O	D		
					3 V	I	L	L	A	G	E
4 A	R	T	S	C	E	N	T	R	E		
		5 F	I	E	L	D					
					6 F	O	R	E	S	T	
			7 T	O	W	N					

Language and culture Step 1:
City, town or village?
(coursebook p. 25)
10– mins

- To be used after the *Round up*, coursebook p. 11.
- Board: c______, t______, v______
  Say: *Berlin is a big … (Name of a town) is a … (Name of a village) is a …* and elicit city, town, village.
- Board: True or false?
  1 A hamlet is bigger than a town. (True.)
  2 All British cities must have a cathedral. (False.)
  3 In some states in the USA 'town' and 'city' mean the same. (True.)

→

- Students read the text to find out if the sentences are true or false.
- Students work in small groups to discuss the questions on page 25 and report back to the class.
  ! If you have students who all live in the same city / town / village, you can ask them to think of another place they have lived in.

Downloads

- There's an activity for Unit 1 Step 1 which you can download from the Internet: www.klett-langenscheidt.de/networknow/activities

FYI Unit 1 Step 2

If you would like to know more about the **Chicken Hotel**, go to www.klett-langenscheidt.de/networknow/fyi.

Preparing Unit 1 Step 2

Test each other
5+ mins

- To be used any time after *Exercise 3a,* coursebook p. 15.
- Students work in pairs. One student closes his / her book and the other says one word / phrase from the left-hand column of *Exercise 3a,* e.g. *airport* and his / her partner has to remember the matching word: *shuttle.*

Top Five facilities
10 mins

- To be used any time after *Exercise 3a,* coursebook p. 15.
- Students work in groups of five.
- Tell students to make a list of facilities which are important to them in a good hotel and then rank these facilities to give them a Top Five hotel facilities.

Tip: Ranking tasks Asking students to rank words in order can help them to personalise the words and internalise them. This personalisation means that they are actively using the vocabulary which helps them to remember it.

- One volunteer from each group then tells the class about their Top Five.

Booking a hotel room
15 mins

- To be used any time after *Exercise 4a,* coursebook p. 15.
- **Photocopy *2 Booking a hotel room*** (p. 103) – one copy for each pair of students.
- Cut along the dotted line so that you have a Partner A role for each A Student and a Partner B role for each B Student.
- Divide the class into two groups, A and B. Give Group A the Partner A role and Group B the Partner B role.
- Allow students a few minutes to read their roles and, if necessary, help each other with vocabulary / questions.
- Put students into A / B pairs. Say: *B Students, phone your partner and ask him / her questions about Regents Hotel and book a room. A Students, answer your partner's questions using the information you have.*
- If time permits, students swap roles.

Partner B:
Possible questions:
– How much is a single / double room? – Is breakfast included in the price? – Is an evening meal included in the price? – Is Internet access available? – Is there a children's play area? – Is an airport shuttle available? Does is cost extra? – Is the hotel close to the centre of London? – Are there things to do nearby?

Partner A:
Possible answers:
– A single room costs £150.00 per night. / A double room costs £200.00 per night. – Yes, it is. – No, it isn't but an evening meal can be ordered separately. – Yes, there is. – No, there isn't, but there is a park with a children's play area near the hotel. – Yes, there is and it's free for hotel guests. – The hotel is a 10 minute walk from the centre of London or two stops on the tube. – Yes, there are lots of things to do nearby. There's a park, an art gallery, a cinema and two museums.

Language and culture Step 2: Pets
(coursebook p. 25)
10 mins

- To be used after the *Round up*, coursebook p. 15.
- Ask: *What do you think are the top five pets in British households?* Ask students to guess and write their ideas on the board. If necessary, help with vocabulary.
- Ask students to read the text silently and see if they were right. (dogs, cats, rabbits, birds, hamsters)
- Put students into groups to discuss the questions on page 25.
- If a lot of students in your class have a pet, then you can do a pets list for your class. Ask students which pets they have and then count how many people have the same pets. Write this on the board, e.g. dogs 2, cats 3, birds 2.
- Encourage students to do the Internet task at home.

Downloads

- There's an activity for Unit 1 Step 2 which you can download from the Internet: www.klett-langenscheidt.de/networknow/activities

FYI Unit 1 Step 3

If you would like to know more about **couch surfing**, check out the Couch surfing website by going to www.klett-langenscheidt.de/networknow/fyi.

Preparing Unit 1 Step 3

What do you think?
10+ mins

- To be used any time after *Exercise 2a*, coursebook p. 18.
- In small groups, students use the types of accommodation in *Exercise 1b* to make their own comparative sentences and give a reason for their choice, e.g. *I think camping is nicer than staying in a motel because you get lots of fresh air and you're outdoors.*
- Monitor and check that their sentences are correct.
- Ask individual students to read two of their sentences out to the class.

Compare it
10+ mins

Tip: Materials Some photocopiable tasks require a lot of cutting up. For these tasks it's a good idea to either copy them onto thin card before cutting, as they last longer or, if possible, to laminate the paper before you cut. This means you can use the cards again and again.

- To be used any time after *Exercise 2a*, coursebook p. 18.
- **Photocopy *3 Compare it*** (p. 104) – one pack of cards for each pair. Cut up the cards to make a set of 6 cards.
- Students play in pairs. Give each pair a set of cards, placed face down on the desk, and tell them they need a piece of paper to write on.
- Tell the class that they have ten minutes to write as many comparative sentences as possible about the information on the cards.
- Students turn over the first card and write sentences (e.g. Couch surfing is cheaper than / not as comfortable as staying in a hotel. / ... more dangerous than staying with friends.). When they run out of ideas for that card, they move on to the next, and so on.
- Stop the activity after ten minutes and ask students to read out their sentences. For every correct sentence they get a point. The team with the most points wins.
- It doesn't matter how many of the cards students write about, most important is the number of correct comparative sentences.

Possible answers:

1 Couch surfing is cheaper than / not as comfortable as staying in a hotel. / ... more dangerous than staying with friends.
2 Museums are not as interesting as / more interesting than art galleries. / ... not as exciting as theme parks. / ... cheaper than going to the cinema.
3 A beach holiday is not as interesting as / not as exciting as / more relaxing than / nicer than a city break.
4 Cities are bigger than / more interesting than towns / villages.
5 Hiking is not as dangerous as / more tiring than swimming. / ... better than skiing.
6 A four-star hotel is more expensive than / more comfortable than / not as nice as camping. / ... safer than couch surfing.

→

3c Now you: Your guests
(coursebook p. 19)

Tip: Pair / Group work (2)

Pair work:
- Half of the class are As, the other half Bs – tell the As to find a B to work with.
- If you have a class of, for example, 16 students, count round one half of the class from 1 to 8, then count again from 1 to 8 for the other half. Say: *The same numbers work together.*
- Choose a vocabulary set (e.g. jobs) and make pairs of cards (2x 'policeman', 2x 'nurse' etc.). Give each student a job card. Tell them they mustn't show their cards to the other students. Students stand up and find their partner by asking questions (e.g. Where do you work?). Tell students they can't ask: What do you do? / What's your job?
- Take lengths of wool or ribbon into the class (about 90 cm long and all the same colour) – you need one piece for each pair of students. Hold the bunch of ribbons in the middle. Ask each student to take hold of the end of one ribbon. When everyone is holding an end of a ribbon, let go of the bunch. The students who are holding the ends of the same ribbon work together.
- Say: *Work with a student who has something in common with you. Who has a birthday in October?* (When students put their hands up, pair them off.) – *Who has a white car? Who has a grandchild? Who has a nice boss? Who has two mobile phones? Who has a cat / dog? Who has ...?*

Group work:
- Ask your students to put themselves into a line based on the first letter of their names (A is the beginning, Z is the end), or on their birthday months (January at one end, December at the other). Count down the line (1, 2, 3, ...) to make group sizes of your choice.
- Cut up a selection of postcards (e.g. for groups of 6 cut the postcards into 6 pieces). Mix the pieces and hand them out to the class. Tell students to stand up and find the other students with pieces from the same postcard. Students then sit down together and put the postcard together (like a jigsaw puzzle).

Texting abbreviations
5+ mins

- To be used any time after *Exercise 4b,* coursebook p. 19.
- Ask students how often they send text messages and if they ever use abbreviations. If yes, ask for some examples. (e.g.: 8ung – Achtung, Gute N8 – Gute Nacht, AKLA – Alles klar, BB – Bis bald, DD – Drück Dich, WTEL – Wir telefonieren, GNGN – Geht nicht gibt's nicht, ...)
- Board: gr8, 2moro, 2nite, B4, hand, cu, atm, lol Say: *Guess what these abbreviations mean.*
- Students work in pairs to see if they can guess what they mean. (gr8 – great, 2moro – tomorrow, 2nite – tonight, B4 – before, hand – have a nice day, cu – see you, atm – at the moment, lol – laugh out loud).
- Ask students if they know any other text abbreviations.

Language and culture Step 3: Web addresses
(coursebook p. 25)
10– mins

- To be used at the end of the lesson.
- Board: www Ask students what this means. (world wide web)
- Board: 1 .com, 2 .ed, 3 .gov
  Say: *These are all part of web addresses. Read the text and find out what they mean.*
- Then read out the instructions for the web country code task.
- Students work in pairs to match the country codes to the countries.
- If there are students in class whose country code is not included, ask them to say what it is.

Listen in
1/23

- Encourage students to do the *Listen in* task at home. **!** They hear an unscripted conversation and are encouraged to understand the gist of this conversation. The transcript can be found online.

Reading: First night in London
(coursebook p. 21)

- The Reading page can be done as selfstudy or read in class. You'll find ideas on how to exploit the text in class on page 120.

Downloads

- There's an activity for Unit 1 Step 3 which you can download from the Internet: www.klett-langenscheidt.de/networknow/activities

FYI Unit 1 Now I can

To find out about some of the **world's top hotels**, go to www.klett-langenscheidt.de/networknow/fyi.

Preparing Unit 1 Now I can

Note: As the *Now I can* pages are revision and consolidation, you can use any of the optional and additional materials suggested for Steps 1–3.

Choose your hotel
5 mins

- To be used with *Exercises 1a–2b*, coursebook p. 22/23.
- Take a selection of pictures of hotels into class (you could use travel brochures or print some pictures off the Internet).
- Students choose a hotel picture to represent their hotel and use this in the planning and presentation phases of the *Now I can* section.

Template 1: Word diagrams
15 mins

- To be used any time after *Part 3*, coursebook p. 23.
- **Photocopy Template 1: *Word diagrams*** (p. 114). Write a vocabulary topic from Unit 1 (e.g. In and around town, Hotel facilities, Places to stay) in the box in each word diagram. Photocopy the page so that you can cut out one diagram for each group of three or four students.
- Students work in their groups to think of as many words as possible linked to the topic and write them in their word diagram.
- Students put the word diagrams on their desks, stand up, walk around and look at the word diagrams made by the other groups.
- If there are any words students don't understand, ask them to write these on the board.
- When students have finished, ask them to sit back down. Look at the words on the board and ask the students to explain what they mean in English.
- This template can be used to recycle unit vocabulary from any unit at all levels.

Downloads

- There's an activity for Unit 6 *Now I can* which you can download from the Internet: www.klett-langenscheidt.de/networknow/activities

Getting ready for Unit 2

Preparing Unit 2 Step 1

Word stress
5 mins

- To be used with *Exercise 1b*, coursebook p. 28.
- Draw a table on the board with these headings: O | Oo | Ooo | oOo | oOoo | ooOoo
- Ask students to copy the table onto a piece of paper.
- Remind students that each bubble represents a syllable and that the larger one is the stressed syllable in the word.
- Demonstrate the task by saying one word, e.g. *college*. Say: *How many syllables?* (Two.) *Where's the main stress?* (On the first syllable.) Write *college* under the Oo stress pattern.
- Ask students to work in pairs. Tell them to say the words from *Exercise 1b*, work out how many syllables they have and write them on their piece of paper in the correct columns.

O	Oo	Ooo	oOo	oOoo	ooOoo
learn work course	college study homework lesson student subject	doctorate	apprentice diploma	apprenticeship certificate	university

Person, thing, place
15+ mins

- To be used any time after *Exercise 2a*, coursebook p. 29.
- **Photocopy *4 Person, thing, place*** (p. 104) – one copy for each group of four students. Cut out the word cards, one set of cards for each group.
- Students work in groups of four.
- Place the set of cards face down in the middle of their table.
- Player 1 takes a card and defines the word on it, using *who, that / which* or *where*. If he / she doesn't know the word, and therefore can't define it, it is returned to the bottom of the pile and the same player takes another card.
- The student who guesses the word correctly keeps the card and takes the next card from the pile.
- The winner is the player with the most cards.

Optional & additional materials | Getting ready for Unit 2

Language and culture
Step 1: Schooldays
(coursebook p. 43)
10– mins

- To be used after the *Round up,* coursebook p. 29.
- Ask students to read the text.
- Say: *I went to a primary school. Am I American or British?* (British)
- Repeat for the following sentences*: I took A-level exams.* (British) / *I've got a high school diploma.* (American) / *I went to secondary school.* (British) / *I went to elementary school.* (American)
- Students then work in small groups to discuss the two questions and report back to the class.

Downloads

- There's an activity for Unit 2 Step 1 which you can download from the Internet: www.klett-langenscheidt.de/networknow/activities

FYI Unit 2 Step 2

To see some **oshiyas in action**, have a look at www.klett-langenscheidt.de/networknow/fyi.

Preparing Unit 2 Step 2

Use the words
5+ mins

- To be used any time after *Exercise 1b,* coursebook p. 32.

Tip: Personalising vocabulary Asking students to use words in their own sentences can help them to personalise the words and also check that they can actually use them effectively. This increases the chance that this vocabulary will become active, rather than passive, knowledge.

- Students work in pairs. One student chooses a word / phrase from *Exercise 1b,* e.g. *employee* and his / her partner has to make a sentence using this word, e.g. *My company has about 200 employees.*
- They do this until they've made sentences using each word / phrase.

Question tags
15 mins

- To be used any time after *Exercise 3a,* coursebook p. 33.
- **Photocopy *5 Question tags*** (p. 105) – one copy for each group of three students.
- Cut out the cards and make two sets – the statements (e.g. *His brother works in Berlin,*) and the question tags (e.g. *doesn't he?*).
- Students work in groups of three.
- Give out a set of statements to each group. Ask them to spread them out, face down, on the table.
- Give out a set of question tags to each group and ask them to deal them out among themselves so that each student has the same number of tags.
- One student turns over a statement card and reads it out. Each member of the group looks to see if he / she has the question tag for that statement.
- The person who has the correct tag puts it next to the statement, reads out the full sentence and then turns over the next statement card.
- At the end of the game, there will be 15 correctly tagged statements on the table. These can be read out and checked in class.

What's my job?
10 mins

- To be used any time after *Exercise 3a,* coursebook p. 33.
- Students work in pairs. They think of a job, but don't tell anyone what it is.
- Using the phrases in *Exercise 3a* they write sentences which describe their job, e.g. *I work full-time. I work in a hospital. I work with people. It's my job to help people who are ill.* (a doctor)
- When students have finished writing, they read their sentences out to the class.
- The class guess what the job is.

Language and culture
Step 2:
Problematic words
(coursebook p. 43)
10+ mins

- To be used after the *Round up,* coursebook p. 33.
- Board: 1 You mustn't / don't have to speak German in class.
  2 You mustn't / don't have to speak English in the break.
- Ask students to cross out the wrong words. (1 ~~don't have to~~, 2 ~~mustn't~~)
- Ask: *Why do students sometimes confuse 'mustn't' and 'don't have to'?*
- Students read the text to find out. (The English word *mustn't (nicht dürfen)* looks like the German word *nicht müssen (don't have to).*)
- Ask the class the two questions at the end of the text. (I got a cake ... / get and become)
- In pairs, students translate the words in the table in the right column on page 43.

Downloads

- There's an activity for Unit 2 Step 2 which you can download from the Internet: www.klett-langenscheidt.de/networknow/activities

FYI Unit 2 Step 3

The smallest library in Britain is a converted telephone box. Other telephone boxes have been turned into an aquarium, a shower and the home of a cardiac defibrillator! To look at some other **phone box conversions**, go to www.klett-langenscheidt.de/networknow/fyi.

Preparing Unit 2 Step 3

Reading – the same or different?
10 mins

- To be used any time after *Exercise 3d*, coursebook p. 37.
- **Photocopy** ***6 Reading – the same or different?*** (p. 106) – one copy for each pair of students. Cut along the dotted line so that you have a sheet of paper for Partner A / Partner B.
- Students work in pairs. They read the questions and answer them for themselves, writing their answer in the 'You' column.
- Then they interview their partner and write his / her answers in the second column.
- Together they compare their answers and, in the last column, put a tick (✓) if their answers are the same or a cross (**×**) if their answers are different.
- Ask individual students to tell the class what they had in common with their partner: *We both ...*

Language and culture Step 3: ISBNs
(coursebook p. 43)
10– mins

- To be used at the end of the lesson.
- Board: ISBN Say: *Look at the bottom of page 2 of your coursebook. What can you read there?* (ISBN + number) *What is this? Read the text and find out.*
- Students read the text to find out what *ISBN* stands for. Then repeat your question.
- Ask students to write down one question about the information in the text. Then get them to ask their questions to the class.
- Students work in small groups and tell each other about the last book they bought using the questions as prompts.
- Encourage students to do the Internet task at home.

Listen in

1/46

- Encourage students to do the *Listen in* task at home. The transcript can be found online.

Reading: Languages of the world
(coursebook p. 39)

- The Reading page can be done as selfstudy or read in class. You'll find ideas on how to exploit the text in class on page 120.

Downloads

- There's an activity for Unit 2 Step 3 which you can download from the Internet: www.klett-langenscheidt.de/networknow/activities

FYI Unit 2 Now I can

These days gap years are not just for youngsters. To look at some **gap years for 'grown ups'** go to www.klett-langenscheidt.de/networknow/fyi.

Preparing Unit 2 Now I can

Note: As the *Now I can* pages are revision and consolidation, you can use any of the optional and additional materials suggested for Steps 1–3.

My ideal gap year
10 mins

- To be used after *Exercise 1b*, coursebook p. 40.
- Ask students to make some notes about what their ideal gap year would be.
- Students then work in small groups and present their ideal gap year to the group saying why they have chosen it.

→

Template 2: What's your opinion?
15+ mins

- To be used any time after *Part 1*, coursebook p. 40.
- **Photocopy Template 2: *What's your opinion?*** (p. 115). Fill in the topic *gap years* and copy the sheet – one for each student.
- Hand out the sheets and tell students they have five minutes to complete as many of the sentences as they can on the topic of *gap years*.
- When students have finished, ask them to work in groups or with a partner. They should tell their group / partner about their opinions using their sentences to help them.
- Other students should agree, or disagree politely! Remind students of some polite phrases to disagree, e.g. *I see what you mean, but …* or *That's a good point, but …*
- This template can be used to recycle topics from any unit at all levels.

Downloads

- There's an activity for Unit 2 *Now I can* which you can download from the Internet: www.klett-langenscheidt.de/networknow/activities

Getting ready for Unit 3

Preparing Unit 3 Step 1

What can you do on holiday?
10+ mins

- To be used after *Exercise 2a*, coursebook p. 49.
- Students work in small groups.
- They have five minutes to make a list of all the activities you can do on holiday.
  Possible answers: **swim, sunbathe, sleep, read, play volleyball / table tennis / football, take photos, hike, ski, eat, drink cocktails, relax, buy souvenirs** (Accept a range of answers here.)
- Ask individual students to read out their lists and then ask the other groups if they have anything to add.
- Then ask volunteers to make a sentence with one of the words.

Holiday decisions
15+ mins

- To be used any time after *Exercise 3b*, coursebook p. 49.
- **Photocopy *7 Holiday decisions*** (p. 107) – one copy for each group of four students.
- Tell students that they have won a holiday. They all have to travel together.
- Hand out the information sheet about the holidays.
- Students read the information, discuss the options and decide which holiday to go on.
- Each group then reports back to the class which holiday they chose and why.

Language and culture Step 1: Holidays
(coursebook p. 63)
10 mins

- To be used after the *Round up*, coursebook p. 49.
- Board: What are bank holidays? How many bank holidays are there in England?
  What are these days called in the USA? When is Independence Day?
  When is Thanksgiving?
  Ask students to read the text and find the answers. (public holidays – they are called 'bank holidays' because all the banks were closed on the first public holiday in 1871, federal holidays, 4th July, fourth Thursday in November)
- Students then work in small groups to discuss the question after the text on p. 63 and report back to the class.
- Encourage students to do the Internet task at home.

Downloads

- There's an activity for Unit 3 Step 1 which you can download from the Internet: www.klett-langenscheidt.de/networknow/activities

FYI Unit 3 Step 2

To see more **animals using public transport**, have a look at www.klett-langenscheidt.de/networknow/fyi.

Preparing Unit 3 Step 2

What's the word?
10– mins

- To be used any time after *Exercise 1b*, coursebook p. 52.
- Ask students to close their books. Read out the text on p. 52, one sentence at a time. When you get to the end of each sentence, leave out the final word and invite students to call out the word.

In the office
10 mins

- To be used as extra grammar practice any time after *Exercise 2b*, coursebook p. 53.
- First brainstorm what people do in offices, e.g. read emails / the newspaper, drink tea / coffee, talk to colleagues / customers, etc.
- Divide the class into two groups – hard-working office workers and lazy office workers. Give them a minute to think what they were doing when the boss arrived.
- One student tells the class what he / she was doing when the boss arrived and then asks a student from the other group: *And what were you doing when the boss arrived?*
- If you have a class that enjoys acting things out, ask students to mime what they were doing when the boss arrived. Leave the room briefly and come back into the room as the 'boss'. Individual students make sentences about their co-workers: *Klaus was playing cards when you came in.*

When I saw you, ...
15+ mins

- To be used any time after *Exercise 4b*, coursebook p. 53.
- **Photocopy *8 When I saw you, ...*** (p. 107) – one copy for each group of three students.
- Cut up the cards so that you have one set for each group of three students.
- Students work in groups of three and have the set of cards face down on the table.
- One student picks up a card and reads it to the other two students. (e.g. When I saw you, you were talking to a policeman.)
- One of the other two students has to give a reason why he / she was doing that. (e.g. I was visiting an old school friend in his new house – but I didn't know where the street was so I stopped a policeman and asked him.)
- The student who gives the reason keeps the card and picks up the next card to read out.
- If both students give an explanation for the activity, the reader chooses which is the better / more entertaining reason.

It happened to me ...
10+ mins

- To be used any time after *Exercise 4c*, coursebook p. 53.
- On the board, write down three events in your life – two must be true and one not true, e.g.
  Board: I rode an elephant when I was a child.
  I ate snails in France.
  I saw Angelina Jolie in London.
- Tell the class that one of these events is not true and they can question you about each event for one minute.
- After three minutes, the class votes on which event didn't really happen to you.

Language and culture Step 2: Queues
(coursebook p. 63)
10+ mins

- To be used after the *Round up*, coursebook p. 53.
- Tell students that *to queue* is used in BE and *to stand in line* is used in AE.
  Board: BE: to queue AE: to stand in line
- Ask students: *What do you think 'to queue-jump' means? Read the text and find out.*
- Students read the text to find out the answer. (To push in front of anyone in the queue.)
- In class, answer the two questions at the end of the text.

Downloads

- There's an activity for Unit 3 Step 2 which you can download from the Internet: www.klett-langenscheidt.de/networknow/activities

FYI Unit 3 Step 3

If you want to read more about this trend of **animal station masters in Japan**, go to www.klett-langenscheidt.de/networknow/fyi.

Preparing Unit 3 Step 3

What time ...?
10– mins

- To be used to practise the *And now* grammar any time after *Exercise 3*, coursebook p. 56.
- Give the class prompt words so students can ask questions about timetabled events in the future. Volunteers can give the answers.
  Board: What time does ...?
  Prompts: lesson – end, lesson – start next week, bank – close tomorrow, bank – open at the weekend, last tram / bus – go tonight, the news – start tonight

→

Travelling by train
10+ mins

- To be used any time after *Exercise 5a*, coursebook p. 57.
- **Photocopy *9 Travelling by train*** (p. 108) – one copy for each pair of students.
- Cut up the cards so that you have one set for each pair of students. Ask students to work in pairs. Give out a set of cards to each pair of students and ask them to put them face up on the table.
- Together, students place the appropriate answer next to the question.
- Check the answers in class by having one student read out a question and a student from another pair answer it.
- Then have students role-play the situation of asking for train information, with one student as the passenger and one as the ticket seller, using some of the questions and answers on the cards.

What can you remember?
10– mins

- To be used any time after *Exercise 5c*, coursebook p. 57.
- Ask students to close their books and tell you as much information as they can about the article 'Animal station masters'.

Language and culture Step 3: Uniforms
(coursebook p. 63)
10– mins

- To be used at the end of the lesson.

NB: Point out that *a*, not *an*, is used before words beginning with *uni*: a uniform, a university.

- Students read the text.
- Ask students to close their books and, with a partner, write the answers to the questions which are on the board.

Board:		
	What is a typical school uniform in the UK?	(a blazer or pullover and tie in the school colours)
	What variations are usually allowed?	(headscarves, full-length skirts or trousers, a hijab, a turban)

- Ask the question at the end of the text.
- Finally, ask the class to write down the advantages and disadvantages of wearing school uniforms and encourage a class discussion when answers are compared in class.

Listen in
2/27

- Encourage students to do the *Listen in* task at home. The transcript can be found online.

Reading: I want to complain about our holiday
(coursebook p. 59)

- The Reading page can be done as selfstudy or read in class. You'll find ideas on how to exploit the text in class on pages 120/121.

Downloads

- There's an activity for Unit 3 Step 3 which you can download from the Internet: www.klett-langenscheidt.de/networknow/activities

FYI Unit 3 Now I can

If you want more information and a panoramic view of **Corfe castle**, go to www.klett-langenscheidt.de/networknow/fyi.

Preparing Unit 3 Now I can

Note: As the *Now I can* pages are revision and consolidation, you can use any of the optional and additional materials suggested for Steps 1–3.

Substitution
10+ mins

- To be used after *Exercise 1a*, coursebook p. 60.
- Ask students to underline the following adjectives in the text: 1 award-winning, 2 unique, 3 beautiful, 4 magnificent.
- Ask students to think of adjectives they could use to replace the underlined ones – they don't have to have the same meaning. After five minutes, ask for suggestions.
  Possible answers: **1 wonderful, amazing; 2 (an) exciting, brilliant; 3 lovely, fantastic; 4 wonderful, old**

Summary
10+ mins

- To be used after *Exercise 2b*, coursebook p. 61.
- Give the class a short writing exercise – ask them to write a summary of the end of the story in their own words. Students can work alone or in pairs.

A postcard
10+ mins

- To be used after *Exercise 3*, coursebook p. 61.
- Give out postcard-size cards or small pieces of paper.
- Ask students to write a postcard telling someone what happened on their day out in *Exercise 3b*.
- Students 'send' it to another student to read out to the class.

Template 3: Question time
15+ mins

- To be used any time after *Part 3*, coursebook p. 61.
- **Photocopy Template 3: *Question time*** (p. 116) – one copy for each pair of students.
- Cut out the cards so that each pair of students has one set.
- Students work in pairs – one is the interviewer and one is the holiday maker.
- Give each pair a set of cards. They put the cards into two piles (15 cards in each pile) and put them face-down on the table.
- Explain to students that they are going to be interviewed about their favourite holiday so they should each think of a really good holiday they had.
- The interviewer picks up a card from one pile and asks the holiday maker a question using the word or phrase on the card – and the holiday maker answers the question.
- Demonstrate the activity by picking up a card and making a question with the word or phrase on the card. Choose a 'holiday maker' to answer your question.
- The interviewers then do the same, using the words or phrases on the cards. Their partners, the holiday makers, answer their questions.
- When the interview is complete, students change roles and the second pile of cards is used.
- At the end, if there's time, volunteers can tell the class about their partner's holiday.
- This template can be used for holiday / travel interviews at all levels.

Downloads

- There's an activity for Unit 3 *Now I can* which you can download from the Internet: www.klett-langenscheidt.de/networknow/activities

Getting ready for Unit 4

FYI Unit 4 Step 1

To see what **dinner in the air** actually looks like, have a look at www.klett-langenscheidt.de/networknow/fyi.

Preparing Unit 4 Step 1

Gist reading task
5 mins

- To be used before *Exercise 1a*, coursebook p. 66.
- Ask students to read the *What's on Guide* and decide where they would like to eat and which event they would most like to go to.
- Ask students to report back to the class on their decisions and keep a tally on the board of which restaurants / which events are the most popular in the class.

On, at, in
5 mins

- To be used before *Exercise 2c*, coursebook p. 67.
- Board: on at in
  Remind students that we often use these words when talking about times.
- Read out the words and phrases below. Pause after each phrase and ask a volunteer to repeat the phrase with the word *on*, *at* or *in* before it.
  Monday (on), *3 o'clock* (at), *Friday evening* (on), *lunchtime* (at), *the evening* (in), *Tuesday morning* (on), *half past two* (at), *the morning* (in), *four thirty* (at), *the afternoon* (in).

Find the differences
15 mins

- To be used any time after *Exercise 2b*, coursebook p. 67.
- **Photocopy *10 Find the differences*** (p. 108) – one copy for each pair. Cut out the Student A / Student B parts.
- Students work in pairs and ask and answer questions about the calendars to find the missing information, e.g. *What's Rob doing on Tuesday? – He's playing football.*

Language and culture Step 1: Mealtimes
(coursebook p. 81)
10– mins

- To be used after the *Round up*, coursebook p. 67.
- Board: full English breakfast, brunch, afternoon tea
  Ask students what they would expect to get in a hotel that offered these meals.
- Students then read the text to check their ideas / find out more information.

→

- Ask students to work in pairs and answer the question on page 81. If you have a mixed nationality group, try to pair different nationalities for this task.

Downloads

- There's an activity for Unit 4 Step 1 which you can download from the Internet: www.klett-langenscheidt.de/networknow/activities

FYI Unit 4 Step 2

Reaching 100 can be quite a milestone. To read about how the Queen responds to this, go to www.klett-langenscheidt.de/networknow/fyi.

Preparing Unit 4 Step 2

What's your favourite?
5+ mins

- To be used any time after *Exercise 1b,* coursebook p. 70.
- Students work in pairs to say which type of parties, from the list in *Exercise 1b,* they like, which they don't like, and why.

Muddled invitations
10 mins

- To be used before *Exercise 2b,* coursebook p. 71.
- **Photocopy *11 Muddled invitations*** (p. 109) – one copy for each pair of students.
- Cut out the cards.
- Students work in pairs.
- Tell students they have an invitation and an acceptance letter, but the sentences have got mixed up. They need to sort them out and put them in the correct order.
- Give each pair a set of cards. Ask them to spread them out, face up, on the table.
- Together they have to find the invitation sentences and the acceptance letter sentences.
- Once they have done this, they need to put the sentences of the invitation and acceptance letter into the correct order.

Invitations
10 mins

- To be used with *Exercise 2b,* coursebook p. 71.
- Look online and find a selection of party invitation templates. Photocopy one for each pair of students.
- Students then use the templates to write their invitations.

Language and culture Step 2: Party gifts
(coursebook p. 81)
10+ mins

- To be used after the *Round up,* coursebook p. 71.
- Ask individual students the following questions:
  What was the last party you went to? What did you take for your host? What was the last party you gave? What did your guests bring for you?
- Board: house-warming party, engagement party, potluck supper
  Say: *Read the text and find out what you could / should take to each of these parties.*
  (plant / candle, champagne glasses, food or drink)
- In small groups, students then answer the question *What gift would you take to ...?* on page 81.

Downloads

- There's an activity for Unit 4 Step 2 which you can download from the Internet: www.klett-langenscheidt.de/networknow/activities

Preparing Unit 4 Step 3

What's just happened?
10 mins

- To be used any time after *Exercise 2a,* coursebook p. 74.
- **Photocopy *12 What's just happened?*** (p. 109) – one copy for each pair of students.
- Students work in pairs. They look at the pictures and choose 5. They then write one 'just' sentence for each picture, e.g. She's just failed an exam. She's just won the lottery.
- Then they read out their sentences to the class and the other students try to guess which picture the sentence is about.

  Possible answers:
  1 She's just dropped her mobile phone and it's broken. 2 She's just seen an accident. 3 She's just watched a boring film. 4 She's just forgotten where she put her key. 5 She's just met her boyfriend. 6 She's just won £20,000. 7 She's just had an idea. 8 She's just remembered she's got English homework to do for tomorrow. 9 She's just missed her train.

Language and culture Step 3: American place names
(coursebook p. 81)
10– mins

! You can refer students to the vocabulary section on p. 196 to check the pronunciation of the place names.

- To be used at the end of the lesson.
- Ask students to read the text and find out how the following American cities got their names. Board: 1 San Francisco 2 Louisiana 3 Utah 4 Michigan
- Students read the text to find the answers. (1 After Saint Francis of Assisi, 2 After King Louis XIV of France, 3 Native American name meaning *people of the mountains*, 4 Native American name meaning *great lake*)
- In pairs, students do the task and match the state names to their origins.
- Encourage students to do the Internet task at home.

Listen in
2/51

- Encourage students to do the *Listen in* task at home. The transcript can be found online.

Reading: Where shall we meet?
(coursebook p. 77)

The Reading page can be done as selfstudy or read in class. You'll find ideas on how to exploit the texts in class on page 121.

Downloads

- There's an activity for Unit 4 Step 3 which you can download from the Internet: www.klett-langenscheidt.de/networknow/activities

FYI Unit 4 Now I can

If you're a **detective fan**, go to www.klett-langenscheidt.de/networknow/fyi.

Preparing Unit 4 Now I can

Note: As the *Now I can* pages are revision and consolidation, you can use any of the optional and additional materials suggested for Steps 1–3.

Making arrangements
10 mins

- To be used before *Exercise 1b*, coursebook p. 78.

Board:

S_______ we go to the ...?	(Shall)
Yes, that's a _______ idea.	(good / great)
What time do you p_________?	(prefer)
I'd p_____________ ..., if that's ok with you?	(prefer)
Yes, that's f_______.	(fine)
Where shall we m_______?	(meet)
How a___________ outside of the ...?	(about)
Ok, then I'll see you t________.	(there)

- Elicit the gapped words from the students. Encourage students to use the phrases in *Exercise 1b* when making their arrangements to meet.

Your favourite detective
10 mins

- To be used before *Exercise 2a*, coursebook p. 78.
- Search on the Internet and print off some images of famous detectives (e.g. Miss Marple, Sherlock Holmes, Columbo). Show them to the class and ask the class who they are, and what they know about them. Alternatively you could give students five facts about famous detectives and get them to guess which detective the facts relate to.
- Then ask students to think about their favourite detective and make some notes about him / her.
- Students use their notes to tell the class about their famous detective.

Solution to the crime
5 mins

- To be used after *Exercise 4b*, coursebook p. 79.
- Tell the students you have the answer to the crime. Encourage them to ask you Yes- / No-questions to find out what really happened. (Sir Roderick was in the garden. He was smoking. The cook came out. He offered her an apple. She took it and ate it. They talked and then started kissing. The gardener saw them together. The cook was the gardener's fiancé. He was very angry. He went to the gun room and took a gun. He shot Sir Roderick. The cook went back into the house and say she had found a body.)

→

Template 4: Snakes and ladders
15+ mins

- To be used any time after *Starter,* coursebook p. 78.
- **Photocopy Template 4: *Snakes and ladders*** (p. 117).
- Fill in ten of the blank squares (see examples below) and copy the game board – one for each group of students. You will also need a dice and counters for each group of students.
- Students play in groups of three or four.
- Hand out the game board, dice and counters.

Tip: Alternative dice If you don't have a dice, you can take a 6-sided pencil or felt tip and use a board pen to put dots on it (1 dot – 6 dots). Students then roll the pencil / pen and use it as a dice. Alternatively, cut up six pieces of paper and write the numbers 1–6 on them (one number per piece of paper). Fold the pieces and mix them up. Students then pick one piece of paper and move forward the number of spaces written on the paper.

- Students play the game by throwing the dice and moving forward that number of squares on the board. When they land on a square with a sentence / question beginning or topic on it, they have to finish the sentence / question or talk about the topic. If they land on a ladder, they move up. If they land on a snake, they go down.
- The winner is the person who finishes first.
- This template can be used to recycle topics from any unit at all levels.

Examples for filling ten of the blank squares:
You need 10 tasks linked to Unit 4, which you have just covered, for the blank squares, e.g.:
5x Finish the sentences / questions *(I've just ..., I've already ..., I've never ..., I haven't ... yet, Have you ever ...?)*
5x Talk about ... *(dinner in the air, the last party you went to, your favourite film, your favourite restaurant, your favourite type of party)*

Downloads

- There's an activity for Unit 4 *Now I can* which you can download from the Internet: www.klett-langenscheidt.de/networknow/activities

Getting ready for Unit 5

Preparing Unit 5 Step 1

Name parts of the body beginning with ...
5 mins

- To be used after *Exercise 1b,* coursebook p. 86.
- Divide students into teams.
- Board:

- Tell each team they need to draw a bubble man and label it.
- Monitor while students are working and check they have the correct spellings of the body parts.
- When students have finished, stick the bubble men on the board and see which group has labelled the most body parts.

Half a crossword: Illness
15 mins

- To be used any time after *Exercise 3b,* coursebook p. 87.
- **Photocopy *13 Half a crossword: Illness*** (p. 110) – one copy for each pair. Cut out the two parts, for Student A and for Student B.
- Students work in pairs. Tell them they are going to get a crossword with some missing words. They need to ask their partners questions to find the missing words: *What's 3 across?* or *What's 1 down?* Their partner answers by describing the word, by miming it or by saying a sentence with the word missing. They mustn't show their part of the crossword to their partner.

What's wrong with me?
5 mins

- Extension idea for *Exercise 5a,* coursebook p. 87.
- Look at the list of ailments on p. 170. Fold a piece of paper in half 3 times so that you get 8 rectangles. Write an ailment in each rectangle. Photocopy the paper so you have one for each group, then cut out the rectangles so that each group has a pile of eight cards.

- Students work in small groups. Each group gets a pack of ailment cards and places them face down in a pile on the table.
- The first student picks a card, without showing it to his / her group. The other students ask questions to find out what the ailment is, e.g. Have you hurt yourself? Have you cut your hand? Is it an illness?

Language and culture Step 1: Thanksgiving in America
(coursebook p. 101)
10– mins

- To be used after the *Round up,* coursebook p. 87.
- Ask students what they know about Thanksgiving in America. Write their ideas on the board.
- Tell students they are going to read a text about how Thanksgiving started.
- Board: 1620, December 1620, Spring 1621, 1863
- Say: *Read the text and find out what happened on these dates.* (1620 – The year the Mayflower set sail with the Pilgrims. December 1620 – They arrived in America. Spring 1621 – Native Americans offered to help them grow food. 1863 – Abraham Lincoln made Thanksgiving a national holiday.)
- Ask students to tell the class about a special day in their country.
- Encourage students to do the Internet task at home.

Downloads

- There's an activity for Unit 5 Step 1 which you can download from the Internet: www.klett-langenscheidt.de/networknow/activities

FYI Unit 5 Step 2

Feel like trying out an **office workout** in the classroom? If you do, have a look at some office workout by going to www.klett-langenscheidt.de/networknow/fyi.

Preparing Unit 5 Step 2

Mime it
5+ mins

- To be used any time after *Exercise 2c,* coursebook p. 91.
- Demonstrate the task by miming an activity in a particular way, e.g. eating spaghetti quickly, writing slowly or singing loudly. Ask students to guess what you are doing (they need to get the activity and the adverb).
- Write the following onto 8 cards: swim quickly, do the dishes happily, bake a cake slowly, read a book carefully, eat soup quickly, drive fast, take a photo carefully, write a letter slowly.
- Students work in groups. Give each group a pack of cards. One student takes a card and mimes the activity to his / her group. The student who guesses the activity wins the card, and then picks the next card to mime.

Matching
10 mins

- To be used after *Exercise 4a,* coursebook p. 91.
- **Photocopy *14 Matching*** (p. 111) – one copy for each pair of students.
- Cut out and mix the cards.
- Give each pair a set of cards.
- Students work together to match the advice to the problem.
- When students have finished, check that they all have the correct pairs – ask one student to read out a problem, and another student to read out the appropriate advice.
- Then tell the students to put the advice cards face down on the desk but leave the problem cards visible.
- Using the problem cards, students give more advice.

Language and culture Step 2: Active or not?
(coursebook p. 101)
10+ mins

- To be used after the *Round up,* coursebook p. 91.
- Ask students how active they are in their free time and how much exercise they do.
- Board: Britain
  – _______ of men get enough exercise.
  – _______ of women get enough exercise.
  – Children spend _______ minutes per day, if not more, on social networking sites.
  – _________ of children are overweight.
- Ask students to read the text and find the statistics (see key on page 96).
- Check the answers and write them on the board.
- In small groups, students then discuss the questions under the text.

→

- Refer students to the information on the board and then rub out the numbers and replace *Britain* with *Germany*.
- With a partner, students write down what they think the German equivalent statistics is.
- Compare answers in class, then tell students the actual figures by writing them in the gaps on the board.

Britain	Germany
– 40% of men get enough exercise. – 28% of women get enough exercise. – Children spend 60 minutes per day, if not more, on social networking sites. – 27% of children are overweight.	**– 15.5% of men get enough exercise. – 25.4% of women get enough exercise. – Children spend 66 minutes per day, on average, on social networking sites. – Between 10% and 20% of children are overweight.**

Downloads

- There's an activity for Unit 5 Step 2 which you can download from the Internet: www.klett-langenscheidt.de/networknow/activities

FYI Unit 5 Step 3

Ever wondered where your favourite film was shot? To find out about **key film locations**, go to: www.klett-langenscheidt.de/networknow/fyi.

Preparing Unit 5 Step 3

A sleep survey
15 mins

- To be used any time after *Exercise 3b,* coursebook p. 95.
- **Photocopy *15 A sleep survey*** (p. 111) – one copy for each group of students.
- Students work in groups of 5–6 to complete the survey.
- Hand out the survey and tell students they should take it in turns to ask and answer questions about their group's sleeping habits.
- Students write the number of people in the brackets.
- Once they have completed this, they use the phrases from Step 3 to write five sentences about their group, e.g. *Only a few of us get up before 8 am on Sundays.*
- Finally, they take it in turns to tell the class about their group's sleeping habits.

What's the question?
10 mins

- To be used with *Exercise 4a,* coursebook p. 95.
- Board: Some young people. Playing chess. In Greece. In Japan. From India.
  Ask students to read the text and then write five questions which match these answers.
  Possible questions: **Who enjoys extreme sports? What can help you forget your worries? Where do people play with kolomboi? Where can you go to a 'cat café'? Where does Yoga come from?**

Nouns ending in *-y*
5 mins

- To be used with *Exercise 5,* coursebook p. 95.
- Write the first letters of nouns ending in *-y* on the board and ask volunteers to complete the words, e.g. Board: pa _ _ y (party). (baby, hobby, day, holiday, family, city, gallery etc.).
  If students can't guess, add another letter.
- ↑ Invite students to add other nouns to the board.

Extension task
5 mins

- To be used with *Exercise 5,* coursebook p. 95.
- Students write sentences with five of the plural nouns and then read them to the class.

Language and culture Step 3: Therapies
(coursebook p. 101)
10– mins

- To be used at the end of the lesson.
- Ask students to read the text and then close their books.
- Tell them you want to know what they can remember about the text.
- Read out the text slowly, sentence by sentence, with some words missing (see page 97). Stop after each missing word and ask the students to try to remember and write down the word.

Some people go to counsellors or __________ (therapists) when they have stress-related __________ (problems). For more serious problems, they may visit a __________ (psychoanalyst). Perhaps the most __________ (famous) psychoanalyst was Sigmund Freud, an __________ (Austrian) neurologist who emigrated to __________ (London) in 1983. His influence was so strong that many of his native __________ (German) words were adopted by __________ (English)-speaking therapists. *Angst, gestalt* and *weltschmerz* are just some of the terms which are used in this __________ (field) today.

- Check answers in class by asking individuals to read out one sentence each.
- In groups, students discuss the question, *What do you do to cope with stress?*.

Listen in

3/23

- Encourage students to do the *Listen in* task at home. The transcript can be found online.

Reading:
A body of stories
(coursebook p. 97)

- The Reading page can be done as selfstudy or read in class. You'll find ideas on how to exploit the text in class on page 121.

Downloads

- There's an activity for Unit 5 Step 3 which you can download from the Internet: www.klett-langenscheidt.de/networknow/activities

FYI Unit 5 Now I can

If you'd like to see a **green gym** in action, go to www.klett-langenscheidt.de/networknow/fyi.

Preparing Unit 5 Now I can

Note: As the *Now I can* pages are revision and consolidation, you can use any of the optional and additional materials suggested for Steps 1–3.

Template 5:
Climbing
15+ mins

- To be used any time after *Starter,* coursebook p. 98.
- **Photocopy Template 5: *Climbing*** (p. 118).
- In each rock, write one of the following words / phrases linked to Unit 5, e.g.:
  1st line (at the bottom, the two end blocks are empty): choose four parts of the body from: arm, finger, foot, leg, mouth, neck, nose
  2nd line: How much ...?, How many ...?, not much / a little / a bit of, not many / a few, a lot of
  3rd line: headache, toothache, backache, stomach ache
  4th line: cold, temperature, pain in my ...
  5th line: Why don't you ...?, If I were you, I'd ...
  6th line: You should ... – You shouldn't ...
- Copy the game sheet so that you have one for each pair of students.
- Hand out the sheets and ask students to read the rules of the game on the sheet.
- This template can be used to recycle topics from any unit at all levels, e.g. write verbs in the rocks and players must make a sentence or ask their partners a question with that verb in a specific tense.

Downloads

- There's an activity for Unit 5 *Now I can* which you can download from the Internet: www.klett-langenscheidt.de/networknow/activities

Getting ready for Unit 6

FYI Unit 6 Step 1

To see some **Freegans** in action and hear more about the roots of Freeganism, go to www.klett-langenscheidt.de/networknow/fyi.

→

Preparing Unit 6 Step 1

Spider diagrams
10 mins

- To be used any time after *Exercise 1b,* coursebook p. 104.
- Create a spider diagram on the board with the class by writing: *glass* and then collecting ideas for things which are made of glass, e.g.:
  Board:
  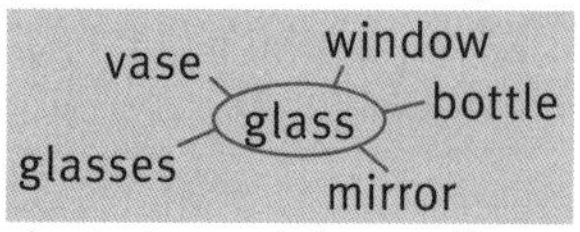

- Ask students to work in small groups. Allocate each group a material: fabric, metal, paper, plastic, wood.
- Give each group a piece of A4 paper and ask them to create a spider diagram for their material. They need to think of as many things which are made of this material.
  Possible answers:
  fabric: (any) clothes, curtains, towels, cushions
  metal: pans, coins, bikes, scissors, jewellery
  paper: newspaper, notebooks, books, receipts, pound / euro notes, envelopes
  plastic: credit cards, chairs, tables, packaging
  wood: rocking horses, tables, chairs, floors, pencils

Grammar consolidation
10 mins

- This can be used with *2 Grammar,* coursebook p. 105 if students need more consolidation of the grammar point.
- Draw two stick men on the board, Tom and Rob.
  Say: *Here are two people, Tom and Rob. Tom is very busy, he never has any time. Rob is retired and has some free time.*
- Board: A: If I have time, I'll do the garden.
  B: If I had time, I'd do the garden.
  Ask: *Which sentence does Tom say?* (B) *Why?* (Because he doesn't have any time, so it isn't possible for him to do the garden.)
  Which sentence does Rob say? (A) *Why?* (Because he has time, so it is possible for him to do the garden.)
- Get students to work in pairs and take the roles of No-time Tom and Retired Rob. Tom begins his sentences with: If I had time, I'd … . Rob begins his sentences with: If I have time, I'll … .
  Write some 'housework' prompts on the board, e.g.:
  Board: shopping, dishes, lunch, ironing, windows, car, cook, clean, wash, go
- Then get them to adopt different roles – No-time (Tina) and Retired (Renate) – and write different prompts on the board, e.g.:
  Board: friends, Spanish course, book, on holidays, party, do, organise, go, meet, write
- Students tell the class about their partner.

What would you do if …?
15 mins

- To be used any time after *Exercise 2c,* coursebook p. 105.
- **Photocopy *16 What would you do if …?*** (p. 112) – one copy for each group of students and cut out the *What would you do if …?* cards.
- Students work in small groups.
- Give each group a set of *What would you do if …?* cards. Place them face down on the table.
- In their groups, one student picks up a card and asks the question on it to another student. The student who answers the question picks up the next card and asks a different student. Continue until all of the questions have been answered.

Language and culture Step 1: Too much bread
(coursebook p. 119)
10– mins

- To be used after the *Round up,* coursebook p. 105.
- Board: True or false:

1 Over forty million tons of food is thrown away in Britain.	(False (over four million).)
2 The most popular food to throw away is bread.	(True.)
3 25% of all bought bread in Britain is thrown away.	(False (32%).)
4 Many British people can't tell the difference between two-day-old and six-day-old bread.	(True.)

- Ask students to work with a partner and decide if these statements are true or false.
- Tell them to open their books at page 119 and look at the first text: *Too much bread.*
- Allow time for the students to read the text silently and find out if they chose the right answers.
- Discuss the task question in class.

! If students have visited Britain and tried the bread there, you can talk about the differences between bread in their countries and the UK.
- Encourage students to do the Internet task at home.

Downloads

There's an activity for Unit 6 Step 1 which you can download from the Internet: www.klett-langenscheidt.de/networknow/activities

FYI Unit 6 Step 2

To test your own knowledge of **food**, go to www.klett-langenscheidt.de/networknow/fyi.

Preparing Unit 6 Step 2

Food flashcards
5 mins

- To be used to introduce the article *The Millionaire's Menu*, coursebook p. 108.
- Look in some magazines or online to find pictures of a selection of the food mentioned in the article and cut them out (e.g. hamburgers, sandwiches, pizza, lemons, onions, sausage, duck, mustard, truffles, mushrooms, chicken, ham, seafood, prawns, caviar).
- Hold the pictures up and ask students to name the food (or you can provide the word if they don't know).
- If possible, stick the pictures up around the board.
- Say: *You are going to read an article with a menu. While you are reading underline the food words you find.*
  ! These pictures can also be used to recycle some food vocabulary before working on *Exercise 2b*, coursebook p. 109.

4 Now you: You and your food
(coursebook p. 109)

Tip: Getting students into groups (1) Here's a suggestion of getting students into small goups:
- Fold a piece of paper in half 3 times so that you have 8 rectangles (fold two / three pieces of paper if you have more than 8 students). If you want groups of three, write 'Lancashire hotpot' on three of the rectangles, 'Sunday roast' on three etc. Cut out the cards and mix them up, then hand them out randomly to the students. Say to the class: *Stand up and find the people with the same pub food as you've got on your card, then sit down together as a group.*

Describe a traditional dish
10 mins

- To be used any time after *Exercise 5a*, coursebook p. 109.
- **Photocopy *17 Describe a traditional dish*** (p. 112) – one copy for each student.
- Allow time for the students to complete the description of a traditional dish, encouraging them to use dictionaries if they have any.
- Once students have finished, ask them to stand up and walk and talk, telling the other students about their traditional dish.

Language and culture Step 2: Haute cuisine
(coursebook p. 119)

- To be used after the *Round up*, coursebook p. 109.
- Board: Find the answer:

When did the Normans invade England?	(The Normans invaded England in in 1066.)
How long was Norman French spoken?	(Norman French was spoken in England for 300 years.)
How many French words are used in English today?	(About 7,500 French words are used in English today.)
What do some people say before they start a meal in England?	(In England people sometimes say *Bon appetit* before they start a meal.)

- Students read the text to find the answers.
- Ask the class if they know which words from other languages are used in their language.

Downloads

- There's an activity for Unit 6 Step 2 which you can download from the Internet: www.klett-langenscheidt.de/networknow/activities

FYI Unit 6 Step 3

Do you think you are a **saver** or a **spender**? To check, go to www.klett-langenscheidt.de/networknow/fyi. →

Preparing Unit 6 Step 3

3b Now you: Your money matters (coursebook p. 113)

Tip: Getting students into groups (2) Here's a suggestion of getting students into small goups:
- Collect a selection of coins. If you have 12 students in your class and want groups of four, you will need 3 sets of 4 identical coins, e.g. 4 x 1 cent, 4 x 2 cent, 4 x 10 cent.
- Put all of the coins into a bag. Move round the room asking each student to take one coin out of the bag.
- Then tell students to stand up and find the other students with the same coins. When they have found them they should sit down together.

Spend your coupons! 15 mins
- To be used any time after *Exercise 4b,* coursebook p. 113.
- **Photocopy *18 Spend your coupons!*** (p. 113) – one for every group of students.
- Students work in small groups. Give each group a copy of the coupons website and tell them they have 5,000 coupons to spend. However, they must talk together and agree as a group what they are going to buy.
- Allow time for the students to read the information and discuss the options.
- Monitor and help with any vocabulary.
- Once the groups have decided, ask them to tell the class how they are going to spend their coupons.

Numbers – an alternative idea 10 mins
- To be used as an alternative idea for *Exercise 4c,* coursebook p. 113.
- Students work in pairs. One student closes his / her book. The other keeps his / her book open.
- The student with the open book asks his / her partner what he / she can remember about the first three numbers and checks his / her answers by referring back to the text.
- Students then swap roles for the last three numbers.

Language and culture Step 3: Coupons (coursebook p. 119) 10– mins
- To be used at the end of the lesson.
- Say: *Read the text and then close your book.*
- Allow students time to do this. Then say*: Work with a partner. How much of the text can you remember? Write down the main points.*
- Allow time for the students to do this. Then ask the class to tell you what they have written down and write the main points on the board.
- Students then open their books. Ask volunteers to read out the text sentence by sentence, and as they are doing this tick off the points which are on the board and add anything which is missing on the board.
- In pairs, students then discuss the questions.

Listen in 3/47
- Encourage students to do the *Listen in* task at home. The transcript can be found online.

Reading: I'm not selling anything! (coursebook p. 115)
- The Reading page can be done as selfstudy or read in class. You'll find ideas on how to exploit the story in class on page 121.

Downloads
- There's an activity for Unit 6 Step 3 which you can download from the Internet: www.klett-langenscheidt.de/networknow/activities

FYI Unit 6 Now I can

To find out more about **Cajun food**, go to www.klett-langenscheidt.de/networknow/fyi.

Preparing Unit 6 Now I can

Note: As the *Now I can* pages are revision and consolidation, you can use any of the optional and additional materials suggested for Steps 1–3.

What's on your menu?
20 mins

- To be used instead of or after *Exercise 2c*, coursebook p. 117.
- Divide the class into groups of three. Give each group a piece of A4 paper.
- Tell the groups they have just bought a new restaurant. They need to decide on a name and create a menu. They need to include two starters, three main courses and two desserts.
- Students work in their groups to design their menus.
- When they have finished, ask one member of each group to be the waiter. Ask all of the waiters to stand up with their menu and move to another group.
- Students then use the menus to role play ordering a meal with one waiter and two guests.
- If times permits, you can change roles several times.

Template 6:
Tell me about it
15 mins

- To be used after *Part 4*, coursebook p. 117.
- **Photocopy Template 6: *Tell me about it*** (p. 119) and write one of the following on each rock:
  – I think the most interesting text in the book is ... because ...
  – I liked the Globetrotter section on ... because ...
  – My favourite unit was ... because ...
  – The way I learned vocabulary was ...
  – The blog I most enjoyed writing was ...
  – The thing I have enjoyed most about the course was ...
  – I think the most useful Language and culture text was ...
  – I have / haven't used the Dictionary section at the back of the book because ...
  – I think the most interesting topic in the book was because ...
  – During the course I have read ... in English.
  – I think I've learned ... new words. The words I've found most useful are ...
  – I now find it easier to ...
  – I still want to improve my ...
  – The way I learned grammar was ...
  – I feel more confident now when ...
  – When I finish this course, I plan to ...
- Copy the sheet so that you have one for each pair of students.
- Ask students to work with a partner.
- Each pair needs a coin. Students flip the coin – heads move forward one space, tails move forward three spaces.
- When they land on a rock, they must talk for 30 seconds on that topic.
- The game is over when the first person reaches *Finish*.
- This template can be used in a variety of ways to practice talking about different topics.

Downloads

- There's an activity for Unit 6 *Now I can* which you can download from the Internet: www.klett-langenscheidt.de/networknow/activities

1 In and around town (Unit 1 Step 1)

Partner A

- Work with Partner B. Ask him / her about your missing words. Ask: *What's number ...?* Your partner will give you a *definition* of the word. Guess what the word is and write it in your puzzle.

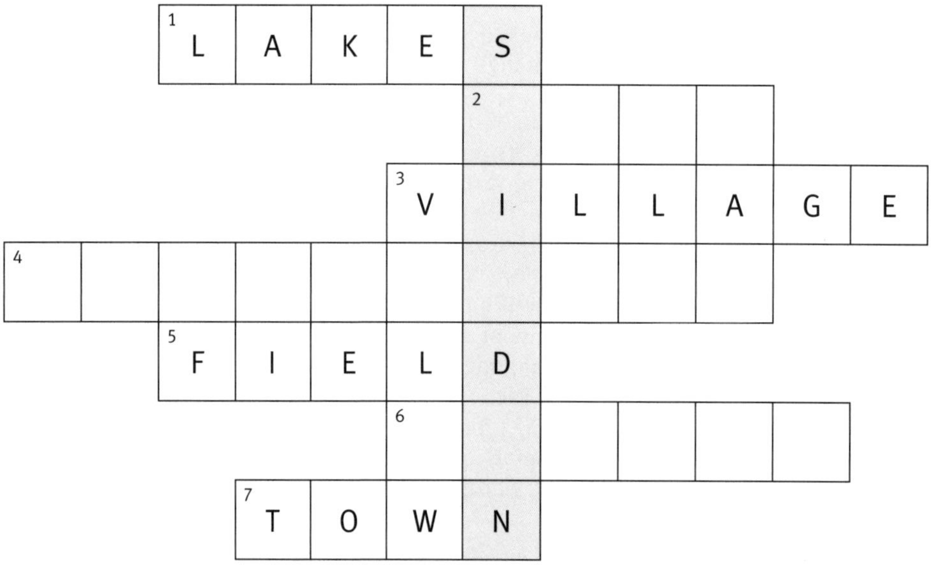

What's the mystery word? ____________________

✂ -

Partner B

- Work with Partner A. Ask him / her about your missing words. Ask: *What's number ...?* Your partner will give you a *definition* of the word. Guess what the word is and write it in your puzzle.

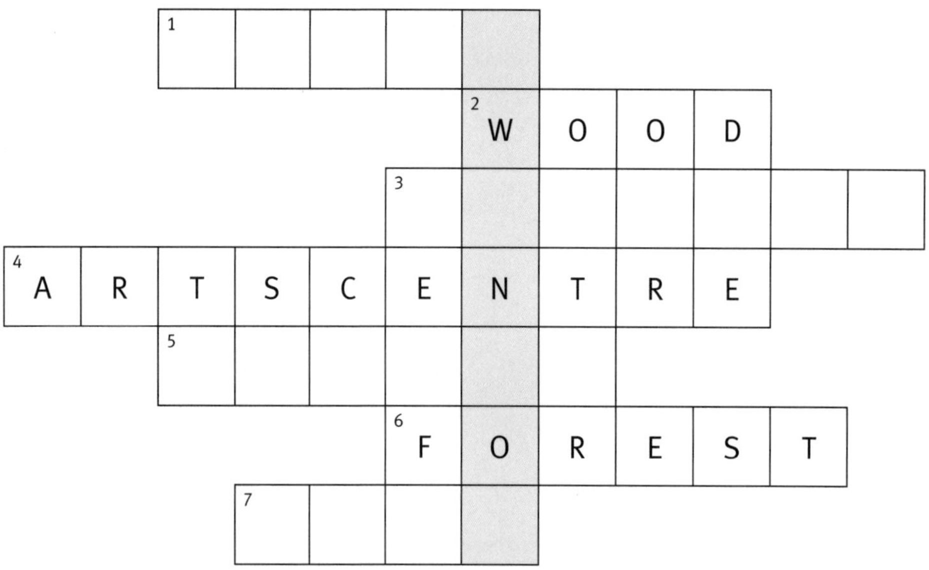

What's the mystery word? ____________________

2 Booking a hotel room (Unit 1 Step 2)

Partner A

- You work at Regents Hotel in London. Read the information below about the hotel's prices and facilities.

REGENTS HOTEL

- Price list:
  Double: £200.00 per night
  Single: £150.00 per night
- Facilities: Internet, cable TV, car parking, 24-hour reception, free airport shuttle, restaurant (breakfast is included in the price, evening meal can be ordered separately)
- Nearby: a park, an art gallery, a cinema and two museums
- Getting to the city centre: 10 minute walk / take the tube (two stops)

- Partner B is going to phone you and ask about booking a room at your hotel. Answer the phone by saying: *Good morning, Regents Hotel. How can I help?*

Partner B

- You are going to London for a weekend (Friday – Sunday). You want to book a hotel. Using the notes below, write down some questions to ask.

price - how much (single / double)? ______________________________?

breakfast included? ______________________________?

evening meal included? ______________________________?

Internet? ______________________________?

children's play area? ______________________________?

airport shuttle? cost extra? ______________________________?

how close to centre of London? ______________________________?

things to do nearby? ______________________________?

- Then call Partner A, who is the receptionist at the Regents Hotel in London, to book a room. Start by saying: *Hello. I'm calling to book a room for ...*

3 Compare it (Unit 1 Step 3)

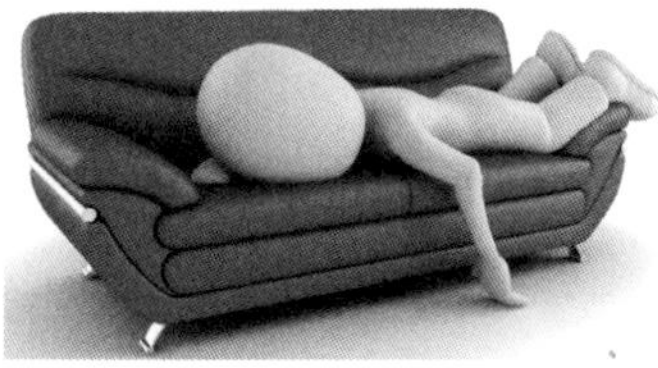

Couch surfing is ...

Cities are ...

Museums are ...

Hiking is ...

A beach holiday is ...

A four star hotel is ...

4 Person, thing, place (Unit 2 Step 1)

church	canteen	receptionist	cook	plane	coursebook
school	car park	air steward	employee	baggage	handbag
college	cinema	bus driver	mechanic	beer	jacket
university	hospital	car dealer	firefighter	breakfast	fridge
village	library	cleaner	journalist	guide book	magazine
airport	petrol station	electrician	dentist	dictionary	money
town	theatre	hairdresser	optician	passport	photocopier
art gallery	museum	doctor	teacher	newspaper	pillow

5 Question tags (Unit 2 Step 2)

His brother works in Berlin,	doesn't he?
He doesn't work full-time,	does he?
You aren't retired,	are you?
You're a teacher,	aren't you?
They don't work in the evening,	do they?
She deals with customers,	doesn't she?
It's her job to deal with customers,	isn't it?
Your brother is unemployed,	isn't he?
Her sister works part-time,	doesn't she?
She's a sales assistant,	isn't she?
His office is on the second floor,	isn't it?
They aren't responsible for sales,	are they?
You work full-time,	don't you?
They don't share an office,	do they?
You don't work in an office,	do you?

6 Reading - the same or different? (Unit 2 Step 3)

- **Partner A,** answer the questions for yourself in the 'You' column. Then ask your questions to Partner B. Write his / her answers in the 'Partner B' column. If you have the same answers, put a ✓ in the final column, if not, put a ✗.

	You	Partner B	✗ / ✓
How often do you read books?	______	______	______
When do you usually read books?	______	______	______
What's your favourite kind of book?	______	______	______
What was the last book you read?	______	______	______
Do you ever go to the library?	______	______	______

✂ -

- **Partner B,** answer the questions for yourself in the 'You' column. Then ask your questions to Partner A. Write his / her answers in the 'Partner A' column. If you have the same answers, put a ✓ in the final column, if not, put a ✗.

	You	Partner A	✗ / ✓
Do you enjoy reading?	______	______	______
What's your favourite book?	______	______	______
Do you have an e-book reader?	______	______	______
What do you read most: newspapers / magazines / books / other (what?)?	______	______	______
What did you read yesterday?	______	______	______

7 Holiday decisions (Unit 3 Step 1)

- Your group has won a group holiday. Read the descriptions of holidays which you can choose from. Then talk together and decide which holiday you want to go on and why. Then tell the class which holiday you've chosen and give your reasons.

Caribbean family resorts

Looking for the ideal family holiday with perfect weather and sandy beaches?

Then spend a holiday at one of our all-inclusive clubs. Land and water sports, children's club, excellent food and lots of fun activities for the whole family.

***Walk Britain* holidays**

We are the specialists for walking tours in Britain. We offer over 50 walking routes from the Cornish coast to the castles of Scotland.

Comfortable accommodation in four-star B&Bs.

You can book two-day to two-week trips. We do all the hard work, you just do the walking.

Cruisewithus.uk

Welcome aboard! Join us on one of our exclusive international cruises. Routes include Scandinavian fjords, the Irish and Scottish coastlines and the West Indies.

All meals and snacks provided. Our spa and fitness centre is included in the price. Children's activities all day every day.

Cruises available from 7 days to 10 weeks.

Swiss Mountain Spa

Enjoy the combination of a winter holiday and a spa experience in one of our luxury chalets.

All chalets are located near the ski slopes, have five-star accommodation, full board and spa and sauna facilities. The main hotel also has a thermal pool.

Skiing equipment and tuition available.

8 When I saw you, ... (Unit 3 Step 2)

When I saw you, you were running after a car.

When I saw you, you were wearing a Pippi Longstocking costume.

When I saw you, you were talking to a policeman.

When I saw you, you were waiting for a bus.

When I saw you, you were swimming in a river with your clothes on.

When I saw you, you were eating tomatoes.

When I saw you, you were climbing a tree.

When I saw you, you were singing in the town centre.

When I saw you, you were running after a dog in the park.

When I saw you, you were queueing outside the football stadium.

9 Travelling by train (Unit 3 Step 3)

Excuse me. When's the next train to Leeds?	The next one leaves at 3.35.
How long does it take from York to Leeds?	It takes forty-five minutes on the fast train.
What does a day return cost?	It costs £35.
When does the train arrive in Leeds?	It arrives at 4.20.
Which platform does the train go from?	The Leeds train leaves from platform 2.
Is there a buffet car?	There isn't, but there's a trolley service.
Do I have to change?	No – it's a direct train.
Can I take my bike on the train?	Yes, but there's an extra charge.
Is the train to Leeds delayed?	Yes, it is. But it'll be here in 20 minutes.
Can I use an off-peak ticket on this train?	No, sorry, they're only valid after 9.15.

10 Find the differences (Unit 4 Step 1)

Student A

- Look at Rob's diary for next week. You can't read some of the information. Ask Student B questions to find out the missing information and write it in the diary. Answer Student B's questions.

Monday	*job interview at 4.00*
Tuesday	*at club. 6.00 start.*
Wednesday	*lunch with Sam and Kate 12.30*
Thursday	*with Jack*
Friday	*Cinema with Jay, Chris and Mac. Meet at 6.30 outside Odeon Cinema.*
Saturday	*in Crofton. Kick off at 9.30. Set alarm!*
Sunday	*Sunday dinner at mum's 12.30 … – don't be late!!*

Student B

- Look at Rob's diary for next week. You can't read some of the information. Ask Student A questions to find out the missing information and write it in the diary. Answer Student A's questions.

Monday	*at 4.00*
Tuesday	*Playing football at club. 6.00 start.*
Wednesday	*with Sam and Kate 12.30*
Thursday	*dinner with Jack*
Friday	*with Jay, Chris and Mac. Meet at 6.30 outside Odeon Cinema.*
Saturday	*Football match in Crofton. Kick off at 9.30. Set alarm!*
Sunday	*at mum's 12.30 … - don't be late!!*

11 Muddled invitations (Unit 4 Step 2)

Dear Sue and Richard, We'd like	Dear Cate and Allan, Thanks
to invite you to	for the invitation. We'd
our house-warming party on	love to come. Do we
Saturday, 5th October, at 7 o'clock.	need to bring anything? Looking forward
We hope you can come.	to seeing you and your new house on the 5th.
Love, Cate and Allan	Love, Sue and Richard

12 What's just happened? (Unit 4 Step 3)

- Work with a partner. Look at these pictures. Choose five and say what you think has just happened. Write one sentence with 'just' for each picture.
- Then read your sentences out to the class. See if the other students can guess which picture your sentence is about.

13 Half a crossword: Illness (Unit 5 Step 1)

Student A

- Work with a partner. You have a crossword and the words across (→) are missing. In your partner's crossword, the words down (↓) are missing. In turn, ask each other for a clue so that you can write in the missing words. To give a clue, you can give a definition, mime the word or make a sentence with the word missing.

You can ask: *What's (3) across?*

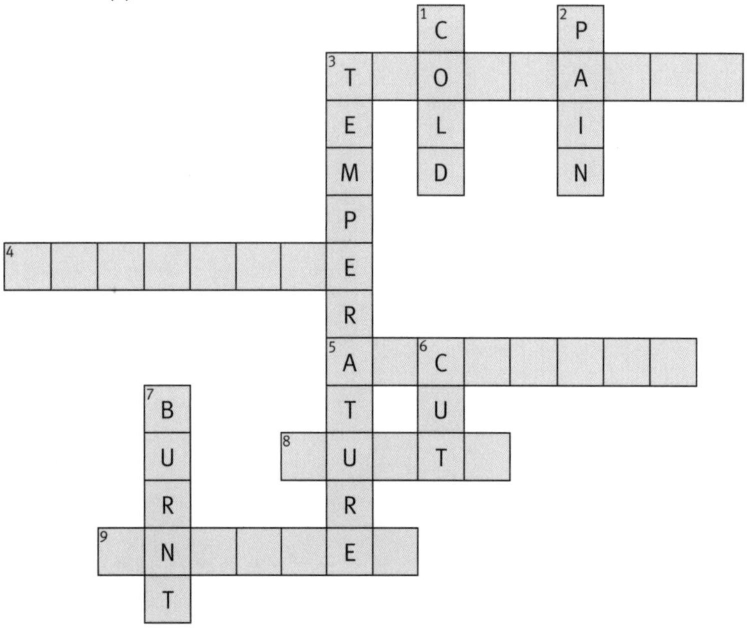

Student B

- Work with a partner. You have a crossword and the words down (↓) are missing. In your partner's crossword, the words across (→) are missing. In turn, ask each other for a clue so that you can write in the missing words. To give a clue, you can give a definition, mime the word or make a sentence with the word missing.

You can ask: *What's (1) down?*

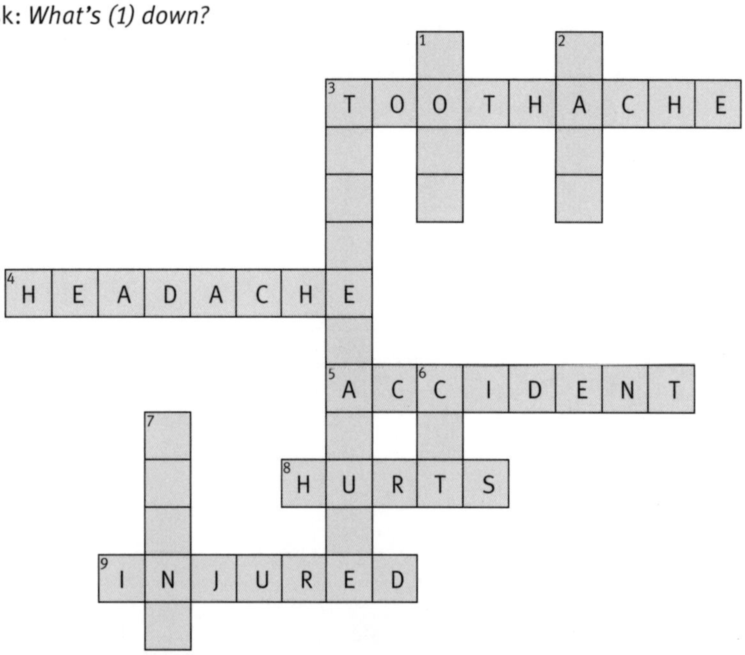

14 Matching (Unit 5 Step 2)

I've got a headache.	You should take a paracetamol.
Ouch, I've burnt my hand!	You should run your hand under cold water.
I've cut my finger badly.	I think you should go to hospital.
I need to lose some weight.	If I were you, I'd go to a diet club.
I need to stop smoking.	Why don't you talk to a doctor about stopping?
I'm stressed at work.	Why don't you talk to your boss?
I feel dizzy.	I think you should lie down.
I'd like to do more exercise.	Why don't you take up running?

15 A sleep survey (Unit 5 Step 3)

- Work together. Take it in turns to ask and answer questions to find out the following information about the people in your group. Write down the number of people in the brackets ( ).

1 How many people normally sleep
  a) less than 5 hours? (__) b) between 5–8 hours? (__) c) more than 8 hours? (__)
2 How many people get up before 8am on Sundays? (__)
3 How many people regularly remember their dreams? (__)
4 How many people often wake up during the night? (__)
5 How many people go to bed after 10 o'clock every night? (__)

- Now write five sentences about your group's sleeping habits using some of the words / phrases you have learned:
  All / Most of us ..., A lot of us ..., Quite a lot of us ..., Only a few of us ..., Not very many of us ..., Nobody..., None of us ...

1 ______________________________.

2 ______________________________.

3 ______________________________.

4 ______________________________.

5 ______________________________.

- Take it in turns to tell the class about your group's sleeping habits.

16 What would you do if ...? (Unit 6 Step 1)

What would you do if you won £10,000?	*What would you do if you found a wallet in the street?*	*If you invited a vegetarian to dinner, what would you cook?*	*What would you do if someone queue-jumped in front of you?*
What would you do if you saw an accident?	*What would you do if you lost your purse?*	*If you could have tickets for any concert, what would you choose?*	*What would you do if your passport was stolen?*
If you could buy one new thing for your home, what would you buy?	*Where would you go if you could choose one place in the world to visit?*	*Who would you choose if you could meet one famous person?*	*If you had a free day next week, how would you spend it?*
If you had coupons for 1000 euros, which shop would you spend them in?	*Where would you go if you had to move to another town / city?*	*If your neighbours' dog barked a lot at night, what would you do?*	*If you wanted to give a surprise party for your best friend, who would you invite?*

17 Describe a traditional dish (Unit 6 Step 2)

- Think of a traditional dish from your country. How would you describe it? Use the sentences below to help you to write a description of it.

______________________ (name of dish) is a traditional dish from ______________ (your country).

It's made with ____.

It's got ____ in it.

It often comes with ____.

We eat it (is there a special time of year when you eat it?) ______________________

______________________.

- Now walk and talk and tell the other students about the traditional dish.

18 Spend your coupons! (Unit 6 Step 3)

- Work in small groups. Your group has 5,000 coupons to spend. Talk together and decide what you are going to spend your coupons on. Try to use some of the agreeing and disagreeing phrases in your coursebook on page 105.

Sparkles cleaning services.
For only **1,000 coupons** you and your friends can hire a cleaner for the day (all participants must live within 10 miles of each other).

Need to get fit? Then try our Green Gym experience, for only **100 coupons per person** for your first session.

The ultimate meal deal. For only **1,500 coupons** you and up to 5 friends can enjoy a 4 course meal at our modern Japanese restaurant. All food freshly cooked.

Paintballing. The most exciting thing to do at the weekend. Paintballing for up to 8 people including equipment hire, lunch and 100 paintballs for only **2,500 coupons.**

Creative writing course. Have you ever wanted to write a book? Now is your chance to try with our four hour writing course. Only **1,000 coupons per person**.

Group photo. Do you want to remember your friends? Then book a two hour photo session with our professional photographer. Only **2,500 coupons.**

English for tourists. Going on holiday and want to practise your English? Then try our thirty hour online course. **300 coupons** needed for this great deal.

English cooking is no good? Who said so? Find out how to cook traditional English food in our modern kitchens with top Chef Tim Morgan. This Saturday course costs **750 coupons** per person.

Template 1: Word diagrams

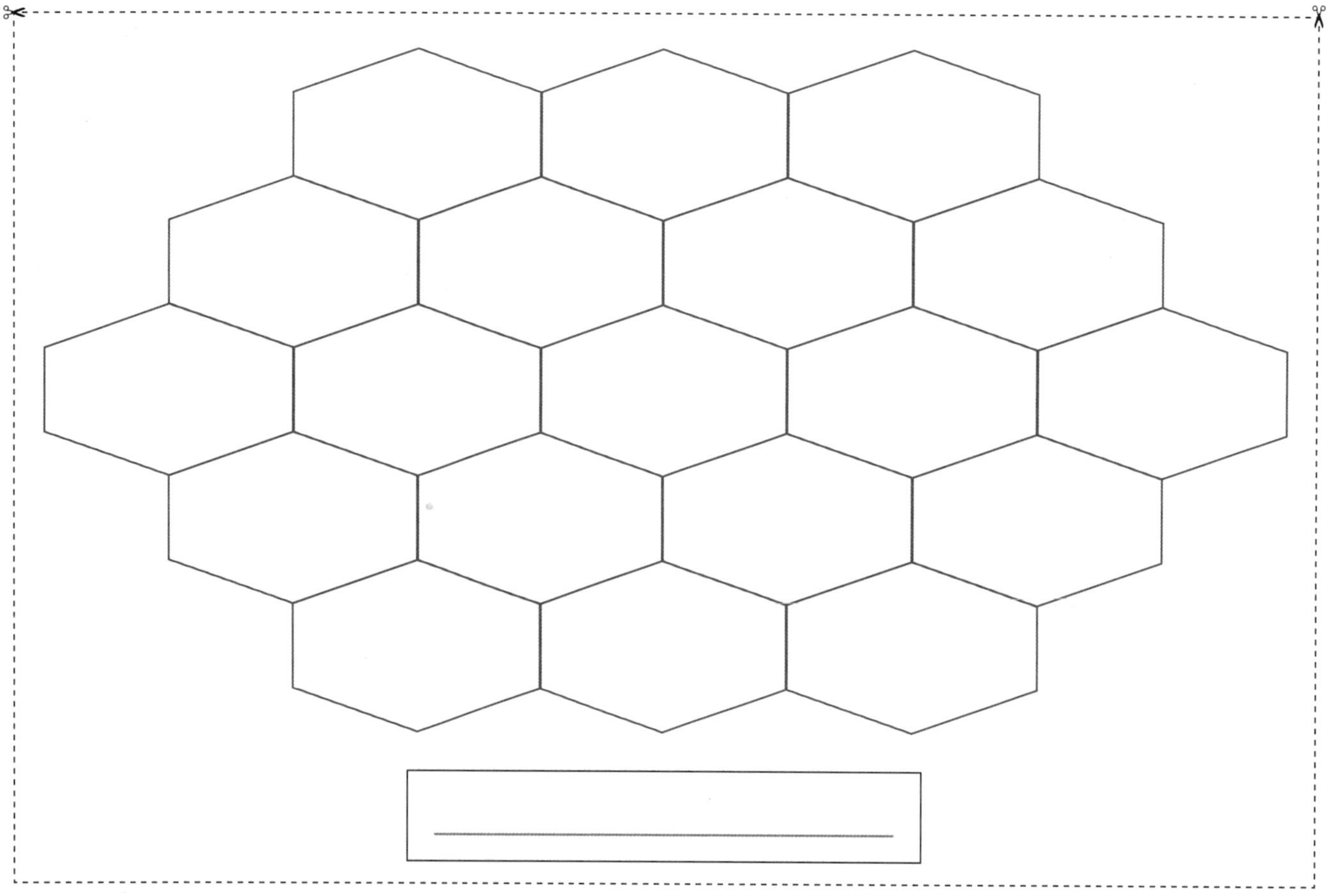

Template 2: What's your opinion?

What's your opinion on ______________________________?

- Complete as many of the sentences as you can.

In my opinion ... ______________________________ ______________________________.	I think that ... ______________________________ ______________________________.
One positive thing about ... is ... ______________________________ ______________________________.	One negative thing about ... is ... ______________________________ ______________________________.
I think everyone should ... ______________________________ ______________________________.	If more people ... ______________________________ ______________________________.
I think more people in my country should ... ______________________________ ______________________________.	I would / wouldn't be interested in ... ______________________________ ______________________________.
All you need ... ______________________________ ______________________________.	You can ... ______________________________ ______________________________.
You don't have to ... ______________________________ ______________________________.	Everyone can ... ______________________________ ______________________________.

Template 3: Question time

Who ...?	Where ...?	When ...?	Why ...?	What ...?
How ...?	How many ...?	How did ...?	How long ...?	Which ...?
Was ...?	Were ...?	Did ...?	Did you have ...?	Did you see ...?
Did you go ...?	Was there a ...?	Were there any ...?	see	buy
enjoy	eat	drink	go	do
souvenirs	weather	journey	hotel	food

Template 4: Snakes and ladders

- Finish the sentences / questions and talk about the topics.

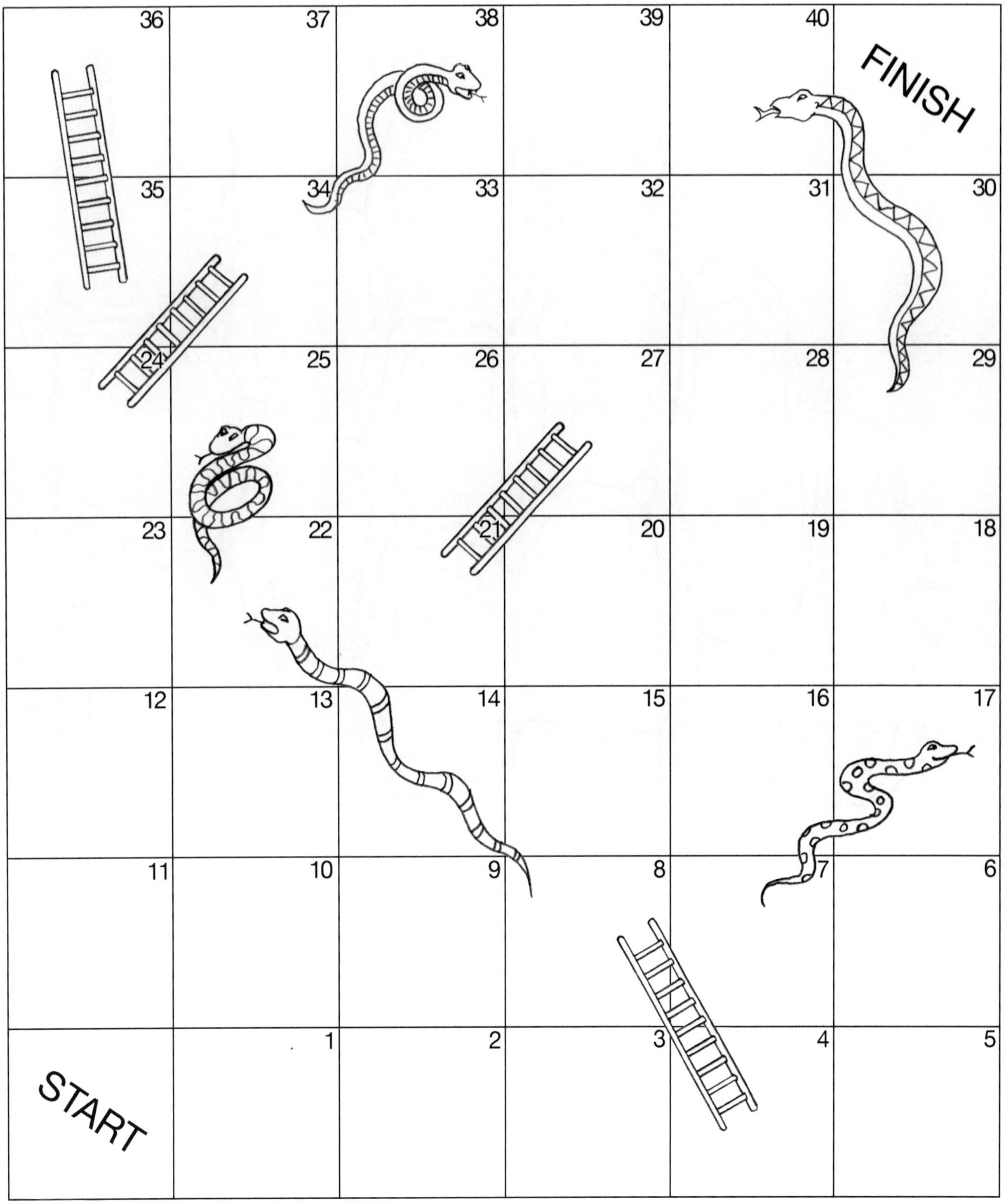

Template 5: Climbing

- Partnerarbeit:
  Beide Partner benötigen eine Spielfigur, z. B. eine Münze.
  Beginnen Sie am Fuß des Berges und steigen Sie bis zur Spitze hoch.
  Sie können immer nur zu einem verbundenen Felsen weitergehen.
  Auf jedem Felsen (außer dem Gipfelfelsen) darf nur eine Spielfigur stehen.
  Wenn Sie auf einem Felsen angekommen sind, bilden Sie einen Satz oder eine Frage mit den Wörtern, die auf diesem Felsen stehen.

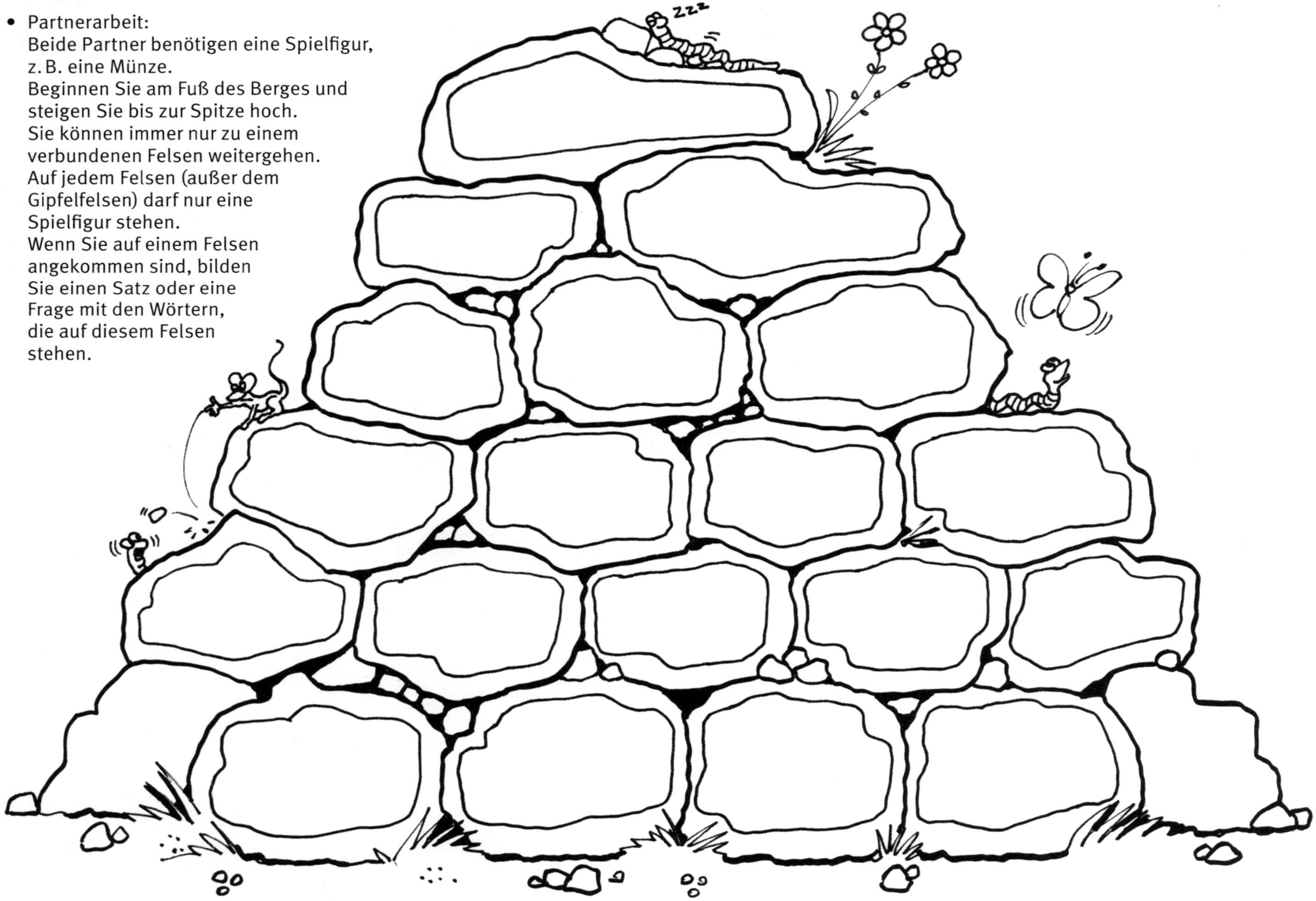

Template 6: Tell me about it

- Work with a partner. Flip a coin – heads move forward one space, tails move forward three spaces. Talk for 30 seconds about the topic you land on.

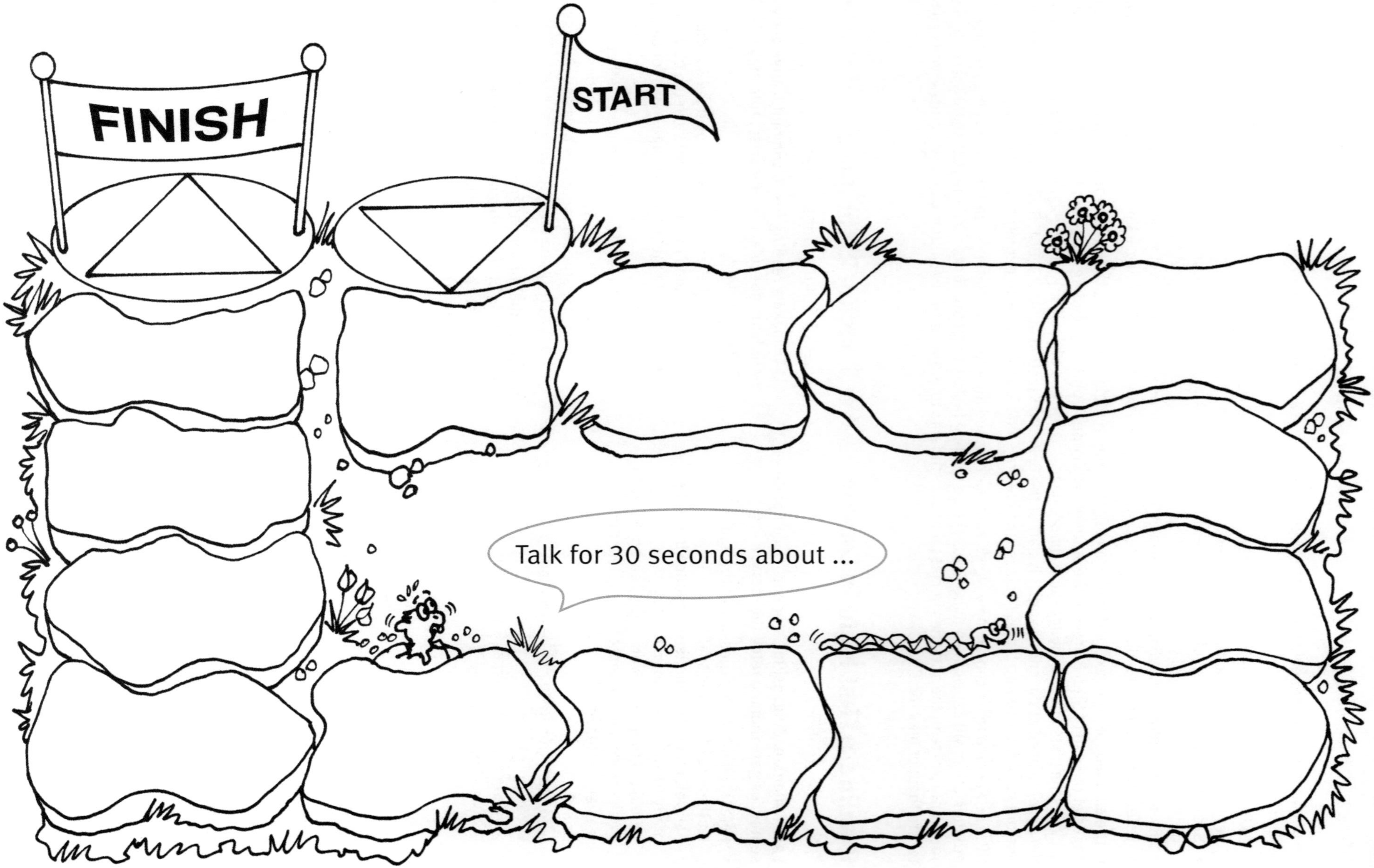

Reading

Ideas for dealing with the *Reading* pages at the end of Step 3

Throughout the coursebook, students are given texts to read and are presented with various tasks to practise different reading skills:

- **Skimming** – reading rapidly for the main points – for example, when you quickly read the front page of a newspaper to get the gist of what's in the news today
- **Scanning** – reading rapidly to find a specific piece of information – for example, when you read a train timetable in order to find the time of your train
- **Intensive reading** – reading a short text for detailed information – for example, when you read a contract
- **Extensive reading** – reading a longer text with emphasis on overall meaning – for example, when you read a novel

In the coursebook, the texts in Steps 1 and 2, the *Reading* texts in Step 3, the *Language and culture* texts and the *Reading* pages at the end of Step 3 provide the students with opportunity for reading longer texts. Each step has a text for reading in class; the texts on the *Language and culture* pages, at the end of each unit, are designed for home or classroom use; and the *Reading* page at the end of Step 3 is part of the Selfstudy section of Step 3. But, if you have time, you might like to do one or two of the *Reading* pages in class, so here are some ideas on how to exploit the texts.

NB: The *Reading* texts contain new words so it isn't a good idea to have students read the texts aloud at first – unknown pronunciation will cause them to hesitate. A true reading task is to let students read the text silently and then do a task. If you want to extend the activities in class and get students to produce the vocabulary and structures, you can read out the text to them or play the CD.

Reading 1: First night in London

1/20 (coursebook p. 21)

! After silent reading, asking students to complete sentences gets them to retell the story.

- Refer students to the Glossary at the end of the text and let them read the text silently.
- Ask volunteers to complete the following sentences orally (in their own words).
  ↓ Weaker groups can work with their books open.
  ↓ Ask the weaker students to complete the earlier (easier) sentences.
  Board:

– Jon flew from New York to ____.	– (London)
– He was lucky because a lot of flights were ____.	– (cancelled)
– He saw a taxi driver with the sign: ____.	– ('Mr J Gardener, Analytica, NYC')
– The taxi took him to ____.	– (the hotel / the Plaza)
– When he was in his room, he ____.	– (ordered a bottle of wine (from the room service))
– The next morning, before he packed, he ____.	– (swam in the hotel pool / enjoyed a big breakfast)
– He checked out and he heard the receptionist apologise to a guest: ____.	– ("I'm sorry, Mr Gardener. The computer shows that you checked in yesterday. We sent a taxi to the airport and it brought you back here. There must be a mistake.")
– Jon quickly ____.	– (walked out into the street)

- ↑ As a possible follow up, set a writing activity by asking students to complete the (above) sentences, which you have written on the board.

Reading 2: Languages of the world

1/42 (coursebook p. 39)

! To make a reading text a communicative activity, have students speculate, summarise, role play – in this case, they speculate.

- Before the lesson, photocopy page 39. Blank out the ABC options in questions 1–9 in the quiz.
- Then copy the prepared page – one for each pair of students.
- Read the first third of the page together – up to and including the *Did you know ...?* section.
- In pairs, students read the quiz and discuss possible answers to the ten questions.

Tip: Mediation You needn't insist that they discuss in English. In order to discuss the question, they will have to translate parts of it into their own language. This in itself is a useful skill. In business or holiday situations where English is the lingua franca, the students will be in a situation where they have to relay information which they've heard or read in English to other people in their group.

- In class, ask for possible answers to the ten questions. If someone offers the correct answer, praise them.
- Then ask students to open their books at page 39 – here they can see options and they choose an answer to the remaining questions.
- To check the answers, have a volunteer read out the answers from the key on page 127.

Reading 3: I want to complain about our holiday

2/22 (coursebook p. 59)

! A reading text can be exploited for vocabulary work – finding synonyms, opposites or rhyming words; you can also make gap-fill exercises with missing prepositions or – in this case – missing verbs. →

- Before the lesson, photocopy page 59.
- Blank out the following verbs:
  The beach was too sandy. – There were too many Spanish people. The receptionist spoke Spanish. The food was Spanish. – The sand on the beach wasn't like the sand in the brochure. Your brochure shows the sand as yellow, but it was white. – I compared the size of our one-bedroom apartment to our friends' three-bedroom apartment and ours was much smaller. – We had to wait outside without air conditioning. – I was shocked to learn that Spanish pesetas were no longer accepted. – No-one told us there would be fish in the sea. The children were frightened. – We bought Ray-Ban sunglasses for five euros from a street trader, but we later found out that they weren't real Ray-Bans. – I was bitten by a mosquito. No-one said they could bite. – On our Christmas holiday to Lapland, the reindeer couldn't fly. The children were very disappointed. You should state this clearly in your brochure. – Your brochure says that the local Slovanian tour guides speak English, but you didn't say anything about their Slovenian accents. – We booked an excursion to a water park but no-one told us to bring our swimming costumes and towels.
- Then copy the prepared page – one for each pair of students.
- Write the Glossary on the board.
- Tell the class that some verbs are missing from the texts.
- ↓ Write the blanked out verbs on the board in random order.
- In pairs, students discuss appropriate verbs and write down their choices.
- In class, compare the options.
- Students check their answers by listening to the CD. Play ▶ 2/22.
- ↓ Students check their answers by looking at the texts on page 59 while listening to the CD. Play ▶ 2/22.

Reading 4: Where shall we meet?

2/47 (coursebook p. 77)

! Matching titles to paragraphs shows that students understand the text – and this is a *telc* and *KET* exam skill at this level.

- Before the lesson, photocopy page 77.
- Delete the age in the 8 rectangles, so that it reads: *At the age of ...* and then the text.
- Copy the prepared page – one for each pair of students.
- Cut out the 8 rectangles and the Glossary strip.
- In class, give each pair of students the set of 8 texts + Glossary.
- Explain that each text refers to the same group of friends at different stages in their lives. On the board, write: At the age of 20 ... 30 ... 40 ... 50 ... 60 ... 70 ... 80 ... 90
- Ask students to read the texts and put them in chronological order.
- Play the CD ▶ 2/47 so that students can check / rearrange the order of the texts.

Follow up activity:

- Copy page 77 and cut out the 8 rectangles – without the titles *(At the age of ...)*.
- Give the eight texts (in random order) to eight students so they each have a different text.
- Ask two students to read out their texts.
- The class, working with closed books, should listen and then position the two students in their chronological order.
- A third student reads his / her text and the class positions this person chronologically.
- This continues until the 'story' is in the right order.
- Encourage the class to ask the texts to be re-read if they are undecided about the positioning.
- The eight students read out the texts in the right order.
- ↑ Students can read the texts with the CD playing at the same time. Play ▶ 2/47.

Reading 5: A body of stories

3/19 (coursebook p. 97)

! Getting students to retell what they have read to other students activates the vocabulary from the text.

- Copy page 97 four times and cut out the 5 texts + the attached Glossaries (this will be enough for a class of 20).
- Tell the class that they're going to read some unusual texts about parts of the body.
- Divide the class into five groups and allocate one of the five texts to each group. Give each person in the group a copy of the text. Allow students time to read the text and talk about it amongst themselves and ask you for any help with pronunciation or vocabulary.
- Then get the class to walk and talk. They walk around and find someone from another group and they tell each other about what they've read – without referring to their texts.
- After they have spoken to two or three people, ask them to sit down in their groups. One person from each group tells the class what his / her group learned from a member of another group.
- Play ▶ 3/19 so that students then listen to the texts.

Reading 6: I'm not selling anything!

3/42 (coursebook p. 115)

! Jigsaw reading shows that students understand the text.

- Before the lesson, photocopy page 115 – one copy for each pair of students.
- Cut up the story into 8 or 10 pieces, plus the title and the Glossary, and prepare a set of papers for each pair of students.
- ↓ If you have a weaker class, cut the story into fewer pieces.
- Refer students to the title and the Glossary and have them speculate about what the story could be about.
- Students work in pairs and reassemble the story.
- When most students have finished the task, play ▶ 3/42 so that they can check their story.

Lesson notes for the optional *Globetrotter* (*Work* and *Travel*) pages

After Units 2, 4 and 6 there are two optional pages: *Globetrotter Work* and *Globetrotter Travel*. The three *Globetrotter Work* pages focus on work situations. Here the students are presented with language and situations relevant to a working environment. The three *Globetrotter Travel* pages present students with language and situations which they meet when they're on holiday.

Each of these pages provides 45 minutes of classroom material, and a further 45 minutes of material can be found online. There's a code given under the title of each *Globetrotter*, e.g. www: A2.2GTAW (Coursebook A2.2, *Globetrotter A: Work*) which will take you directly to the activities online.

The *Globetrotter* pages allow for flexibility. Depending on the interests of your class, you may want to focus on just the *Work* page or just the *Travel* page; you could have a lesson consisting of both *Globetrotter* pages; or you may prefer to use just one of the *Globetrotter* pages and supplement the remaining 45 minutes with your own materials, or other optional materials from the previous units.

NB: It's a good idea to work out the number of lessons in your course to make sure that the basic 24 lessons (Units 1–6, Steps 1–3 + *Now I can*) can be covered before including the optional *Globetrotter* materials.

Globetrotter A: Work (coursebook p. 45)

Contents

Focus on Time management

Lesson notes

Further classroom materials can be found online: www: A2.2GTAW

Starter: It's time to get up 5 mins

- Read out the instructions and the clock times. Students write their ideas next to each clock. Check answers in class.
  Possible answers: **1 6:01 – teacher, doctor, businessperson, farmer; 2 12.00 – night shift worker, actor, student, tennis trainer, tour guide, chauffeur, scientist, sculptor, cook; 3 21.00 – security guard, nurse, night shift worker**

Extension idea: Make a list of the jobs on the board. Ask one student to choose a job but not say which one. The class then ask questions, to which the student can give only short answers (Yes, I do. / No, I haven't. etc.), to try and guess the job.

Exercises 1a 1/47, **1b** 1/48, **1c** 20+ mins

- **1a** Read out the instructions. Play ▶ 1/47. Students listen and tick the subjects mentioned.
  ✓ 1, 2, 4, 5

(A = Angela, B = Barbara)
A: OK, Barbara, I've got the coffees.
B: Oh, thanks, Angela.
A: Thank goodness it's Friday, I've had a terrible week at work. My boss is really difficult.
B: What *is* the problem with your boss?
A: Well, for one thing, he gets to work late every day. The company rule is that everybody starts work at eight-thirty and I'm usually there by twenty past eight. But *he* often comes to work at half past nine ...
B: Why is that a problem? I always do a lot more work when my boss isn't in the office!
A: Well yes, but people ring and want to talk to him first thing in the morning and I don't know what to say to them. And he only lives five minutes away – he walks to work so he doesn't have to wait for a bus or find a parking space or anything. I know he's the boss, but I think he should follow the rules like everybody else.
B: Well ... some people don't know the difference between work time and free time. Do you know, there's a woman in our office who never does *any* work – she sends private emails in company time and she's always on the phone to her friends. This morning I walked past her desk and she was using the Internet to book a holiday – and this is all in the company's time.
A: Oh, I know – we have a woman like that in our office.
B: And you know that guy I work with, Dave?
A: Yes.
B: Well, Dave smokes, and every time I look for him, he's gone to have a cigarette. He goes for a cigarette break about ten times a day. I can't take a five-minute coffee break every hour, but he can take lots of cigarette breaks. It's so unfair.
A: Yes, you're right. Goodness! Is that the time? I'm really sorry, Barbara, but I have to go now.
B: Oh, is it time to pick up your little boy? How old is he now?
A: He was three last week. And that's another thing my boss doesn't understand – I have to collect Jake from playschool at four thirty every afternoon. It doesn't matter if there's still work to do, I have to be there, and that means I have to leave work punctually at four o'clock.
B: Huh! Bosses! They just don't understand!
A: No, they don't!

- **1b** Divide the class into two groups. Group A: 'Angelas', Group B: 'Barbaras'. Tell students to listen and make notes about their person. Play ▶ 1/48. Then ask students to get into A/B pairs and role play the conversation that they've just heard.
  Possible answers:
  Partner A: Angela's boss – really difficult, gets to work late every day, not in the office when people want to talk to him first thing in the morning, only lives five minutes away, walks to work, should follow the rules like everyone else;
  Partner B: Barbara's colleague – some people don't know the difference between work and free time; one woman never does any work, sends private emails, is always on the phone, books her holiday on the Internet; Dave smokes and has a cigarette break about ten times a day.

Audio script: see above in *Exercise 1a.*

- **1c** Follow coursebook instructions.

Exercises 2a, 2b 20 mins
- **2a** Follow coursebook instructions.
- **2b** Read out the instructions. Once students have finished, ask them to share their tips with the class.
  Possible answers: **11 Use a calendar in your computer / phone. Set reminders. 12 Have a clock in front of you – this will help you keep to the allocated time for tasks.**

Globetrotter A: Travel (coursebook p. 46)

Contents

Focus on Jet lag

Lesson notes

Further classroom materials can be found online: www: A2.2GTAT

Starter: Three hours away 5 mins
- Ask individual students the *Starter* question.

Exercises 1a, 1b 15– mins
- **1a** Hold up your open book and point to the picture. Ask students what they think the text is about. Write their ideas on the board (travel, spending time in airports, jet lag). Students read the text to see if they were right. Check answers in class.
  It's about tips to help you to avoid jet lag.
- **1b** Follow coursebook instructions.
  1 When they travel long distances across the world's time zones.
  2 – before you travel?: You can change your body rhythms – for a few days before you fly.
  – on the flight?: You can drink water, don't have caffeine or alcohol and try to sleep. You can break up very long journeys with an overnight stopover.
  – when you arrive?: Change the times you eat and go to bed to the local time. Stay outdoors when you can.

Exercises 2a 1/49, **2b** 1/50, **2c** 25– mins
- **2a** Read out the instructions. Play ▶ 1/49. Students listen and say which continent they are flying in.
  North America

(CS = chief steward)
CS: Well, ladies and gentlemen, we've now landed at Oakland airport. Please remain in your seats, keep your seat belts fastened and do not turn on telephones or electronic devices until you're in the airport building. I'm pleased to tell you that we're twenty minutes ahead of schedule today – that's because of the tail wind on our flight from New York. As you can see, it's a fine afternoon here, and the weather report says it will be warm and sunny for the rest of the week. Remember to change the time on your watches – here in San Francisco it's now five-thirty Pacific Standard Time, and that's three hours behind New York time. For those of you planning to travel into the city today, there's an airport bus that goes from outside the terminal every twenty minutes. That takes you straight downtown. On behalf of Captain Cochran and all of the crew, I'd like to thank you for flying with California Airlines and wish you a very pleasant stay in San Francisco.

- **2b** Play 1/50. Students listen and complete the information.
  twenty minutes, it will be warm and sunny, five-thirty (Pacific Standard Time), three hours (behind), twenty minutes

Audio script: see above in *Exercise 2a.*

- **2c** In groups, students talk about their experiences using the questions as prompts.

Globetrotter B: Work (coursebook p. 83)

Contents

Focus on — Clothes for work

Lesson notes

Further classroom materials can be found online: www: A2.2GTBW

Starter: Things to wear 5 mins
- Read out the first part of the instructions. Allow students time to write. Then follow coursebook instructions.
  Possible answers: **trousers, skirt, suit, pullover, tie, socks, T-shirt, jacket, jeans, dress**

Exercise 1 5 mins
- Students look at the pictures and say which job each person does.
  1 a lawyer, 2 a nurse, 3 a fireman, 4 a ballet dancer

! Refer students to the *Info box* and tell them that words beginning with *uni* take *a* not *an* despite 'u' being a vowel (this is because the first sound is pronounced as a [j], which is a consonant sound).

Exercises 2a, 2b 2/52–53, **2c** 20 mins
- **2a** As a class, discuss the importance of appearance for the listed jobs.
- **2b** Read out the instructions. Play ▶ 2/52. Students listen and answer the gist question.
  Because his clothes are not suitable for work.
  Play ▶ 2/53. Students listen and tick the phrases they hear.
  ✓ 1, 2, 3, 6

(H = Helen, T = Trevor)
H: Trevor, could I have a word with you, please?
T: Oh, OK Helen. What's it about?
H: Well, it's about what you're wearing to work today. It's OK for staff to wear casual clothes on Fridays, but there are standards ...
T: Oh. Is there something wrong with how I'm dressed?
H: I'm sorry I have to say this, but it's not really suitable for work.
T: But it's Friday today.
H: Well, I know it's Friday, but that doesn't mean you can wear just anything. It means you don't have to wear a tie, and you can wear jeans – if you don't have to meet clients.
T: Well, I don't have to meet clients at all – I work on the computer all day.
H: But that still doesn't mean you can wear ... things like that. It isn't appropriate!
T: But I thought it was OK – and I'm going straight on to a party after work.
H: Well, why didn't you bring clothes to change into after work?
T: I thought these clothes were OK.
H: No, I really think you should go home and change your clothes.
T: OK, Helen. Sorry. It won't happen again.
H: Thank you. Trevor, it might be a good idea to look at what other people are wearing next Friday.
T: Yes, I'll do that, too. See you later.
T: See you later, Trevor.

- **2c** Students work with a partner to role play the conversation. If time permits, swap roles and partners.

Exercises 3a, 3b 15+ mins
- **3a** Students read the letter and responses and underline or highlight the words they think are best.
  ! The answers in the key are possible answers, there is no wrong or right answer as this is a matter of opinion.
  Dear Yvonne: classic, white; smart, dark / conservative; scarf / bag
  Dear Alan: formally; open-necked shirt; jacket and open-necked shirt; black leather shoes
- **3b** Follow coursebook instructions.

Globetrotter B: Travel (coursebook p. 84)

Contents

Focus on — Clothes for travelling

Lesson notes

Further classroom materials can be found online: www: A2.2GTBT

Starter: Holiday clothes 5 mins
- Encourage students to discuss the *Starter* question and make a list for each holiday.

Possible answers: **a skiing holiday: ski suit, thick socks, jeans, gloves, jumpers, T-shirts, thermal underwear / a walking tour: trousers, jeans, shorts, T-shirts, shirts, jumper, hiking boots / a city break: trousers, skirts, shirts, T-shirts, jumper, evening dress / a beach holiday: bikini, swimming trunks, shorts, T-shirts, skirts, jeans, trousers, dress, sunhat**

Exercises 1a 2/54–55, **1b** 15+ mins
- **1a** Play ▶ 2/54. Students answer the gist questions.

A sunhat for her daughter. Ten euros.
Play ▶ 2/55. Students listen and tick the sentences they hear.
✓ 1b), 2a), 3b), 4b), 5a), 6a), 7b)

(A = shop assistant, S = Sarah, K = Katy)
A: Hola!
S: Oh, hello – do you speak English?
A: Yes, I do.
S: OK – we'd like a sunhat.
A: We've got some very nice sunhats! What size do you want?
S: Er – a child's size. It's for my little girl, Katy.
K: Hello.
A: Oh, isn't she pretty! How old is she?
S: Six.
A: I have a daughter just the same age. And a sunhat is a very good idea – children can burn very easily when the sun is strong. Now, we have some children's sunhats here in different colours. What colour would you like? We have pink, blue, orange ...
K: I want the one with the little cat on it!
S: Can she try it on?
A: Yes, of course. Here you are.
S: Try this on, Katy. Um ... that's a bit too big. Do you have a smaller size?
A: Let me see ... yes, this one is the same hat, but a size smaller.
S: Come here, Katy, and let me change your hat. Oh, that looks good. Do you have a mirror?
A: Yes, it's just here.
S: Oh, yes. Have a look in the mirror, Katy.
K: I like this one mummy.
S: OK, Katy. How much is it?
A: It's 12 euros.
S: Oh – that's a bit too expensive.
A: Well, the light blue ones are only eight euros.
S: Katy, do you like this blue hat?
K: No! I want the cat hat!
S: Oh ...
A: Well, the little girl wants the hat. You can have it for ten euros.
S: Thanks, that's great. Oh ... I've only got five euros. Can I pay with a credit card?
A: Yes, of course. Is there anything else? Maybe a sunhat for you?
S: No, I've already got one. But that blue scarf is beautiful. Is it silk?
A: Yes it is. Feel it! So soft ...
S: Hmmm – I'll think about it, and maybe I'll come back tomorrow. I'll just take the sunhat today.
A: Yes, of course. Now, please can you put your card in the machine here ...

- **1b** Students work with a partner to role play the conversation. If time permits, swap roles and partners.

Exercises 2a, 2b, 2c 25 mins
- **2a** Students read the text.
- **2b** Using the text students complete the sentences. Check answers in class.
  1 ... what your luggage allowance is, 2 ... half as many clothes and twice as much money as you think you'll need / old clothes with you and then throw them away at the end of the week, 3 ... clothes that are unique to the country you're visiting, 4 ... about local clothes sizes before you travel
- **2c** Students work in small groups and discuss the questions.

Globetrotter C: Work (coursebook p. 121)

Contents

Focus on Money

Lesson notes

Further classroom materials can be found online: www: A2.2GTCW

Starter: Fair play 5 mins
- Ask individual students the *Starter* questions.

Exercise 1 10 mins
- Follow coursebook instructions.
  1 SN16 6AZ; 2 March 30; 3 6000; 4 £9.99; 5 17,5; 6 £473,20; 7 within 30 days

Exercise 2a 3/48–49, **2b** 15 mins
- **2a** Play ▶ 3/48. Students listen and answer the gist question.
  There's a stop on the account because a bill hasn't been paid.
  Play ▶ 3/49. Students listen and underline the words / phrases they hear.
  1 order | invoice, 2 14 | 30, 3 23rd | 29th, 4 next week | tomorrow, 5 second | third, 6 goods | items
- **2b** In pairs, students role play the situation. If time permits, swap roles and partners.

(E = employee, C = customer)
E: Good morning, Swindon Office Supplies.
C: Oh hi. This is Andy King from Andy's Electrical Services. I'm phoning about my order – you haven't delivered it yet.
E: Oh, I'm sorry about that. Can you give me the order number please, so I can check?
C: Yes, it's AES/1577. It was for board pens and flip-chart paper – and photocopying toner for our office.

→

E: One moment, please, I'll just check. Oh, there's a 'stop' on your account.
C: I don't understand – what does that mean?
E: Well, it usually means there's an invoice that you haven't paid.
C: Really?
E: I'm just checking ... Yes, I'm afraid we haven't received payment for your last order yet, Mr King – order AES/1576. We sent you the invoice on the 30th of March and we expect to be paid within 30 days.
C: Oh, I'm sorry ... can you tell me when the payment was due for that invoice?
E: It was due on the 29th of April, and that was three weeks ago. That's why we haven't sent your new order out. We sent you a reminder.
C: Oh ... um ... my wife usually deals with payments. I'll need to check with her. Can you send my order and I'll pay you next week?
E: I'm sorry, Mr King, but this is the third time this has happened. And I'm afraid that's company policy. If you don't pay for your last order, we can't send you any more goods.
C: OK – I'll speak to my wife and phone you back ... maybe this afternoon.
E: That's fine Mr King – talk to you soon.
C: Well, er – thanks for your help. Goodbye.
E: Goodbye.

Exercise 3a, 3b 15 mins
- **3a** Read out the instructions. Students complete the task, then check answers in class.
  (1) e), (2) f), (3) d), (4) g), (5) c), (6) b), (7) a)
- **3b** Students work in small groups to discuss the questions.

Globetrotter C: Travel (coursebook p. 122)

Contents

Focus on Money

Lesson notes

Further classroom materials can be found online: www: A2.2GTCT

Starter: Holiday spending 5 mins
- Ask individual students the *Starter* questions.

Exercise 1 5+ mins
- Briefly tell the class about a bad experience you had using the sentence headers provided. Then follow coursebook instructions.

Exercise 2 5+ mins
- Students work in pairs and role play the situation. If time permits, swap roles and partners.

Exercises 3a, 3b 3/50 20 mins
- **3a** Follow coursebook instructions.
- **3b** Play ▶ 3/50. Students listen and say which tips were followed.
  Speaker 1: Don't carry large amounts of cash around with you. Have some 'emergency cash' in a separate bag. Speaker 2: Carry your cash in a money belt if you have to travel in high-crime areas. Speaker 3: If there isn't a safe in your room, ask the receptionist to put your valuables and passport in the hotel safe.

1
S1: Of course, it was difficult when I lost my wallet. I don't think it was stolen – I was wearing shorts and I think it just fell out of my pocket. Nobody handed it in, of course – I checked at the police station. There wasn't a lot of money in the wallet, but all my credit cards were in it, so I had to cancel them. It took a few days for the bank to send me new cards, but I always hide a $100 bill in my suitcase. I think it's important to have ...
2
S2: Well, it was a real adventure travelling round South America with my boyfriend, but it wasn't always safe – sometimes we were in quite dangerous situations. The worst thing was when we were on a bus, and some guys stopped it and robbed everyone. I had to give them my bag, with my purse in it, but they didn't find the rest of my money! I was wearing it! Yes, I was really glad I was wearing my ...
3
S3: I travel a lot for work, and of course, I have money with me – quite a lot of cash and company credit cards, but I also have to take my laptop, my passport and lots of important papers. I never feel very comfortable when I leave things in my room – and some rooms don't have a safe. I really don't like just leaving things in my room, so I hand my things in at the reception. I'm only comfortable when I know that my things are ...

Exercises 4a, 4b 10 mins
- **4a** Individually or in pairs, students see how many countries and currencies they know. Refer students to the key on p. 128 when they have finished.
- **4b** Follow coursebook instructions.

Christmas lesson – activities

If you'd like to do something a bit different in the lesson before Christmas, here are some ideas for activities. You can also find Christmas activities online in the *Network Teachers' Club* (www.klett-langenscheidt.de/network/club).

Activities from Section 1 can be used after completing Unit 2; **Activities from Section 1 + 2** can be used after completing Unit 4; **Activities from Sections 1, 2 + 3** can be used after completing Unit 6.

Section 1:

Activity 1a: Christmas anagrams

- Write the following anagrams on the board:
  etre, adtsycisamhr, tepsresn, dgpudin, asnta
  (tree, Christmas Day, presents, pudding, Santa)
- In pairs, students work out what the words are.
- Give students five minutes to think of their own Christmas anagrams. Then ask volunteers to come up to the board and write their anagrams for the class to guess.

Activity 1b: Christmas dinner guests

- Tell students to write the initials of a famous person (dead or alive) they'd like to invite to their Christmas dinner on a piece of paper.
- Students then work in groups of 4. Tell them they are the people written on their paper. They put their paper with the initials on it in front of them on the table. Then they need to make polite conversation and try to find out who the other people are. They can't ask directly!
- Once students have finished, ask them to guess who the other 'mystery guests' are and introduce them to the class by saying something about them.

Activity 1c: Christmas, define it!

- **Copy Activity 1c** (p. 128) – one for each pair of students, and cut out the A / B parts.
- Ask students to work in A / B pairs and hand out a Student A or Student B copy to each student.
- Students work in their pairs and define the words for each other without saying the word. Their partner must guess what the word is. Remind them to use the relative pronouns *who, which, where*.

Section 2:

Activity 2a: Presents

- Briefly tell the class about the best present you've ever received and why it was so special.
- Board: – What's the best present you've ever received?
  – Why was it so special?
  – What would you like to receive for Christmas?
  – Where and when do you open Christmas presents?
  – Who do buy presents for?
- Students work in small groups to discuss the questions.
- Then think of someone you know who is difficult to buy a present for (or make someone up). Describe him / her to the class and say a bit about his / her interests and hobbies. Ask the class for ideas for presents.
- In their groups, students then do the same.

Activity 2b: Whose Christmas list is this?

- Board: What do you want for Christmas?
- Tell students they have five minutes to write a Christmas list – they can have anything they want.
- Then collect in the lists and redistribute them to other students. Individual students then read out the lists and the class guesses who wrote the list.

Activity 2c: Have you done it yet?

- **Copy Activity 2c** (p. 128) – one for each student.
- Hand out one copy to each student.
- Students walk around the class and ask each other questions. They should talk to as many different students as possible. When they get a *Yes* answer, they should write the student's name next to the question.
- Volunteers then report one fact about someone in the class, e.g. (Jan) has already (got a Christmas tree).

Section 3:

Activity 3a: Christmas food

- Tell the class about your ideal Christmas dinner, what you like to eat and drink and where you like to be for Christmas dinner.
- Ask students to think about their ideal Christmas dinner.
- In small groups, students talk about their ideal Christmas dinner.

Activity 3b: Christmas *Ifs*

- **Copy Activity 3b** (p. 128) – one for each group of students. Cut out the cards.
- Divide the students into groups of three or four.
- Put the piles of cards face down on their desks.
- One student takes a card and reads out the *if*-clause and completes the sentence.

Activity 3c: Christmas game

- **Copy Activity 3c** (p. 128) – one for each group of students.
- Board:

24th December	Boxing Day
25th December	Christmas Eve
26th December	Christmas Day

Ask students to match the dates to their names. (24th December – Christmas Eve, 25th December – Christmas Day, 26th December – Boxing Day)

- Divide the students into groups of four or six.
- Each group needs a coin. Students flip the coin – heads: move forward one space, tails: move forward two spaces.
- When they land on a square, they must talk for 30 seconds about that topic.
- If they can't think of anything to say, they miss a turn.
- The game is over when the first player reaches *Finish*.

Christmas lesson – photocopiable materials

Activity 1c: Christmas, define it!

Student A

- Define these Christmas items for your partner. Your partner should guess what it is:

  a Christmas card
  a Christmas tree
  a turkey
  a Christmas carol
  Father Christmas
  Bethlehem

- You can use these phrases:

  This is something which ...
  This is a person who ...
  This is a place where ...

Student B

- Define these Christmas items for your partner. Your partner should guess what it is:

  Glühwein
  a Christmas present
  Santa Claus
  a Christmas pudding
  a Christmas market
  a star

- You can use these phrases:

  This is something which ...
  This is a person who ...
  This is a place where ...

Activity 2c: Have you done it yet?

- Walk around the class and ask the other students questions using *Have you ... yet?* If someone says *Yes, I have.*, write his / her name on the line. Report one fact about someone in class to the other students: *(Jan) has already ...*

Have you ...	Name:
• bought all of your Christmas presents yet?	______________
• got a Christmas tree yet?	______________
• planned what to eat yet?	______________
• wrapped your Christmas presents yet?	______________
• been to a Christmas market yet?	______________
• had any Glühwein yet?	______________
• put any decorations up yet?	______________

Activity 3b: Christmas *Ifs*

If I met Santa Claus, I'd ...	If it snows at Christmas, I'll ...	If I could have any present at all, I'd have a ...
If I make a cake at Christmas, I'll ...	If I visit a Christmas market, I'll ...	If I had one wish at Christmas, I'd wish for ...
If you bought me a Christmas present, I'd ...	If I cook dinner on Christmas day, I'll ...	If you tell me a Christmas joke, I'll ...
I'll sing you a Christmas carol if ...	I'd be very happy at Christmas if ...	When I've bought all of my Christmas presents, I'll ...

Activity 3c: Christmas game

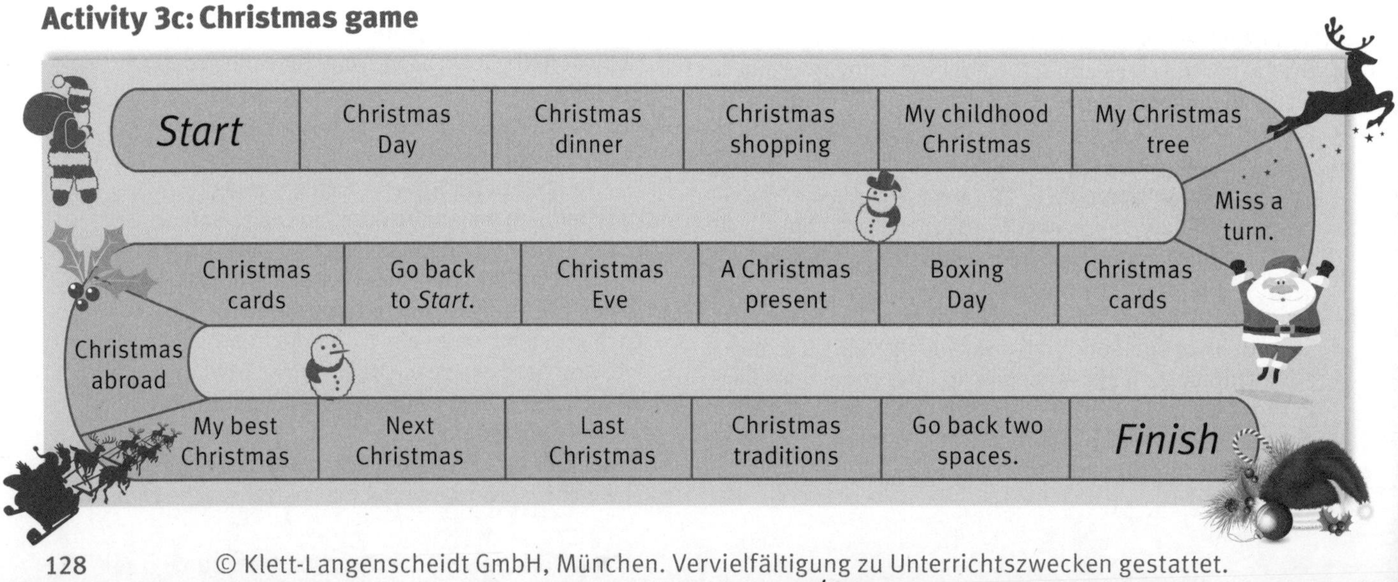

